DATE DUE No.

ELARD

The Great Educators

EDITED BY NICHOLAS MURRAY BUTLER

ABELARD

AND

THE ORIGIN AND EARLY HISTORY OF UNIVERSITIES

27473

BY

GABRIEL COMPAYRÉ

RECTOR OF THE ACADEMY OF POITIERS, FRANCE

NEW YORK

CHARLES SCRIBNER'S SONS

1910

PREFACE

THE present essay has no pretension — as its size sufficiently indicates — to be a complete and thorough history of the universities of the Middle Ages.

To write that history with all its details, several volumes would be necessary, volumes rivalling in their dimensions the enormous folios in which the erudite have massed the documents relating to each university — as, for instance, the *Chartularium* of the University of Paris, by Père Denifle.

I have merely sought, in a sketch which touches on all questions pertaining to this vast subject without exhausting any of them, to give an idea of what these great associations of masters and students which played such an important part in the past, must have been in their beginnings, in their internal organization, their programmes of study, their methods of instruction, and, finally, in their general spirit and external influence.

In spite of the bad reputation given to the old universities by the Humanists of the Renaissance, it is impossible to ignore the services that they rendered in their time. They constitute an epoch, and a characteristic epoch, in the history of education; and I hope that the young and brilliant universities of

v

America will not find it uninteresting to glance backward at the history of their predecessors in ancient Europe.

In any case, I trust that my readers may find as much pleasure in running through this little book as I have had in writing it. I trust also, that the literary dictionaries of the future, if they should grant me a place in their pages, will have the goodness when they mention my name to follow it with this notice: Gabriel Compayré, a French writer, whose least mediocre work, translated into English before being printed, was published in America.

POITIERS, October 17, 1892.

CONTENTS

Part I

THE ORIGINS OF THE UNIVERSITIES

Chapter I — Abelard the Forerunner of the Universities

Chapter II — The General Causes of the Rise of Universities

PART II

THE ORGANIZATION OF THE EARLY UNIVERSITIES

CHAPTER I—PRIVILEGES OF THE UNIVERSITIES

CHAPTER II — NATIONS AND FACULTIES

CHAPTER III — GOVERNMENT OF UNIVERSITIES

CHAPTER IV — SYSTEM OF GRADUATION

Part III

THE COURSE OF STUDY AND THE METHODS OF TEACHING

Chapter I — The Faculties of Arts

Part IV

GENERAL SPIRIT AND INFLUENCE OF THE EARLY UNIVERSITIES

Chapter I — Manners and Habits of Students and Teachers

Chapter II — External Influence of the Universities and their Spirit of Freedom

PART I

THE ORIGINS OF THE UNIVERSITIES

ABELARD

CHAPTER I

ABELARD THE FORERUNNER OF THE UNIVERSITIES

I. Testimony to the influence of Abelard — The transmission of learning from Charlemagne to Abelard — II. The life of Abelard — His character, his eloquence, his method of teaching — His audiences the first great assemblages of students — III. Abelard's doctrines and point of view — Freedom of inquiry and of reason — His method followed in the schools of Paris.

ABELARD was born in 1079; he died in 1142. The University of Paris was not formally constituted until sixty years later, in the first years of the thirteenth century. And yet Abelard has been, and should be, considered as the real founder of this university, which served as model and prototype of most of the other universities of the Middle Ages. There is here an apparent paradox which must first be resolved and explained, if the title given to this treatise is to be justified.

I

Let me begin by establishing the fact that I am in accord with all serious authorities in attributing to Abelard a pre-eminent part in the foundation of the

3

great Parisian University. "The man," Victor Cousin has said, "who, by his qualities and his defects, by the audacity of his opinions, the éclat of his life, his inborn passion for controversy, and his rare talent for instruction, contributed most to increase and expand the taste for study and that intellectual movement from which the University of Paris issued in the thirteenth century, was Peter Abelard."[1] In England the same opinion is held. "The name of Abelard is closely associated with the commencement of the University of Paris," says Cardinal Newman in his interesting essay on *The Strength and Weakness of Universities.*[2]

In order not to multiply testimony, I shall content myself with invoking finally, that of Père Denifle, the learned editor of the *Chartularium Universitatis Parisiensis.* "Although Abelard," he says, "taught long before the constitution of the University of Paris, his method of instruction for the sciences, and above all for theology and the liberal arts, nevertheless remained the model which the future university was to follow."[3]

It is no longer a question whether to accept as true the fabulous origins attributed to the University of Paris by its earliest historians, by Du Boulay[4] or by

[1] *Ouvrages inédits d'Abélard*, publiés par V. Cousin, 1836. Introduction.

[2] Cardinal Newman, *Historical Sketches*, vol. iii, p. 192. London, 1889.

[3] *Chartularium Universitatis Parisiensis.* Paris, Delalain, 1889, t. i, Introduction, p. xvi.

[4] Bulæus, *Historia Universitatis Parisiensis ab anno circiter 800.* Paris, 1665–1673. 6 vols.

Crevier, who does not hesitate to say: "The University of Paris, as a school, goes back to Alcuin; . . . Charlemagne was its founder." [1]

Doubtless, there is no absolute breach of continuity either in the history of the progress of human thought, or in the evolution of scholastic studies. The three centuries which separate Charlemagne from Abelard were not a period of complete inertia, of intellectual slumber, of absolutely obscure night. And it would even be possible to establish, as has been attempted by ingenious and learned men, a sort of filiation from Alcuin to Abelard, which would demonstrate that laborious and instructed men had not ceased to pass the torch of studies from hand to hand.[2] Borrowing the biblical style, we might say, *Alcuinus genuit* Rabanum,[3] *Rabanus autem genuit Lupum servatum;*[4] . . . and continue thus down to Roscelinus and William of Champeaux, who were Abelard's masters.

It is incontestable, on the other hand, that important schools were flourishing in the ninth, tenth, and eleventh centuries; those of Rheims, Tours, Angers, and Laon; that of the Benedictines of Cluny, under Odo (879–942) and his disciples; that of the Benedictines of Bec in Normandy, with Lanfranc (1005–1089) and St. Anselm (1033–1109) at its head; and an obscure multitude of episcopal or monastic schools,

[1] Crevier, *Histoire de l'Université de Paris*, 1761, t. vii, pp. 92–162.

[2] Monnier, *Alcuin et son influence*, p. 189.

[3] Rabanus Maurus (776–856), a pupil of Alcuin, opened a celebrated school at Fulda in Germany.

[4] Loup de Ferrières (805–882) taught at Fulda.

established sometimes under the patronage of bishops in the chapter-houses of cathedral churches, sometimes under the protection of monasteries, in which elementary instruction was given. These schools had succeeded to the Schools of the Palace of Charlemagne, "a great but transitory creation."

But neither in the existence of these schools, nor in the hereditary transmission from one individual to another of what then constituted the light luggage of human science, is it possible to see anything more than the remote preparation for the universities of the Middle Ages, and not their direct and immediate origins. The various schools which maintained themselves after the unfruitful efforts of Charlemagne, served no purpose save that of preventing the complete shipwreck of intellectual culture. They might be compared to a Noah's ark, launched upon that sea of ignorance and increasing barbarism, to preserve the sacred deposit of letters and sciences, until the day when the carefully collected germs might again, under circumstances more favorable and a more clement sky, find a soil to fertilize. The episcopal and monastic schools were the cradle of the universities in appearance only.

Abelard, it is true—when, about the year 1100, he arrived at Paris for the first time, at the age of twenty—was a pupil of the episcopal school of the cloister of Notre Dame, which was annexed, as was customary, to the cathedral church. But, though he attended the lectures of William of Champeaux[1] for

[1] William of Champeaux, who died in 1121, was one of the most brilliant champions of Realism. See the Abbé Michaud's work:

a time, it was only to separate from him almost immediately, to attack his doctrines, to set himself up as an independent opponent, and, changing from pupil to master, to open in 1102, a school at Melun, and then another at Corbeil, until such time as he should establish himself, "until he should pitch his camp," as he said in his boastful speech on the heights of Ste. Geneviève.[1] This single episode in Abelard's life is, as it were, the symbol, the striking image, of the relations subsisting in general between the episcopal schools and the universities; the latter supplanting the former and installing themselves in their place, or at any rate, relegating them to obscurity or to a secondary position while awaiting the time when they should absorb them completely. "The monastic and episcopal schools," says an English writer,[2] "continued to exist long after the rise of the universities; but it is obvious that if the former represented merely the stationary and conservative element, while the latter attracted to themselves whatever lay beneath the ban of unreasoning authority — all that widened the domain of knowledge or enriched the limits already attained — the comparative importance of the two agencies could not remain the same."

Victor Leclerc says rightly, that the schools of the bishops and the cloisters "continued to flourish at the same time as the new societies of studies,"[3] that

Guillaume de Champeaux et les écoles de Paris au XIIe Siècle, Paris, 1867.

[1] ". . . in monte S. Genovefæ scholarum nostrarum castra posui," *Abelardi Opera*, édition Cousin, 1849, t. i, p. 6.

[2] Mullinger, *The University of Cambridge*. Cambridge, 1873, p. 70.

[3] Leclerc, *État des Lettres au XIVme Siècle*, i, p. 302.

is to say, the universities. The truth is that, without disappearing, they declined. The universities, protected alike by popes, kings, and emperors, replaced them in the favor of both the civil and the religious powers; and, drawing to themselves the very great majority of students, (they were destined to represent increasingly, in opposition to the immobile tradition of the older schools, the forward march, the movement of ideas, the progress of thought.) If one desires to know the real heirs of the monastic and episcopal schools, it is not in the universities that he must seek them, but in the congregations, and the various religious orders, with which precisely it was that the universities had so many struggles to undergo, and whose members they never admitted within their precincts save with suspicion and unwillingly.

II

To prepare the great movement from which the universities were to proceed something different from the passive transmission of certain beliefs accepted with docility was needful, something other than certain schools of theology or timid dialectics piously sleeping within the bosom of the Church. To begin with, a man, a scholar, must be found sufficiently Catholic not to quarrel with the received dogmas, but nevertheless bold enough to open new paths for himself, and, at the same time, powerful enough, both in speech and in thought, to move minds, arouse the taste for study, assemble great audiences, and finally, by his success as an instructor, establish a great intellectual movement. A short sketch of the life and work of Abelard will show how this programme was accomplished.

It is difficult, by a mere perusal of Abelard's works, to understand the effect he produced upon his hearers by the force of his argumentation, whether studied or improvised, and by the ardor and animation of his eloquence, and the grace and attractiveness of his person. But the testimony of his contemporaries is unanimous; even his adversaries themselves render justice to his high oratorical qualities. No one ever reasoned with more subtlety, or handled the dialectic tool with more address; and assuredly, something of these qualities is to be found in the writings he has left us. But the intense life, the enthusiastic ardor which enlivened his discourses, the beauty of his face, and the charm of his voice cannot be imparted by cold manuscripts. Héloise, whose name is inseparably linked with that of her unfortunate husband, and whom Charles de Rémusat does not hesitate to call "the first of women"; [1] who, in any case, was a superior person of her time; Héloise, who loved Abelard with "an immoderate love," [2] and who, under the veil of a *religieuse* and throughout the practice of devotional duties, remained faithful to him until death; Héloise said to him in her famous letter of 1136: "Thou hast [3] two things especially which could instantly win thee the hearts of all women: the charm

[1] Charles de Rémusat, *Abélard*. Paris, 1845. t. i, p. 262

[2] ". . . te immoderato amore complexa sum," *Abelardi Opera,* édition Cousin, t. i, p. 74.

[3] ". . . dictandi videlicet et cantandi gratia," *Ibid.*, p. 76.

thou knowest how to impart to thy voice in speaking,
and in singing."

External gifts combined with intellectual qualities
to make of Abelard an incomparable seducer of minds
and hearts. Add to this an astonishing memory, a
knowledge as profound as was compatible with the resources of his time, and a vast erudition which caused
his contemporaries to consider him a master of universal knowledge.[1] It was not merely the weapons of
a skilful but barren logic that he had recourse to when
he desired to convince; nourished on the perusal of
Latin orators and poets, he embellished his discourses
with literary digressions, classical allusions, and quotations from Horace or from Vergil. A poet himself
when at forty years of age he fell in love with
Héloise, renewing his youth through love and repeating the drama of *Faust*, he composed love-songs in
the common tongue, which became very popular.

We must not omit to signalize the intrepidity of his
ardent character, always ready to attack or to defend,
provoking controversy rather than seeking to appease
it; in a word, the adventurous and militant temper
wherein one recognizes the innovator. Charles de
Rémusat represents Abelard before he was twenty,
as "wandering over the provinces, seeking masters
and adversaries, going from controversy to controversy, a veritable knight-errant of philosophy."[2]

[1] Abelard avowed, however, that he did not know Greek and
that he had failed in the study of mathematics.

[2] Abelard, in his first letter to Héloise, which is like the history
of his life, *historia calamitatum*, himself writes: "*Diversas dis-
putando perambulans provincias, peripateticorum æmulator fac-
tus sum,*" *Abelardi Opera*, p. 4.

Later on, when in 1101 he dared to contradict and succeeded in refuting William of Champeaux, then at the height of his power and reigning as a sovereign in the school of the cloister of Notre Dame; and when, in 1114, he went to attack on his own ground, in his school at Laon, in the midst of his pupils, stupefied at such audacity, the old Anselm of Laon, himself a pupil of St. Anselm, and who at this epoch held "the sceptre of theology," was he not armed with extraordinary courage, this young philosopher who, without other title than his genius, endowed by no one with the right to teach, avowing himself without a master, — *sine magistro*, as his enemies reproached him with being, — found in himself the needful inspiration to undertake the most formidable controversies and to triumph in them?

Victory then accompanied and encouraged his efforts. But, when the hours of his disgrace arrived, when the hostility of churchmen whom he had affrighted and troubled in their repose, arraigned him successively before two Councils, that of Soissons in 1121, and that of Sens in 1140, to listen to the condemnation of his heresies; did he not give proof even in his defeat, of an energy, a force of soul, rare at all times, but almost unknown in epochs of blind submission and theocratic terror?

At Soissons he was not disconcerted, even in the midst of a fanatical populace who accused him of having preached that there were three Gods, on account of the interpretation he gave to the dogma of the Trinity, and who were on the point of stoning some of his disciples; and he embarrassed his accusers by the

boldness of his replies and his haughty countenance.
Condemned notwithstanding, obliged to burn his books
with his own hands, confined as a prisoner in the convent of St. Médard, it was only in appearance that he
bowed before the indisputable authority of a sovereign
tribunal; in reality, trembling with rage under the
yoke imposed upon him, "bound," according to the
expression of an author of the day, "like a wild rhi-
noceros," he persevered in his independent thought
and his personal faith; just as, though shut up in the
cloister of Argenteuil, Héloïse persevered in her love.

At Sens, grown old and tired, at odds with St.
Bernard who occupied a commanding position in the
Church, — with that man, superior likewise, but superior solely by the sanctity of his life and the
ardor of his devotion, and who was, in a word, only
"a monk," — Abelard, it is true, appeared to fail.
Instead of defending himself, he retired, restricting
himself to declaring that he recognized no judge but
the Roman Pontiff. His persecutors published that
he had been intimidated, seized with a miraculous confusion. Is it not more likely that, feeling himself
condemned in advance before an assembly of openly
hostile prelates, and unwilling to confess himself de-
feated, the rationalistic Christian, were it merely to
retard his discomfiture, appeals to the Pope, as the
rationalistic philosophers appeal later on to eternal
truth and justice?

The sketch I am making would be incomplete if
it failed to note a final trait of Abelard's character:
his confidence in himself, his presumptuous assurance.
Abelard is not a studious man, devoting himself to

the search after truth in the silence and solitude of his chamber; he is a combatant, eager for glory and for power. After the scandal of his amours with Héloise, after the atrocious mutilation to which he had been subjected, another man, less strongly tempered, would have thought of nothing but hiding his shame in retreat. But Abelard, in his ambitious activity, could not resign himself to repose, and a year after his cruel adventure, in 1120, he opened a new school in Champagne and there won again his past victories. "There was in this man," says Charles de Rémusat, "somewhat of the insolence of those natures born for command and royalty." Greatly attached to his opinions, greatly in love with his own discernment, intoxicated moreover, as it were, with the enthusiastic homage of his pupils, he had none of the humility, nor even of the modesty which the habit of intellectual docility rendered easy to his contemporaries. He went so far as to write that he considered himself the only philosopher of his time; [1] but for that matter, if he was wrong to say it, perhaps he was right in thinking it.

How can one be astonished that with such qualities Abelard gained an extraordinary ascendency over his age; that, having become the intellectual ruler and, as it were, the dictator of the thought of the twelfth century, he should have succeeded in attracting to his chair and in retaining around it thousands of young men; the first germ of those assemblages of students who were to constitute the universities several years later?

[1] " . . . quum jam me solum in mundo superesse philosophum æstimarem," Abelardi Opera, t. i, p. 9.

Abelard, in spite of the vicissitudes of his existence, was, above all things, a professor.[1] Let me recall in a few words, the principal stages in his career. I have already stated that by 1102 he had taught at Melun, then at Corbeil, from whence, nearer to Paris, "he delivered the assault, so to say, on the citadel of the school of Notre Dame." This assault became still more vigorous when, in 1108, he established himself in Paris on the Mount of Ste. Geneviève, "that hill destined to become the Sinai of university instruction," where schools were already in existence which competed freely with the official school of the city. It was at this period that William of Champeaux, discouraged by the growing success of his pupil, definitely quitted the cloister of Notre Dame, at first to found, at the gates of Paris, a congregation which became the celebrated Abbey of St. Victor, but afterwards to become the Bishop of Châlons-sur-Marne. He left the place free to his rival, and it is about 1113 that we find Abelard at last installed in the school of the city, reigning as master of instruction in a town which was already the intellectual capital of Europe, and realizing thus the dream of his youth: *ad scholarum regimen adolescentulus aspirabam.*[2]

This was the most brilliant period of his life: it lasted but a few years, being interrupted after 1118

[1] It is not known at what date Abelard became a priest. He was probably not one at the time of his marriage with Héloise; this is not proved, however. He has himself expressed the opinion that a priest may marry. *Abelardi Opera,* t. i, p. 16.

[2] "He obtained the chair of the cloister, to which he had long aspired, and he taught there at the same time theology and philosophy. Crevier, *op. cit.,* t. i, p. 127."

by the scandal of his *liaison* with Héloise.   But from 1120, after some months of meditation spent at the Abbey of St. Denis, he felt again the need for action; he installed himself in the Priory of Maisoncelle, in Champagne, where, it is said, he was surrounded by three thousand students.   Then, after new disturbances, after the condemnation pronounced by the Council of Soissons, after a veritable Ulysses's journey from convent to convent, he obtained from the King, Louis the Fat, and from his ministers, Stephen de Garlande and Suger, permission to establish himself in a retreat of his own choice.   Royalty in the twelfth century, resuming the rôle and experiencing anew the inspirations of Charlemagne, seems from this period to have been conscious of its duties towards learning and scientific men; and the protection granted by the ministers of Louis the Fat to Abelard, persecuted by the Church, is the prelude to the privileges granted to the universities by the princes of the thirteenth century.

Thanks to the royal favor, Abelard was able to fix his residence without hindrance in a desert place belonging to the territory of Troyes, and there, in some fields which were given him, he built an oratory of stubble which he called the *Paraclete*, the *Comforter*.   He had come there alone, save for one pupil. But his retreat was soon known; students flocked to him anew, pursuing their regretted master even to the wilderness where he had hidden himself.   "Cities and castles were deserted for this Thebaid of science. Tents were set up; mud walls, covered with moss, rose to shelter the numerous disciples who slept on the grass and nourished themselves with rustic dishes and coarse bread."[1] The instruction given at this School of the Paraclete, marvellously opened in the midst of fields, was continued from 1122 to 1125. But this new success called forth new attacks which saddened all the latter part of Abelard's life. He was to reappear only once more, in 1136, in his chair at Paris, the first theatre of his glory, ardent as ever, in spite of his fifty-seven years, and followed still by the sympathy of his hearers. It was at this epoch that he had John of Salisbury[2] as a pupil, whose testimony is precious to recall. "I repaired," he says, "to the country of the Palatin[3] peripatetic, who was then presiding on Mount Ste. Geneviève, an illustrious doctor, admirable for everything. . . . There, at his feet, I received the first elements of the dialectic art, and, according to the measure of my feeble understanding, I gathered up, with all the avidity of my soul, everything that proceeded from his mouth."

Up to the last day of his teaching, then, Abelard was the uncontested master, the professor *par excellence.* In a time when there was neither publicity nor advertising, and renown could only be established slowly and from place to place by conversation and

[1] Charles de Rémusat, *op. cit.*, p. 108.

[2] John of Salisbury (1110–1174), an English monk, became secretary to St. Thomas Becket, afterwards to Alexander III, and finally Bishop of Chartres. He wrote numerous works, among others the *Metalogicus*, which is a plea for literary studies.

[3] Abelard was born near Nantes, in the town of Pallet or Palais, whence the name of Palatin given him by John of Salisbury. It is known that "Abelard" is only a surname, the origin of which is much disputed. See Rémusat, *op. cit.*, p. 171.

oral accounts, he nevertheless acquired both glory and popularity. Wherever he went, says Cousin, he seemed to carry reputation and a crowd along with him. He attracted such a vast number of hearers, not only from all parts of France, but even of Europe, that, as he says himself, the inns were not sufficient to contain them, nor the earth to feed them. "No idea can be given of the effect he produced in teaching philosophy, and never does any science seem to have had a more powerful propagandist. As the head of a school he recalls, if he does not efface, for brilliancy and ascendency the success of the great philosophers of Greece."[1] But however flattering this comparison may be — for nobody dreams of making Abelard equal with Socrates or Plato — it still does injustice, nevertheless, to what was particularly characteristic in the great assemblages of men who thronged about the professor of the Middle Ages. The great philosophers of antiquity had only a very small number of pupils. Around Abelard there was a multitude of human beings; there were more than five thousand pupils in his school at Paris. His school was open to every comer and entered by whoever willed, as is shown by the anecdote of a young student, the pupil of William of Champeaux, of whom the Church has made a saint, St. Gosvin, who, in 1108, desiring to try conclusions with Abelard, bravely entered the school on Mount Ste. Geneviève while the master was speaking, and making a sign that he wished to say something, drew upon himself this apostrophe: "Mind you keep still and don't interrupt my lecture."

[1] Charles de Rémusat, *op. cit.*, p. 31.

III

It is not alone by the outward success of his scholastic apostolate that Abelard merits consideration as the precursor of the modern spirit and the promoter of the foundation of the universities; it is also by his doctrine, or at least by his method. He may, in fact, be counted among the liberators of the human mind, and even, according to the expression of Brucker, "among the martyrs of philosophy."[1]

In what, then, consisted the novelty of his opinions? Abelard remains especially celebrated, among the historians of philosophy, for having taken an intermediate and sound position between the Realists and the Nominalists, between William of Champeaux and Roscelinus;[2] for having maintained that general ideas are neither independent entities nor mere words, but must be defined as concepts of the mind seizing the real relations of things. But whatever may be the value of this theory of Abelard, of this Conceptualism which was the doctrine of good sense, it is not in it that his real originality appears; that consists, above all, in the application he made of reason to theology, in his Christian rationalism, which prepared the way for philosophical rationalism. "What Abelard taught that was most novel for his age," says

[1] Brucker, *Historia critica philosophiæ*, t. iii, p. 704. Cousin does not hesitate to say that Abelard was "leader of a school and almost martyr of an opinion."

[2] Roscelinus, a philosopher of the eleventh century, the chief of the Nominalists, born in Brittany, like Abelard, who had, it appears, followed his lectures: "*Magistri nostri Roscelini tam insana sententia.*" (*Ouvrages inédits*, p. 471.)

Mme. Guizot, "was liberty, the right to consult reason and to listen to it alone. An almost involuntary innovator, he had methods that were still bolder than his doctrines, and principles whose range far outran the consequences at which he himself arrived. Hence, his influence is not to be sought for in the verities which he established, but in the impulse which he gave. He attached his name to none of those powerful ideas which act throughout the centuries, but he imparted to minds that impetus which perpetuates itself from generation to generation." [1]

Assuredly, no one claims that Abelard was the first who, in the Middle Ages, had introduced dialectics into theology, reason into authority. In the ninth century, Scotus Erigena had already said: "Authority is derived from reason." Scholasticism, which is nothing but logic enlightening theology, an effort of reason to demonstrate dogma, had begun before Abelard; but it was he who gave movement and life to the method by lending it his power and his renown. It was he above all who erected it into a principle and gave it a general application.

To estimate the independence of Abelard's thought, to comprehend how far he was in advance of his time, it is sufficient to recall the opposition he encountered among the representatives of tradition. "The human mind," said St. Bernard in his earliest denunciations of Abelard, "the human mind usurps all, no longer leaving anything to faith. . . . It lays hands upon what is most high; it searches that which is stronger

[1] Mme. Guizot, *Essai sur la Vie et les Écrits d'Abélard et de Héloïse*, p. 343.

than itself. It flings itself upon divine things; it forces rather than opens the holy places. Read, if you please, Peter Abelard's book which he calls *theology.*"[1]

It is important to observe that Abelard did not enter upon the study of theology until after he had devoted himself to the study of philosophy. When he presented himself at the school of Anselm at Laon, his fellows reproached with having as yet been initiated only into "the natural sciences." Thus, even in teaching theology, he remains the man who desires to comprehend before he believes. He does not proceed by authority. He appeals to the freedom of the mind. He imagines, no doubt, with a naïve confidence, that this effort to examine will leave the traditional beliefs intact; but he none the less opens the door to all succeeding liberties, to all the heresies of the future; since he wills that everything shall be discussed, everything explained, that there shall be no more secrets, no more mysteries.

Abelard has doubted; he has investigated. One of his books entitled the *Sic et Non,*[2] furnishes the proof of this. He there accumulates the arguments for and against every question. "I expose these contradictions," he says himself, "so that they may excite the susceptible minds of my readers to the search for truth, and that they may render their minds more penetrating as the effect of that search."[3] The reader

---

[1] This is the *Introductio ad theologiam*, composed about 1121. See *Abelardi Opera*, edition Cousin, 1849, t. ii.

[2] The *Sic et Non* has been published by V. Cousin in the *Ouvrages inédits d'Abelard*.

[3] " . . . *Ut teneros lectores ad maximum inquirendæ veritatis*

was to find the solution of these controversies for himself. Thus Abelard gave to the Christian mysteries,
as has been very justly remarked, "the form of a
problem, and to the dogmas the form of a solution."

It was all very well for him to incline for his own
part toward that solution of every question which
was most conformable to authority. It is none the
less true that the provisional orthodoxy of his conclusions, if it dissimulated, did not wholly conceal the
freedom of his method; that it excited the curiosity
of other minds; that it proclaimed the sovereignty of
dialectics; that, consequently, it emancipated reason
by giving it confidence in its own forces; that it authorized, in fine, by its processes of argumentation,
the free solutions which it did not teach and which it
dared not even glance at.

It is the method of Abelard which is the soul of
the scholastic philosophy, of that philosophy which
lasted for five centuries, until the Renaissance, and
which reigned supreme in the University of Paris,
which in early times was merely a great school of
theology and philosophy. "That Abelard's method,"
says Père Denifle, "was introduced into the schools
and never departed thence, can be doubted by none
who will compare the works which preceded Abelard
with those that succeeded him, notably the *Quæstiones*, the *Disputationes*, the *Summæ*, composed by
the professors of those times. . . . We encounter
this method again in the celebrated book which, during several centuries has been, as it were, the text of

*exercitium provocarent et acutiores ex inquisitione redderent."
(Sic et non, prologus.)*

theological instruction, I mean the *Sentences* by Peter Lombard.[1] . . . The influence of the same method is felt even in the famous work which has been like the code of the schools of canon law, the *Decretals of Gratian.*"[2]

It is, therefore, permissible to conclude that we are not deceived in attributing to Abelard the first place in a study of the origin of the universities and the causes which gave them birth. Abelard was the real founder of the University of Paris, and by that fact the promoter of all the universities created in its image. He was its founder in several ways: at first through his reputation, by habituating foreigners to come to Paris for the purpose of studying there, and by assembling vast audiences around him; afterwards by popularizing the studies and the methods which were held in honor for centuries in the Parisian schools. He raised the level of instruction by substituting, in the place of the old routine of the *trivium* and the *quadrivium*, and of purely elementary studies, the lofty lessons of reasoned theology and abstract philosophy. He was the first professor of superior instruction; and he did his work with an incomparable éclat. Among his immediate pupils, says Crevier, were twenty cardinals, fifty archbishops or bishops, and a Pope, Celestin II; and he thus began to make the theological school of Paris the Seminary of Christian Europe. But he also counted among his disciples bold and independent spirits: such as Arnold of Brescia, who was an innovator both in politics and religion, who revolutionized Rome, and who expiated

[1] See Part II, chap. ii. [2] See Part II, chap. iii.

on the scaffold, in 1155, his audacity of thought and deed. In fine, beyond the actual limits of the audiences that followed Abelard's lectures with enthusiasm, it is permissible to say that, in the following centuries, he has had as disciples all those who, in any degree whatever, have maintained the rights of reason and contended for the emancipation of the human mind. One cannot awaken thought without unchaining it; and without wishing to force things, Abelard, the first of French philosophers in the order of time, is, by the intellectual movement which he determined, the precursor of Ramus and of Descartes, in other words, of the Renaissance and the modern spirit.

CHAPTER II

THE GENERAL CAUSES OF THE RISE OF UNIVERSITIES

I. Individual and general causes — Spontaneity of the growth of the first universities — Popes and kings protectors, not founders — Exceptions: University of Palancia (1212), of Naples (1224) — Generally a long local evolution precedes the university constitution — Specialization of studies in the beginning — Progressive extension — Mutual exchanges — II. Original meaning of the terms *universitas, studium generale* — A university is originally an association of students and teachers — General association movement — The Commons — The Crusades — The trade-guilds — III. Equal patronage of the ecclesiastical and civil powers — Universities considered as an instrument for the propagation of the faith — Various citations from pontifical bulls — Universities specially constituted against heresy — IV. Reasons for the royal or imperial favor — Interested motives — Preparation of legists and counsellors for the kings — Universities not only centres of studies, but also of political action.

HOWEVER important the rôle of Abelard may have been, I have no thought of attributing to a single man, or an individual influence, an academic revolution so considerable as that of the foundation of the universities of the Middle Ages. The most brilliant personality can do nothing if the society in which it finds itself is not propitious, if circumstances do not second its action.

Abelard, moreover, is not the only individual whose name should be inscribed on the first page of the Golden Book of the founders of the universities; thus

24

he counts for nothing[1] in the constitution of the great
Italian school, the University of Bologna, the first in
date of all the universities, since its existence was
officially recognized in 1158. The Bolognese legist
Irnerius (1067–1138 or 1150) merits, for his personal
action, a place, if not equal, at least analogous to that
assigned to Abelard.[2]

After bringing into prominence the part played by
the French philosopher, and saluting him as the chief
individual cause of the birth of the universities, it is
important to mention the general causes whose concurrence explains the origin and the development of those
great and powerful scientific associations.

I

It is necessary, in the first place, to discard the
prejudice that the first universities of the Middle
Ages were born suddenly, in a day, at a precise moment whose date it would be possible to fix exactly.
Doubtless the letters-patent of kings, the bulls of
popes, which have for the most part been their con-
stitutive charters, have each their date. But these acts
of formal consecration, coming from the royal or the
pontifical authority, contemplated almost always an
accomplished fact; they simply sanctioned an institution which had formed itself, and whose slow elabora-
tion had been prepared by the spontaneous efforts of
several generations. This is so true that, even for

[1] It is established, nevertheless, that even at Bologna the works
of Abelard were read, studied, and imitated in the time of Gratian.
[2] See Part III, chap. iii.

the universities whose histories are best known, — for the University of Paris, for example, — it is impossible to say exactly at what epoch they commenced.[1] The privilege conferred by Philip Augustus in 1200 on Parisian students and instructors; the regulation of the Cardinal Legate, Robert de Courçon, in 1215; the pontifical charter of Gregory IX, in 1231, — all these documents presuppose the previous existence, the already constituted force, of the Parisian schools of which they undertake to regulate the organization in detail.

In a word, the popes, like the kings, if they were the patrons, the protectors of the first universities, were not their founders. The universities sprang from a spontaneous movement of the human mind.[2] By the very force of things, with the aid of time, and thanks to favorable social conditions, they were the natural result of one of those intellectual movements which, like the Renaissance of the sixteenth century or the Revolution of 1789, after ages of torpor, gain force enough to dominate the human mind. They originated from one of those fortunate crises of growth which are met with, from time to time, in the life of humanity, as in that of individuals, during their adolescence. "The University of Paris," says

[1] "What we know the least about in all our history," said Professor M. Croiset of the University of Montpellier, at the centenary fêtes of 1889, "is the precise moment when it began. Universities do not come into the world with a clatter."

[2] Compare Savigny, *Geschichte des römischen Rechts*, chap. xxx, sect. 60: "It would be altogether erroneous to compare the earliest universities of the Middle Ages with the learned foundations of our own times, established by a monarch," etc.

Thurot, "was born of the need of companionship which men who cultivate their intelligence feel."[1] With still more precision Mr. Laurie has written: "The universities were founded by a concurrence (not wholly fortuitous) of able men who had something they wished to teach and youths who desired to learn."[2]

Doubtless, when once the first universities had found their definitive form, it was easy for popes and kings to decree, at a given date, the creation of a new establishment. The model once fashioned, it became easy to imitate it. Thus it is that numbers of universities, founded in the fourteenth and fifteenth centuries, are merely faithful copies of the University of Paris or that of Bologna. But at the beginning, in the thirteenth century, we see hardly more than two universities which form an exception to the general rule of a more or less long preparation, and which sprang instantaneously from an act of sovereign will: that of Palencia, in Spain, created by Alfonso VIII of Castile in 1212–1214; and that of Naples, constituted in 1224 by Frederic II. It is to be remarked, besides, that these universities, by the very reason of their factitious origin, were scarcely prosperous. That of Palencia, notably, had only a precarious and ephemeral existence.[3] And it is permissible to conclude that the majority of the univer-

[1] Thurot, *De l'organisation de l'enseignement dans l'Université de Paris.* Paris, 1850, p. 3.

[2] Laurie, *Lectures on the Rise and Early Constitution of Universities.* London, 1886, p. 108.

[3] Vicente de la Fuente, *Historia de las Universidades en España.* Madrid, 1884, t. i, p. 76.

sities, even the smallest provincial ones, such as those
of Orleans and Angers in France, have been the pro-
duct of a long local evolution, and thrust their roots
deep into a long past of labor and intellectual culture.

It is only in modern times that flourishing universities may be seen springing out of the earth between
one day and the next, created, so to say, by the stroke
of a magic wand. To make such improvisations possible, two things are needful which were alike unknown to the Middle Ages : either a governmental
centralization sufficiently strong to be able to install
at once, in any given city, a corps of professors, with
the necessary appliances; or such individual munificence as has been witnessed in the United States
many times during this century in the case of such
men as George Peabody, Ezra Cornell, and Johns
Hopkins, — to cite only these, — munificence great
enough to establish complete universities in a few
years, equipped with all their instruments.

Things went otherwise in the Middle Ages. As
has been very justly remarked by an annalist of the
universities of Sicily : "A doctor of some reputation
drew around him a group of disciples eager to be instructed. Their numbers gradually increased; other
doctors, finding an audience all ready, set up their
chairs near his; and thus was founded a school which
went by the name of *Studium*, but which did not
at first embrace the entire body of human learning. The University of Paris began with schools of
theology and philosophy. The school of Salerno, the
most ancient in all Italy, was never anything but
a medical school. The University of Bologna, which

was so greatly renowned, which had eighty professorships, and whither flocked as many as twelve thousand students from all countries, was at first only
a school of Roman law. So, too, the University of
Padua comprised at the beginning only its chairs of
law." [1]

It is impossible, in fact, to avoid the conclusion
that the universities, when they began, did not in the
least resemble complete bodies of instruction. They
began by specialization. "Four cities," wrote St.
Thomas Aquinas toward the middle of the thirteenth
century, "surpass all others, *Parisius in scientiis, Salernum in medicinis, Bononia in legibus, Aurelianis*
(Orleans) *in actoribus*" (pleaders). It was in nowise
necessary that a school, a *studium generale*, desiring
to call itself a university, should be provided with
the four faculties: arts, theology, law, and medicine.
The University of Paris was itself incomplete, since
civil law was not taught there. It was only 1360
that Pope Innocent VI created a school of theology
at Bologna. Orleans was never more than a university of law, to use the expression then in vogue.[2]
The University of Avignon was opened in 1227 by the
establishment of a theological instruction destined to
combat heresy.[3] On the other hand, a great number
of universities either never had professors of theology, or did not have them at first. "Neither at

[1] Aubé, *Étude sur l'instruction publique en Sicile*. Paris, 1872,
p. 4.

[2] Étienne Pasquier, *Recherches de la France*, t. i, p. 989.

[3] Marcel Fournier, *Les statuts et privilèges des Universités françaises*. Paris, 1891, t. ii, p. 301.

Salamanca nor Coimbra, neither at Valladolid nor at Lerida, up to the fifteenth century," says a historian of the Spanish universities, " was there any theological instruction except a few chairs of canon law. It is a mistake to imagine that the point of departure for the universities was the idea of studying ecclesiastical science." [1]

At Paris dialectics and theology were emphasized, by reason of the movement started by Abelard; the study of civil law took the lead in the majority of the Italian universities, through a natural affinity with Rome, and thanks to the most carefully preserved traditions of Roman law; elsewhere, as in the universities of Spain, for example, under the more direct influence exerted in that country by Arabian physicians, the medical sciences came first; everywhere, in fine, for local reasons and particular circumstances, a special instruction is first developed. It stimulates intellectual effort in a limited field; then, little by little, the circle is enlarged; the awakened human mind stretches itself in all directions; studies of another order are grafted on the primitive stem, and new schools are seen to open beside the first.

At the same time exchanges are made, and, as it were, colonizations from city to city. Legists from Bologna introduced the study of law into the French universities, as, for example, at Montpellier. Parisian theologians carried their science and their methods to Oxford. And, thanks to these reciprocal relations, the universities, insensibly aggregating the different

---

[1] Vicente de la Fuente, *op. cit.*, t. i, p. 227.

kinds of studies then known, were for the most part able to constitute themselves with their new *quadrivium*: theology, law, medicine, and arts.

II

One mistake must be avoided. "University," at the outset, is not a synonym of the university of science, but simply of the university of persons, teachers, and students, *doctores et docendi,* who compose a group, an association of studies. The proof of this is that, in all the acts relating to the University of Paris in the thirteenth century, the word *universitas* is always followed by the genitives *magistrorum et scholarium.* In the letter by which Pope Innocent III in 1205, invited the professors of Paris to send some of their number to Constantinople to reform the studies there, these are the opening words: "*Universis magistris et scholaribus Parisiensibus,* to all the masters and scholars of Paris." And a few lines further on, the pope addresses the university in these terms: *Universitatem vestram rogamus.*[1] In the statutes given to the Medical Faculty of Montpellier, in 1220, by Cardinal Conrad, Legate of the Holy See, the author asks the opinion of the "University of the physicians of Montpellier, *tam doctorum quam discipulorum.*"[2] But what use is it to multiply testimony? It is unnecessary to recall that Orleans was never anything but a "University of law"; that at Bologna, in one and the same city, two universities were recog-

[1] *Chartularium Universitatis Parisiensis.*   Paris, 1889, t. i, pp. 62, 63.   [2] M. Fournier, *op. cit.,* t. ii, p. 4.

nized, that of law and that of arts. The question is not a doubtful one. *Universities,* in its primitive sense, merely signifies "association," "corporation." "In the language of the civil law," observes Malden, "all corporations were called *universitates,* as forming one whole out of many individuals. In the German jurisconsults *universitas* is the word for a corporate town. In Italy, it was applied to the incorporated trades in the cities. In ecclesiastical language the term was sometimes applied to a number of churches united under the superintendence of one archdeacon. In a papal rescript of the year 688 it is used of the body of the canons of the church of Pisa."[1]

No use can be made, as against the definition I have given of the word "university," of the ambiguity which might be created by the expression "*studium generale,*" constantly used, from the second half of the thirteenth century, to designate a centre of studies.[2] Nor does *studium generale* mean a school embracing the complete circle of sciences. Bologna, when it was still merely a school of law, Orleans, which has never been anything else, were *studia generalia* as truly as the most complete universities. The epithet *generale* was not applied in view of the extent or nature of the instruction, but simply of the fact that the lectures were public, open to everybody, accessible to students of all countries and all conditions. "The universities," says Laurie, "were *open to all*

[1] Professor Malden, *Origin of Universities,* p. 13.

[2] *Studium generale* should be understood as *congregatio generalis,* the *general* assembly of all the members of the university. Savigny is wrong in suggesting that the adjective *generale* relates to the privilege *docendi hic et ubique.*

without restriction as *studia publica* or *generalia*, as opposed to the more restricted ecclesiastical schools which were under a *Rule*."[1]

The universities then, at their origin, were merely academic associations, analogous, as societies of mutual guaranty, to the corporations of workingmen, the commercial leagues, the trade-guilds which were playing so great a part at the same epoch; analogous also, by the privileges granted to them, to the municipal associations and political communities which date from the same time. It was from the second half of the eleventh century that the Lombard and Tuscan cities rose against their sovereign bishops and formed themselves into a veritable republic, leagued among themselves, but independent and self-governing. If Italy, among all European countries, has been the one that saw the birth of the most universities in the thirteenth century, she certainly owes this to special social conditions, to the republican constitution of the majority of her cities.[2]   In the same way, it is during the twelfth century that the spirit of political liberty began to develop itself in France and the emancipation of the communes was accomplished.

On the other hand, the Crusades, while binding closer the ties and solidifying the relations between the peoples of Western Europe, excited the imagination, brought the Occident into contact with the Orient, with the civilization and science of the Arabs.

[1] Laurie, *op. cit.*, p. 101.

[2] Of the fifteen cities of Northern Italy which in 1226 founded the Second Lombard League, five had universities from the thirteenth century: Bologna, Vicenza, Padua, Vercelli, Plaisance.

They inspired an inclination for adventure and travel, and, in fine, uniting men of all ranks and countries by the impulse of a common enthusiasm, they opened the way to associations of another sort, founded, not for the deliverance of the Holy Land, but for the conquest of knowledge.

It is beyond doubt that the university associations modelled themselves upon the much older associations which sprang from the necessity of protecting commercial and industrial interests; either those which, in the interior of a city, grouped workmen of the same trade; [1] or those which, like the Hanse of Hamburg and of Lubeck (1241), united a certain number of industrial towns for the development of foreign commerce; or, finally, those travelling corporations which, square and trowel in hand, went from province to province, from city to city, to build their cathedrals. [2]

Established for an entirely different purpose, that of preserving and increasing the deposit of learning, the universities had, none the less, their own interests to defend, and a multitude of individuals to protect; and it is natural that, following the example, either of the merchants corporately leagued, or of the communes emancipated by royal charters, they should have sought to strengthen themselves, at first by solidarity, by the mutual assistance of all persons

[1] It was under the same king, Philip Augustus, that the University of Paris began to take form, and that the Parisian Hanse, or association of the water-sellers of Paris, was constituted.

[2] See, concerning this interesting question of the points of agreement between the trade-guilds and the universities, M. Bimbenet's work, *Histoire de l'Université de Lois d'Orléans*. Paris, 1853, p. 59 *et seq.*

composing them; and afterwards by the participation of all their members in the same franchises and privileges.

"I explain to myself," says a French writer, "how a single city could in the Middle Ages bring together bodies of students belonging to different provinces and different countries, by the analogy which this agglomeration of students bears to the agglomerations of traders of different nations in certain cities on the seacoast, where they have their separate banks, and even their separate markets."[1]

III

I have described what there was of spontaneity in the growth of the universities. But it is none the less true that these studious tendencies, these efforts at association, would very probably have resulted in nothing if they had not obtained the co-operation and favor both of the ecclesiastical and civil powers. I shall in the first place show this in relation to the Church and the popes.

It is incontestable that the protection, the kindly aid, of the papacy was gained from the very begin-

[1] Bouthors, *Coutumes de Picardie*, cited by Bimbenet, *op. cit.*, p. 73. Bimbenet reproduces several articles from the statutes of the guilds, the provisions of which are identical with those contained in the statutes of the universities; this, for example: "If one of the associates fall sick, the brethren shall visit him; if he happen to die, four brethren, nominated by the ancient (the dean) shall watch by the dead man, and bury his body; and all the associates shall accompany him. . . ."

nings of the universities.[1] One after another, the
popes granted, with the most cordial alacrity, the bulls
of erection or the confirmations of privileges solicited
by the kings and emperors.

The Church of the thirteenth century was no longer
minded, as a Council of Carthage had been, to pro-
scribe the study of letters. Without claiming that
the court of Rome had become a centre of liberal
ideas, some progress had been accomplished. The
days had gone by when a pope, Sylvester II (999–
1003), was accused by his contemporaries of having
transactions with the devil, because he had acquired,
chiefly in the Arabian schools of Spain, a certain
modicum of science; so that after his death it was
said: *Homagium diabolo fecit et male finivit.* Toward
the close of the twelfth century, the chair of St.
Peter was occupied by such a man as Alexander III
(1159–1181), who deserved to be called the *propug-
nator* of Italian liberties, for his support of the
league of the Lombard cities against the emperor of
Germany; at the commencement of the thirteenth
century, by Innocent III (1198–1216), who needed
nothing to interest him in the beginnings of the University of Paris but the recollection that he had
himself been one of its students;[2] by Honorius III
(1216–1227), who deposed a bishop for not having

[1] From 1200 to 1250 the *chartularium* of the single University of
Paris contains more than one hundred and fifty pontifical letters,
granting privileges, regulating studies, etc.

[2] Not only Innocent III, but Honorius III, Gregory IX (1227–
1241), and still other popes must be reckoned among the students
of the University of Paris. See Budinsky's work, *Die Universität
Paris,* Berlin, 1876, p. 189 *et seq.*

read Donatus, that is to say, for not having studied grammar.[1]

Moreover, the Church had as yet no reason to suspect an intellectual progress whose representatives seemed to have no other object than that of studying the faith, and of submitting themselves intelligently to dogmas henceforward explained and demonstrated by a compliant dialectic. The philosophy of that age was generally humble and modest — Abelard having been scarcely more than an exception — and it did not complain of being called the handmaid of theology (*ancilla theologiæ*). Doubtless the new establishments, thanks to the immunities and privileges whose possession was assured to them by the popes themselves, were more than once destined to be the antagonists of the papacy. But who could then divine, in the obscure beginnings, the éclat and the ambitions of the future? Doubtless the universities, by the intellectual travail they were to excite, bore the germs of the approaching liberty of thought, the Reformation and free philosophy. But who could then suspect that the human mind, encouraged in its efforts by the Church, would one day turn against the Church, that reason would not always be in accord with faith, that science could be something other than the confirmation of the traditional beliefs?

In generously according their patronage to the universities, in favoring the development and diffusion of human learning, the popes certainly believed that they were laboring only for the glory of God and the good of the Church. This conviction is shown in

[1] See Part III, chap. 1.

the almost identical terms by which the different pontifical bulls urge the importance of letters and the sciences. A few extracts will suffice to prove this.

In 1229, Gregory IX wrote to the king of France, Louis IX, to recommend to him the University of Paris, then disturbed by a students' riot. He reminds him that " wisdom is necessary, and that wisdom is nourished by the study of letters." [1] Now, what is wisdom, to a pope, except the Christian faith ? In 1231, in the emphatic language of the time, the same pope writes to the Parisian professors and students : [2] " Paris, mother of sciences, city of letters, . . . where, as in a special factory of wisdom (*in officina sapientiæ speciali*), . . . skilful men ornament and decorate the precious stones of the spouse of Christ. . . ."

The same language occurs in the fourteenth and fifteenth centuries. In 1331, in the bull of the foundation of the University of Cahors, John XXII expresses himself thus : " After having considered how precious is the gift of wisdom and knowledge, and how desirable it is to possess them, since by them the shadows of ignorance are dissipated (*ignorantiæ tenebræ profugantur*) and the obscurities of error dispelled, because they permit the curious intelligence of mortals to order and dispose their acts in the light of truth; . . . we desire ardently and with all our heart that the study of letters should everywhere flourish and be increasingly developed." [3]

In 1422, when he erected the little University of

---

[1] *Chartularium universitatis Parisiensis*, t. i, p. 128.

[2] *Ibid.*, p. 137.

[3] Baudel, *Histoire de l'Université de Cahors*, 1876, p. 10.

Dôle, in Burgundy, Martin V declared that "by the study of letters the worship of divine things increases (*divinorum cultus augetur*) and the Catholic faith is fortified." [1]

In 1431, at the time of the foundation of the University of Poitiers, Eugene IV proclaimed in his turn how well the study of letters, by dissipating the darkness of ignorance, comports with the public and private advantage, both temporal and spiritual, of the entire world. "Thanks to them, the worship of God is increased (*Dei cultus augetur*); they prepare the salvation of souls." [2]

In 1450, Nicholas V, in granting to the University of Barcelona the privileges of the University of Toulouse, considered that, thanks to the new *studium generale*, "the Catholic faith would be extended in that region (*ibidem fides Catholica dilatetur*)." [3]

It would be superfluous to multiply citations. Always and everywhere recur the same expressions, the same eulogies for "the pearl of science," the same homage to the universities considered as instruments for the propagation of faith and piety. It is not the only time in the history of humanity that an established power has been seen to prepare the way for its own decadence by protecting institutions which afterwards rise against it, and little by little promote its ruin. Are we not in our own day witnessing an analogous spectacle, when in every land we see the

[1] Beaune and d'Arbaumont, *Les Universités de la Franche Comte*, 1870: *Pièces justificatives*, p. 3.

[2] *Priviléges de l'Université de Poitiers*, 1726, p. 1.

[3] Vicente de la Fuente, *op. cit.*, t. i, p. 336.

ruling classes rivalling each other in their ardor to
multiply public schools, and thus making ready for
the advent of a new order of things, of a levelling
of society, the result of which, when accomplished,
will be to dispossess the ruling classes of their
privileges?

If a decisive proof is wanted of the part which
the popes expected the universities to play, it will be
sufficient to examine in what circumstances and for
what end one of the most important provincial universities of France, that of Toulouse, was created in
the opening years of the thirteenth century. The
Holy See was at that time occupied with the question of re-establishing the Catholic faith in a region
disturbed by heresy and the Albigensian war. The
creation of the Dominican order (1215) and the foundation of the University of Toulouse were due to the
same purpose. In 1217, in fact, Honorius III wrote
to the professors of Paris to invite them to go and
teach at Toulouse, "in that country," said he, "whose
inhabitants wish to return to God; where it is necessary to prevent venomous serpents from entering, and
where it would be fitting to transplant certain men,
who, by their lectures, their preaching, and their
exhortations, would ardently uphold the cause of
God."[1]   And in 1233, when he confirmed the erection of the new university, instituted by his legate
in 1229, Gregory IX expressed the hope that "the
Catholic faith, which seemed to be completely ruined
in these regions, might again flourish there, if a school
of letters (*studium litterarum*) were established."[2]

[1] M. Fournier, *op. cit.*, t. i, p. 437.   [2] *Ibid.*, t. i, p. 441.

The University of Toulouse then, in the opinion of the popes, was to be a bulwark established against the inroads and progress of heresy, a sort of fortress constructed in a hostile country, wherein to shelter and protect the orthodox faithful. And this idea of seeking a point of vantage in the universities, a counteraction to the heretical propaganda, shows itself again, and more forcibly, when, in the sixteenth century, the popes, in order to combat the Reformation, authorize the foundation of Jesuit universities, that of Pont à Mousson, for example.[1]

IV

By what idea were the emperors of Germany, the kings of France, and the other princes of the Middle Ages moved, when they united with the popes to assist the rising universities by their favor? Assuredly, it was not so much a disinterested affection for the study of science as it was a political forecast. In the first place they proposed to embellish and enrich their dominions by endowing them with public schools whose reputation, once established, might attract thither many foreigners, a source of glory, and of riches as well. But they thought afterwards — and the event more than once proved them to have been in the right[2] — that the universities which they

---

[1] See chap. iii.

[2] In 1688, Louis XIV wrote to the professors of the University of Poitiers: "Having seen the zeal and affection you have, both for our person and for the conservation of our right and those of our States —." . . . More than once the universities took sides for the King of France against the claims of the court of Rome.

called "their very dear daughters," would become,
thanks to the independence they enjoyed, centres of
influence and political action, and a solid support of
the royal power. "The universities," says M. Liard,
"are not merely the homes of science. They are also
schools of public spirit. In all times politicians have
regarded them as such."[1] Finally, the heads of the
State hoped that, recognizing the favors with which
they overwhelmed them, the universities would form
faithful subjects for the crown, just as the popes
expected that they would give good Christians to
the Church; that they would be schools of political
loyalty, as, on the other side, they were to be schools
of religious faith.

When Frederick Barbarossa instituted the University of Bologna, by his decree of 1158, he justified
the protection he promised to masters and disciples
by saying that "their science illuminated the entire
world, and that, thanks to it, subjects learned how
to live in obedience to God, and to the emperors,
who are the ministers of God."[2]

When he confirmed, in 1367, the privileges of the
university of the city of Cahors, then placed under
the domination of the English, Edward, Prince of
Wales, wrote: "It is befitting to crown with all the
gifts of our munificence those who teach how to distinguish the just from the unjust."[3] It is evident
that the study of law was preferred by princes, as
the study of theology was preferred by the popes.

---

[1] M. Liard, *Universités et Facultés.* Paris, 1890, p. 151.
[2] Coppi, *Le Universita Italiane nel medio evo.* Firenze, 1880,
p. 73.   [3] Baudel, *op. cit.,* p. 40.

In 1212, Philip the Fair, regulating the study of civil and canonical law at Orleans, declared that the science of laws and of written law is profitable for the development of reason, directs morals, and by doctrine prepares for the practice of justice and the understanding of what is customary." [1] It is not doubtful that considerations of utility attracted the sympathies of kings toward the juridical studies which would give them prudent counsellors, and legists expert in the management of affairs.

Just as several universities were organized by a *motu proprio* of popes, to combat the progress of heresy, so others were created by the will of kings, to combat the inroads of foreign politicians. It was thus that in 1331, in the midst of the Hundred Years war, the King of France, Charles VII, solicited from Pope Eugene IV the erection of the University of Poitiers. It was a question for him who had been derisively called the King of Bourges, of stirring up national sentiment by constituting, in a province which had remained faithful and French, a new centre of influence. And the proof is, that the King of England, Henry VI, by a sort of retort, hastened to reply to the establishment of the French University of Poitiers, by obtaining from the same pope, Eugene IV, the foundation of the University of Caen for Normandy in 1437, and, in 1441, that of the University of Bordeaux for Guienne. [2] Similar reasons determined Philip II of Spain to install a university at Douai

[1] M. Fournier, *op. cit.*, t. i, p. 36.

[2] See Barckhausen, *Statuts et règlements de l'ancienne Université de Bordeaux*. Bordeaux, 1860.

in 1561.[1] So, too, in the fifteenth century, King Louis
XI and Pope Pius II agreed to authorize the universities of Nantes in Brittany (1460), and of Bourges
in Berry (1463), the two provinces which sent most
students to Paris; they intended, by these creations,
to reduce and counterbalance the importance of the
University of Paris, which had compromised itself
at this epoch by supporting the Pragmatic Sanction
of Bourges.

Interests of every sort, then, have presided at the
formation of the universities. In Italy, says Coppi,
many *studia* were founded by the cities with a view
to increasing the population and the wealth of the
inhabitants.[2] Among this number were Pavia (1361)
and Ferrara (1391). The Republic of Florence
created its university in 1348, to repair the breaches
made by the pest in its population and prosperity.

Thus the most diverse causes contributed to the
birth of the universities and to assuring their success. Nevertheless, that which dominates all the
rest is that, in a society ignorant until then, the universities opened for the first time a free course to
the travail of the mind and the search for truth.
Thenceforward the rude cares of warfare or the prac-
tices of a blind devotion no longer absorbed the life
of the Middle Ages. With bad methods, doubtless,
and within very narrow limits, the universities were,
notwithstanding, superior schools. They responded
after their manner to the travail of the mind, the
vague longing after knowledge which thereafter tor-

[1] See Dehaisnes, *l'Université de Douai.* Douai, 1866.
[2] Coppi, *op. cit.*, p. 116.

ments human consciousness. Between the strong-holds of the nobles and the cathedrals of the bishops, they were the sanctuaries of study. As was eloquently said at the centenary of the University of Montpellier, by Professor M. Croiset: "Everywhere in Europe at that time, the two powers of the world, the Church and feudalism, attracted all attention, one by the boldness of its lofty cathedrals, the other by the massiveness of its dungeons. But between these two and at their feet, an obscure force is already active, composed of ideas in part, and in part of passions, a menacing force, aroused by instinct, and which does not itself know as yet either all that it wishes, or all that it can do."

CHAPTER III

THE RISE OF THE UNIVERSITIES

I

To give a complete idea of the origin of the universities, one should be able to relate the particular history of each of them, and to enter into details incompatible with the plan of this treatise. I must be content with certain general views, and set aside the particulars which abound, and which permit me to say that, during the thirteenth and fourteenth centuries at least, no two universities were founded under identical conditions. It is only in the fifteenth century that the formalities of institution for new universities were regulated. The civil power, a king, an emperor, or some nobleman, took the first steps, and solicited the pontifical power for a bull of erection. This bull, which was never refused, authorized the creation of the university, conceded privileges to it, and determined the number of faculties. Then the civil power intervened anew and confirmed the organization of the university by a definite act.

But in the thirteenth and fourteenth centuries, in the period of hesitancy and of laborious births, we must not expect to find this precision and this regularity of form. Sometimes, and most frequently, it was the pope who took the initiative; sometimes it was the head of the state. Thus John XXII founded the University of Cahors in 1332, and it was only in 1368 that the Prince of Wales, and in 1370 that Louis, Duke of Anjou and lieutenant of the king of France in Languedoc, conferred upon it the favor of a civil institution.[1] By an inverse proceeding, other universities were created by royal decree and waited years for the pontifical consecration. Salamanca was legally established in 1243, by privilege of Ferdinand III, king of Leon and Castile; and did not receive a bull from Pope Alexander IV, approving the foundation, until 1254.[2] So likewise the English University of Cambridge had been already recognized by royal authority in 1217; it is from this year, in fact, that its "earliest authentic legal instrument" is dated, an edict of the king, Henry III, addressed to all clerks of Cambridge; but it was

---

[1] Fournier, *op. cit.*, t. ii, pp. 553–558.

[2] Vicente de la Fuente, *op. cit.*, t. i, pp. 90, 312.

only a hundred years later, in 1318, that Pope John XXII accorded to Cambridge formal recognition as a *studium generale.* Sometimes the civil and the ecclesiastical authorities were not wholly in agreement. For example, Clement V erected the University of Orleans in 1306, through a sentiment of gratitude toward the schools of that city, where he had studied law; and 1312, the King of France, Philip the Fair, issued letters-patent which, while maintaining the University of Orleans, profoundly modified the privileges granted it by the pope.[1]

It is far from true, moreover, that all of the universities have had the double institution; many of them had to be content, some with a papal bull, others with a royal or imperial decree. There are even some, and among the number the most important and the most ancient, which erected themselves, so to speak, and which cannot exhibit in their *chartularium* any written act of institution. "The earliest universities," says Laurie, "grew and were not founded."

This is so true that Père Denifle, in his learned work on the universities of the Middle Ages,[2] has adopted as his principle of classification for the universities, and the basis of his labor, this diversity of origin. He distinguishes, in effect, four categories of universities : 1. The high schools, which organized themselves, without a written act of erection (*ohne Errichtungs-briefe*), — for example, Salernum, Oxford,

[1] Bimbenet, *op. cit.*, p. 15 *et seq.*
[2] *Die Entstehung der Universitäten des Mittelalters bis* 1400, Berlin, 1885.

Cambridge, Angers, Padua, etc.; 2. Those whose establishment was decreed by the pontifical will, — Rome, Pisa, Toulouse, Montpellier, Avignon, Cahors, etc.; 3. Those founded by a king or emperor, — Arezzo, Palencia, Naples, Orange, Salamanca, etc.; 4. Those, finally, and they were the least numerous during the period studied by Père Denifle, — that is to say, up to 1400, — which had the double investiture, — Prague, Vienna, etc.

Very few at the beginning, the universities rapidly multiplied themselves with a prodigious fecundity; and by the end of the fifteenth century there were already nearly eighty institutions of the sort presiding over the intellectual movement of Europe. It is to be remarked, moreover, that during three hundred years this movement went on accelerating from century to century. In the twelfth century there had been but a single official institution, — that of Bologna, in 1158; in the thirteenth century we reckon nineteen or twenty, most of them between 1200 and 1250; in the fourteenth, more than twenty-five; in the fifteenth century, thirty. Here is the list, with the description of their foundation: [1] —

[1] I omit a certain number of *studia* which appear to have claimed, unsuccessfully, the title of university; for example, in Italy, Reggio, where a school of law flourished toward the end of the twelfth century; Modena, which, after obtaining from Honorius III and Frederick III (1225 and 1226) the concession of privileges, was unable to stand the competition of Bologna, and soon disappeared. It was the same with Vicena (1204), etc.

Thirteenth Century

1200, *Paris;* privilege granted by Philip Augustus.

12—, *Oxford;* whose university constituted itself without any official sanction; the first royal recognition, a charter from Henry III, is dated in 1258.[1]

12—, *Cambridge;* which sprang from Oxford, and developed spontaneously like Oxford; letters-patent from Henry III in 1217 and 1231; a bull from Pope John XXII in 1318.

12—, *Arezzo;* which likewise dates from the first half of the thirteenth century; imperial recognition from Charles IV in 1355.

1212, *Palencia;*[2] in Spain, founded by Alfonso VIII, King of Castile.

1222, *Padua;* which arose from an emigration of Bolognese professors.

1224, *Naples;* Frederick II, Emperor of Germany.

1224–1228, *Verceil;* which arose from an emigration of professors from Padua.[3]

1229, *Toulouse;* Pope Gregory IX.

1243, *Salamanca;* Ferdinand III, King of Castile and Leon; confirmation in 1254 from Pope Alexander IV.

1244, *Curia Romana;* Pope Innocent IV; this school followed the popes to Avignon.

1245, *Valencia;* in Spain; James I, King of Aragon.

1248, *Plaisance;* in Italy; Innocent IV; the Duke of Milan, Galeazzo II, confirmed its privileges in 1398.

---

[1] Laurie affirms that Oxford had been "a true university" from 1140, and Cambridge from 1200; but he admits that "their university *organization* took its form about 1230, after the Paris migration." Laurie, *op. cit.*, p. 242.

[2] The university of Palencia had but an ephemeral existence. St. Dominic studied there.

[3] Verceil was never very important, and soon disappeared. On all the Italian universities, see Savigny, *Geschichte des römischen Rechts.*

1254, *Seville;* Alfonso X, the Wise, King of Castile and Leon.

1288, *Lisbon;* Denis, King of Portugal; Pope Nicholas IV transferred it to Coimbra in 1308.

1289, *Montpellier;* Pope Nicholas IV.[1]

1289, *Gray;* Otho IV, Count of Burgundy ; transferred to Dôle in 1423 by Philip the Good.

1293, *Alcala;* Sancho IV, King of Aragon.

1295, *Pamiers;* Pope Boniface VIII.

FOURTEENTH CENTURY

1300, *Lerida;* James II, King of Aragon and Sicily.

1303, *Rome;* Pope Boniface VIII.

1303, *Avignon;* Pope Boniface VIII.

1306, *Orleans;* Pope Clement V ; in 1312, King Philip the Fair.[2]

1307, *Perouse;* Clement V ; in 1355, the Emperor Charles IV.

1308, *Coimbra*, already organized toward the close of the thirteenth century, in 1279; successor to the University of Lisbon.

1310, *Dublin;* Pope Clement V.

1332, *Cahors;* Pope John XXII.

1339, *Grenoble;* the Dauphin, Humbert II ; Pope Benedict XII.

1343, *Pisa;* Pope Clement VI.

1346, *Valladolid;* Pope Clement VI.

1347, *Prague;* Pope Clement VI ; in 1348, the Emperor Charles IV.[3]

1349, *Florence;* confirmed in 1364 by Charles IV.

1349, *Perpignan;* Peter IV, King of Aragon; confirmed in 1379 by Clement VII.

[1] Montpellier had flourishing schools long before 1289. By 1220, the statutes for the teaching of medicine had been drawn up by a papal legate. In 1230 St. Louis regulated by an ordinance the promotions of the faculty of law.

[2] Orleans had been a university of civil law a hundred years before the formal recognition of 1306.

[3] Charles IV took the initiative, and asked the pope to institute this university.

1354, *Huesca;* Peter IV, King of Aragon; re-established in
    1464 by Pope Paul II.
1357, *Sienna;* from 1321, emigration to Sienna of professors
    from Bologna; privileges conceded, 1357, by the Em-
    peror Charles IV.
1361, *Pavia;* Charles IV; in 1389, Boniface VIII.
1365, *Vienna;* the Emperor Rodolphus IV; Pope Urban V.
1365, *Geneva;* the Emperor Charles IV.
1365, *Orange;* Charles IV.
1365, *Cracovia;* Casimir III, King of Poland; Urban V.
1367, *Fünfkirchen,* in Hungary; Urban V.
1367, *Angers;* Louis II, Duke of Anjou.[1]
1379, *Erfurt;* Pope Clement VII.
1385, *Cologne;* Pope Urban VI.
1385, *Heidelberg;* Pope Urban VI.
1389, *Ofen;* Boniface IX.
1391, *Ferrara;* Boniface IX; this university had been estab-
    lished by municipal statutes since 1263.

FIFTEENTH CENTURY

Würzburg, 1403; *Turin,* 1405; *Aix,* in Provence, 1409;
Leipsic, 1409; *St. Andrews,* Scotland, 1412; *Rostock,* 1419;
Dôle, 1423; *Louvain,* 1426; *Poitiers,* 1431; *Caen,* 1436;
Bordeaux, 1441; *Catana,* 1445; *Valence,* in France, 1452;
Treves, Glasgow, 1454; *Freiburg, Greifswald,* 1456; *Basel,*
1459; *Nantes,* 1460; *Besançon,* 1464; *Bourges,* 1469; *Ingol-*
stadt, 1472; *Saragossa,* 1474; *Copenhagen,* 1475; *Upsala,* 1476;
Tübingen, Mayence, 1477; *Parma,* 1482.

Who could deny, after merely glancing over this long
enumeration, the importance of the university movement in the last three centuries of the Middle Ages?
Doubtless among these universities many remained

[1] Angers had flourishing schools in the first half of the thirteenth
century.

obscure or had no effective existence. Occasionally
they were but the ephemeral adornment of over-
ambitious cities which did not possess the resources
necessary to make great schools prosper. Some of
them, born of the favoritism of popes or kings, or
owing their existence to a sort of local vanity, have
inscribed their modest titles for a few years only in
the history of the universities. But, on the other
hand, how many have remained glorious, and maintained to our own day, while undergoing a transformation, their useful and laborious existence?

In the sixteenth century the creations did not
slacken. The age of the Renaissance saw the birth
of more than thirty universities, among them some
which have left a mark in the history of letters
and sciences; for example, Aberdeen (1506), Königs-
berg (1542), Jena (1552), Leyden (1575), Edinburgh
(1582). Two special causes were added during the
sixteenth century to those general ones which, in that
epoch of renovation, were bound to multiply scholastic
foundations. On the one hand, the Reformation gave
rise to the institution of Protestant universities — the
first was that of Marburg, in 1527; on the other, the
creation of the Society of Jesus, among other pedagogic consequences, had that of the establishment of
Jesuit universities — for example, that of Messina,[1]
which Ignatius of Loyola organized in 1547 by send-

[1] The University of Messina was instituted, on paper, in 1459
by King John of Sicily. But it was not until 1550 that Pope Paul
III, at the request of Loyola, granted the bull of erection. The
Jesuits multiplied in Sicily, and in the eighteenth century they were
the masters of instruction throughout the island.

ing several members of his order thither; and that of
Pont à Mousson, also, which dates from 1572.[1]

Between 1600 and 1700, although most of the cities
that were able to support universities were already
provided with them, we see twenty-one more created,
chiefly in Germany and Holland, — France and Italy
having long since attained the maximum that they were
capable of reaching. Finally, in the eighteenth and
nineteenth centuries, without speaking of transatlantic
universities, of those which in America have constituted themselves the fortunate rivals and the vigorous
imitators of the universities of the Old World, more
than forty new universities have seen the light of
day in Europe.[2]

II

But I must go back and keep within the limits of
my subject. From the thirteenth century, England
with Oxford, Spain with Salamanca, France with
Paris, Italy with Bologna, leaving unmentioned the
universities of less importance, had each a focus of
instruction whose brilliancy streamed afar. Germany
was behindhand, — it is true that it has caught up
very well since, — and it was not until the fourteenth
century that it followed the movement. The first

[1] The University of Pont à Mousson in Lorraine was instituted
by Duke Charles III, and Pope Gregory XIII. See, concerning this
university, various opuscules by M. Favier, Nancy, 1878, 1880.

[2] Among this number are Berlin, 1810; Christiania, 1811; St.
Petersburg, 1819; Brussels, 1834; London, 1836; Athens, 1836. In
France the Revolution and the Empire suppressed the ancient universities, and at the present time the law which proposes to re-
establish them is being discussed in the French Senate.

German university, that of Prague, dates, in fact, from 1347. It will be interesting to review rapidly the history of the origins of those great universities of the thirteenth century — which one might call the mother-universities, because from them nearly all the others originated — and to show that similar circumstances presided at their formation.

At Paris the movement created by Abelard survived him. The influx of students from every nation was prodigious during the second half of the thirteenth century, and we are told that it was one of the causes which determined Philip Augustus to enlarge the circumference of Paris.[1] Men who had a great reputation in their time continued Abelard's instruction. Among the number was Gilbert de la Porrée, who taught theology. He also was a heretic, and was persecuted in his turn by St. Bernard, who procured his condemnation by the Council of Rome in 1148.[2] After him I may cite Peter Lombard[3] and Maurice de Sully, who succeeded Peter Lombard as Bishop of Paris in 1150; and who arrived as a mendicant, begging his bread, in the city where he was afterwards to teach philosophy and theology with so much renown, and to occupy its highest ecclesiastical dignity.[4] Popes Adrian IV (1154–1159) and Innocent IV (1198–1216) studied at Paris during

---

[1] Juvenal des Ursins, in 1435, affirmed that there had been from 16,000 to 20,000 students in Paris the previous year. Their number must have been still more considerable in the thirteenth century, when the universities were not yet multiplied.

[2] Gilbert de la Porrée (1070–1154).

[3] See chapter v.

[4] Maurice de Sully (1105–1196).

this period.   An English historian enumerates no
fewer than thirty-two eminent Oxonians who had also
studied at Paris, and among them Robert Grosseteste
and Roger Bacon.[1]   The schools of Mount Ste. Geneviève and of St. Victor had their *clientèle*, and the
cathedral school of Notre Dame continued to flourish.
And it was not from the ancient palatine school, long
before dispersed, but "from the reunion of the schools
of logic established on the mountain with the school
of theology that was in the cloister of Notre Dame,
that the University of Paris was formed." [2]

Bologna, like Paris, laid claim to very ancient
beginnings, and in Dezobry's *Dictionnaire de biogra-
phie et d'histoire* (1857) one may read: "The University of Bologna owes its origin to a school of law
founded by Theodosius II, in 425, and revived by
Charlemagne."   More enterprising still, certain historians of the University of Cambridge trace back
the foundation of their university to the fourth
century before Jesus Christ.   "The year 375 B.C.,"
wrote, in 1574, an adventurous author, "a son of the
king of Spain, named Cantaber, landed in England,
founded the town of Cambridge, and there instituted
a university, composed at first of philosophers and
astronomers whom he had brought with him from
the city of Athens." [3]

Something must be abated from these pretensions
to antiquity.   As a school of law, Bologna does not

---

[1] Mullinger, *op. cit.*, p. 134.   [2] Thurot, *op. cit.*, p. 7.

[3] Concerning these legends, see Mullinger, *op. cit.*, p. 450.   The
fabulous tradition related above proceeds from the English doctor,
John Caye.

appear to date earlier than the twelfth century. In the commencement of that century the professors of jurisprudence occupied an important position there. From 1123 they composed one of the three sovereign assemblies of the city of Bologna, — that which was called the Council of Credence (Consiglio di Credenza). It was in 1137 that Irnerius taught there, and he was the true founder of this university, as we shall see later on.[1]

In England, for the mother-university, that of Oxford, there was a slow and progressive preparation. Here we have not to go back to the remote beginnings, to the influence exercised in the eighth century by the celebrated Bede,[2] of whom an English writer has said that, "in his tomb science was enshrouded during four centuries"; nor to the part played by Alfred the Great, and the efforts to regenerate studies in his realm, which he made in the ninth century in imitation of Charlemagne. I need only say that at that epoch Oxford possessed flourishing schools. They were twice pillaged and destroyed by the Danish invasions, but by the eleventh century they had regained their old position. The rhetoric of Cicero and the logic of Aristotle were studied there.[3] After having suffered further loss at the time of the Norman conquest, Oxford, thanks to the protection of Henry I, third son and second successor of William the Conqueror, again became a centre of studies.

[1] See Part III, chap. iii, where I shall have occasion to return to the founder of the University of Bologna.

[2] Bede, an English monk and historian (673–735).

[3] Vallet de Viriville, *Histoire de l'instruction publique en Europe*, 1869, p. 100.

Undoubtedly there were then none of those scholastic palaces which arose there in the course of time. It is related that the lecture-halls and the houses where the students lodged were built of wood and thatched with straw, and were thus at the mercy of the fire which devoured them in 1130. But students flocked thither none the less. More than elsewhere, perhaps, the protection of the higher clergy was gained in England for the rising universities; and, on the other hand, the religious orders, the Franciscans and Dominicans, played a great part in the revival of studies.

One man who has left many memories of himself in his own country, Robert Grosseteste (1175–1253), contributed particularly toward this movement. The first half of the thirteenth century in England has been designated "the age of Robert Grosseteste,"[1] just as, in France, the first half of the twelfth century might be called the age of Abelard. "He was," says Laurie, "a patriot and a scholar and a humanist."[2] He had studied at Oxford, at Cambridge, and at Paris. After becoming Bishop of Lincoln, he did not cease to foster learning: by his writings he popularized the works of Aristotle. And it was not merely Greek books, in the form of translations, that he introduced into the English schools; Mullinger affirms that he sought to attract Greek scholars to England.

One name will serve to show what the intellectual development of England was in the thirteenth cen-

---

[1] Mullinger, *The University of Cambridge*, 1873, p. 84.
[2] Laurie, *op. cit.*, p. 239.

tury, — that of the monk Roger Bacon (1214–1294).
Roger Bacon, before studying in Paris, had studied
at Oxford; then he established himself in England.
By the freedom of his researches and the boldness
of his experiments he aroused the fanaticism of his
contemporaries, and was accused of magic. At the
same time, uniting a love of antiquity to a taste for
investigation in the natural sciences, he collected the
masterpieces of classic literature at great expense,
and, for his time, became a Humanist of the first
rank.

The University of Salamanca was the queen of
Spanish universities. Founded about the year 1200,
it did not receive its official charter until 1243,
from the hands of Ferdinand III, King of Castile
and Leon. But from its very beginning it took its
place in the first rank, among the great centres of
instruction. It took part in drawing up the celebrated astronomical tables of the King of Castile,
Alfonso X, the Wise. Like the University of Paris,
it was mixed up with the great religious quarrels of the age, and took part in the schism of the
West by pronouncing for the popes of Avignon.[1]
It must not be forgotten that, later on, in the fifteenth century, it lent a courageous support to
Christopher Columbus, that it alone had faith in
the success of his great adventure, and that in the
Convent of the Dominicans of St. Stephen, whose
house is still in existence at Salamanca, the project
of navigation to which the fifteenth century owed

[1] Henry VIII, King of England, consulted it in 1527 concerning
his divorce from Katharine.

the discovery of America, was discussed and approved. In the sixteenth century the University of Salamanca was teaching the Copernican system, while Galileo was in prison. More than once it gave professors to Bologna and to Paris.[1] The bachelors of Salamanca remained celebrated up to the eighteenth century. All through the Middle Ages, more than four thousand students pursued there a course of instruction as complete and as various as that imparted at Paris.

The question has been much discussed in Spain as to whether or no the University of Salamanca was derived from that of Palencia, which was founded some years earlier, in 1212.[2] What is certain is that in the twelfth century there were important schools in Salamanca, schools which, like those of Paris, were installed in the cloister of the cathedral. It is also established that, from the beginning, medical studies took an important place in the University of Salamanca; and that the inspiration of these schools came from Arabian physicians. In the tenth century, Gerbert, before becoming Pope Sylvester II, went to seek in the Mohammedan academies in the south of Spain more thorough instruction than he had been able to find in the Christian schools of France. The presence of the Moors and the brilliancy of Arabian science, the philosophy of Averroes, and the medicine

[1] In the sixteenth century, a canon of Salamanca, Peter Cizuelo, taught mathematics at Paris; and, at the same epoch, Bologna borrowed Ramos de Pareja, who passes for the inventor of modern music, from Salamanca.

[2] Vicente de la Fuente, *op. cit.*, t. i, p. 76.

of Avicenna, exercised a manifest influence on the development of studies at Salamanca. Here, then, as elsewhere, there was a scholastic movement which preceded royal ordinances; although the individual action of sovereigns particularly favorable to the sciences, of a king who was a mathematician and astronomer, for example, like Alfonso the Wise, may have contributed much to the development of the University of Salamanca.

III

The example once given by the "mother-universities," the foundation of other universities was merely a question of imitation. Paris especially was imitated. "The Universities of Oxford and Cambridge in England, of Prague, Vienna, Heidelberg, and Cologne in Germany, derived their formal constitution, the tradition of their education, and their modes of instruction from Paris. The influence of this university has indeed emboldened some writers to term her 'the Sinai of instruction' in the Middle Ages."[1]

When the Emperor Charles IV organized, in 1348, the first German university, that of Prague, which had been authorized in 1347 by a bull of Clement VI, he drew upon his memories as a former student of the University of Paris. As Döllinger says, "in memory of his student life in the Rue de Fouarre, he wished to have a copy of the University there in his

[1] Mullinger, *op. cit.*, p. 74.

hereditary kingdom of Bohemia."[1] So, too, in 1385,
when Pope Urban VI organized the University of
Heidelberg, still so flourishing, the pontifical bull
states that the new *studium generale* would be established according to the hallowed formula, *ad instar
studii Parisiensis.*[2] Vienna, for its part, whose university dates from 1365, claimed to continue the traditions of Athens, of Rome, and of Paris.[3] Paris had
succeeded to the literary capitals of the ancient world.
Paris, said St. Bonaventura, is the source whence the
streams of science spread over the whole world.

In England, French influence shone with no less
brilliancy. Oxford, which according to Laurie "was
entitled to the name 'Universitas' about 1140,"[4] and
which in any case comprised a great number of students at the end of the twelfth or the beginning of the
thirteenth century, since in 1209, says a contemporary
chronicler, when an emigration to Cambridge occurred,
*recesserunt ab Oxonia tria millia clericorum tam magis-
trorumquam discipulorum,*[5] — Oxford was several times
stimulated and improved by the coming of foreign
professors from Bologna, and especially from Paris.
It was Vacarius, a Bolognese, who in 1149 tried to
install the study of Roman law there; but it was a
former student of Paris, an Englishman by birth,

[1] Charles IV, says an author of his time, ordained that " *Studium Pragense ad modum et consuetudinem studii Parisiensis,
in quo olim ipse rex in puerilibus constitutus annis studuerat, in
omnibus et per omnia dirigeretur et regeretur,*" Denifle, *Die Entstehung der Universitäten,* etc., p. 588.

[2] Denifle, *op. cit.,* etc., p. 382.   [3] Denifle, *op. cit.,* etc., p. 605.

[4] Laurie, *op. cit.,* lecture xiii, Oxford and Cambridge.

[5] Denifle, *op. cit.,* p. 242.

moreover, Robert Pulleyne, who in 1130 "endeavored
to revive the teaching of theology, and succeeded in
infusing a higher spirit into the Oxford schools." [1]
Later, in 1228, when, after a students' riot and the
reprisals provoked by it, the masters and students of
Paris emigrated in great numbers, it was not only in
the studious towns of France, in Angers, Orleans, and
Rheims, that they took shelter, but also in Oxford and
Cambridge. Henry III, King of England, had invited
them thither in a letter the text of which has been
preserved : *"Duximus vestræ Universitati significandum
quod si vobis placeat ad regnum nostrum Angliæ vos
transferre . . . civitates, burgos vel villas quascumque
velitis eligere vobis ad hoc assignabimus."* [2] This appeal
was listened to. The migrating masters repaired in
part to Oxford, and, says Laurie, "they would carry
the genius of Paris with them."

It is hardly necessary to say that the provincial
universities of France have been, for the most part,
faithful copies of the University of Paris ; Montpellier must be excepted, since it drew its inspiration
partly from Bologna. It is true that, in the papal
bulls relating to the universities, it is almost invari-
ably written that they should be organized *ad instar
studii Tolosani.* But the University of Toulouse itself,

[1] Robert Pulleyne wrote a book of *Sentences*, which is thought
to have suggested that of Peter Lombard, which became the hand-
book of theology in the schools of the Middle Ages.

[2] *Chartularium Univ. Paris.*, t. i, p. 119. The University College was founded at Oxford four years later, in 1232. In 1240,
Robert Grosseteste ordered the professors of theology at Oxford
to conform, in their lectures, to the usages followed at Paris.
Ibid., p. 169.

the most ancient after Paris, was modelled after the
great Parisian school; the privileges were the same,
and, due allowances being made, the studies were
similar. Through Toulouse, then, it was Paris which
was copied everywhere, at Orleans, Angers, Poitiers,
Caen, Bordeaux, etc.

Even in Spain, where, nevertheless, Bologna and
Montpellier had much influence, a strictly French
influence made itself felt. When the King of Aragon, James II, established the University of Lerida
in 1300, he affirmed in his decree that "the Holy
See granted to the new *studium* the same indul-
gences, immunities, and favors already granted to the
Studium of Toulouse." [1] In the previous century,
Alfonso VIII, King of Castile, had constituted the
University of Palencia by inviting "masters of theology and the liberal arts from France and Italy, to
whom, in order to retain them, he assigned large salaries " (*Sapientes e Gallia et Italia convocavit, quibus
magna stipendia est largitus*).[2] So, too, it was the
privileges of the University of Toulouse that Pope
Nicholas V conceded in 1450 to the University of
Barcelona. When Pope Paul II restored the University of Huesca in 1464, he gave it Toulouse, Montpellier, and Lerida as models. Finally, in the bull of
Sixtus IV, in favor of the University of Saragossa
(1474), it is said that the *studium generale* would be

---

[1] Vicente de la Fuente, *op. cit.*, t. i, p. 304.

[2] Denifle, *op. cit.*, p. 474. The *stipendia*, the appointments, naturally played a great part in the prosperity of universities. An
inscription, which may still be seen at Salamanca, says of the university of that city: *illa deficientibus stipendiis defecit*, — until it
was reorganized by Alfonso X.

founded there *ad instar* of the Universities of Paris and of Lerida.

It was from France, again, that Portugal borrowed in part the first elements of university organization. At the close of the thirteenth century, King Alfonso III, who had travelled in France, brought back with him two scholars, Domingos Jardo, a Portuguese, but a doctor of canon law in the University of Paris, and Aymeric d'Hébrard, a nobleman of Quercy.[1] It was with the aid of these two advisers that the kings of Portugal proceeded to the establishment of their national university, installed successively at Lisbon and at Coimbra.

Next to Paris, the University of Bologna had most imitators. The universities of Italy, that of Naples excepted, sprang directly or indirectly from Bologna. That of Padua, in 1222, was founded by a colony of professors from Bologna; so was that of Sienna, in the fourteenth century. "The intellectual movement of the northeast of Italy," M. Renan has said, "is altogether connected with that of Padua. Now the Universities of Padua and Bologna were really only one, at least as far as the philosophical and medical instruction was concerned. The same professors migrated nearly every year from one to the other, to obtain an increase of their salaries." [2] Bologna, however, extended its influence to foreign countries: in

---

[1] Aymeric d'Hébrard was the preceptor of the son of Alfonso III, Denis the Liberal, who founded the University of Lisbon. From 1130 it was customary at Coimbra to send certain canons of the Order of St. Augustine to study in France.

[2] Renan, *Averroés et l'Averroisme*, 1852, p. 258.

France, the Universities of Montpellier and Grenoble were copied after Bologna. It was Placentin,
a Bolognese, who introduced the study of law at
Montpellier.[1]

The multiplication of universities would have been
impossible without these mutual loans and exchanges.
Throughout the entire Middle Ages, there was a perpetual passing to and fro of masters and students
from one country to another, — from France to England, from Italy to France, and back again, — or, in
the same country, going in turn from one city to
another city, from one school to another school. I
may cite some examples. Peter Lombard, the *Master
of the Sentences*, as he is called, the uncontested chief
of theological instruction in the Middle Ages, whose
classic work enjoyed so great an authority that, according to Crevier, — who had counted them, — it has
had 244 commentators — almost as many as Aristotle;
Peter Lombard studied successively at Bologna,
Rheims, and Paris. The successor of Abelard, but
more circumspect than he in the application of dialectics to theology, Peter Lombard did not wholly
escape the criticism of the orthodox, — of theologians
who were alarmed by the freedom of his logic, and
who claimed that the subtleties of dialectics were
"like a fine and minute dust, blinding the eyes of
those who stir it up."[2] Twenty-six erroneous articles are counted up in his doctrines, — making him
quite a "heretic." He maintained that "Jesus
Christ, in so far as he was man, was nothing," — a
proposition from which sprang the sect of "nihilists."

[1] See Part III, chap. iii.   [2] Crevier, *op. cit.*

One was a "nihilist" on easy terms in those days. So, too, a writer justly celebrated in the twelfth century, Peter of Blois, first studied letters and philosophy at Tours and at Paris, then went to Bologna, about 1160, to follow the lectures on law, and afterwards returned to Paris to take up theological studies. He finally ended his career in England.[1] This example is particularly striking, because it shows how, before the foundation of universities which later reunited in the same city and in one centre all sorts of studies, a man eager for learning was obliged to go seeking, from city to city and in special schools, the different branches of human knowledge. John of Salisbury is another example of how these learned peregrinations were then obligatory for all students. Born about 1100, at Salisbury, in England, we have found him in Paris, in 1136, an enthusiastic auditor of Abelard. He spent not less than twelve years in the schools of France, exercising himself in theology, under the direction of Robert of Melun (an Englishman who was teaching at Melun), in grammar with William of Conches (himself a pupil of Bernard of Chartres), and in mathematics and rhetoric under other masters. He taught in Paris about 1145; but he afterwards returned to England, where he was for some time attached to the church of Canterbury. Then he travelled in Italy, and finally returned to France, where he died, Bishop of Chartres, in 1180.

[1] Peter of Blois died about 1198, in England, where he had become an important personage. See the *Histoire littéraire de la France*, t. xv, p. 341 *et seq.*

The beginnings of the University of Cambridge
show plainly how the displacements and migrations
of nomadic professors or members of religious orders,
travelling from one country to another, scattered the
seed of science on fresh soil. Montalembert thus
describes the origin of Cambridge : " Four Norman
monks, transplanted from Saint Evroul, in France, to
Croyland, in England, with the eloquent and learned
Abbot Joffride, formerly professor at Orleans, con-
cluded to open a public course of lectures in a
granary which they hired near the gate of the town
of Cambridge. But, as neither this granary nor other
still larger edifices were able to contain the throng
of men and women who soon hastened to listen to
them, the monks of Croyland conceived the notion
of organizing the instruction given by the professors,
on the plan of the monastic exercises of the order.
Thus, Brother Odo was deputed to teach grammar,
according to Priscian and Remy, at daybreak; at
Prime, Brother Terric taught Aristotle's logic with
the comments of Porphyry and Averroes; at Tierce,
Brother William, the rhetoric of Cicero and Quintilian ; while, on every holiday, Brother Gislebert,
the most learned member of the community, explained the Sacred Scriptures to the priests and to
the scholars, and, moreover, preached every Sunday
to the people, in spite of his unfamiliarity with the
English language. Such was the beginning of the
University of Cambridge, — a feeble rivulet, which
soon became, according to the expression of a French
monk, Peter of Blois, a great stream which fertilized
all England." [1]

[1] De Montalembert, *Les Moines d'Occident*, t. vii, p. 650.

Even after the universities had been constituted, the international exchange of students and of masters did not cease. The papacy, which protected the universities because it counted on directing them, aided by its universal domination in facilitating their relations and the reciprocal services they rendered to each other. It was in vain that certain cities, through self-love and local interests, sought to isolate their universities: Florence, for example, prohibited Florentines to study anywhere but at Florence, under penalty of heavy fines. A current stronger than national rivalry reunited all the universities of Europe in a sort of federation. There was then, in spite of incessant wars, in spite of invasions, in spite of the hatreds between peoples, there was above all the frontiers a European alliance of all the superior schools, a something like the United States of universities. And in this assemblage of almost similar schools, it was Paris that held the leadership. Even at Bologna, the college of theology, annexed to the university by Pope Innocent IV in 1362, was formed on the model of the theological faculty of Paris. Parisian professors were called to the German universities of the fourteenth century. The first rector of the University of Heidelberg, Marsilius de Inghen, had been rector of the University of Paris. It was not a pious illusion, it was truth itself, which inspired Duboulay, when, in the title of his book, he described most of the other universities as daughters of the University of Paris: *quæ ex eadem communi matre excesserunt.*

PART II

*THE ORGANIZATION OF THE EARLY
UNIVERSITIES*

CHAPTER I

PRIVILEGES OF THE UNIVERSITIES

I. The university privileges a derivation from the privileges conceded to the Catholic clergy — Privileges an important cause of the prosperity of the early universities — II. The first university privilege that conferred on Bologna by Emperor Frederick I in the decree *Habita* (1158) — Exceptional or internal jurisdiction of universities — The right of *non trahi extra* — III. Exemption from all personal taxes and contributions and from military service — IV. The right of *cessatio* — Historical examples — V. Other minor privileges — The privileges and immunities extended to all members of a university.

I

ONE might say that there were no privileges, properly speaking, in the Middle Ages; privileges, technically speaking, being abrogations of the common law, and common law, that is to say, a uniform rule for all, not existing at that period. The truth is that there were privileges on all sides; privileges for the clergy, privileges for the nobility, privileges for the communes and for the cities. Every class of men, every community, every city, aspired to live a life of its own, to obtain a relative independence, to have its special system of jurisprudence. Possessing the favor of the spiritual sovereign as well as of the temporal ones, the universities had their share at once, and a very considerable share, of exceptional

73

immunities and franchises. They formed little republics, states within the state, using, and sometimes abusing, the very rights which they held from
kings and from the Holy See, to enter into conflict
with kings and with the Holy See. Almost exclusively ecclesiastical at the outset, — for the majority
of their members belonged to the clergy, — they were
naturally admitted to a participation in the privileges
already enjoyed by the religious orders and the members of the Church in general. "The whole body of
the Catholic clergy," says Gibbon, "was exempted
from all service, private or public, all municipal
offices, and all personal taxes and contributions which
pressed on their fellow-citizens with intolerable weight,
and the duties of their holy profession were accepted
at a full discharge of their obligations to the republic." So it was that when popes or kings extended
these exemptions to the rising universities, the city
governments took no umbrage at it.

And these privileges, granted in the first place to
semi-ecclesiastical academic corporations, were preserved by the universities as, little by little, they
were secularized. The importance of higher study
justified the favors which had originally been authorized by religious sentiment. The language of
the Middle Ages affords proof of this: the word
clericus, clerk, at first signified one who was studying
in order to enter the ecclesiastical state. It was
afterward applied to any learned or educated person.
The immunities, likewise, which none but ecclesiastics
had previously profited by, were granted in the twelfth
and thirteenth centuries to all whom the universities
sheltered under their patronage.

It is to be remarked, moreover, that as a favor accorded to the taste for study, the university privileges of the Middle Ages were not altogether a novelty. "At the time of Vespasian, certainly not long after," says Laurie,[1] "immunities were granted. The Medici and the professors of liberal, arts, who taught in the Roman capital and large provincial towns, were exempted from imperial taxes, from service in war, and from discharging municipal duties, except when they were desirous to do so. These privileges were, of course, extended to the University of Constantinople. Constantine, in his edict of A.D. 321, continues and confirms past privileges as they had existed in all parts of the Empire (*vide* Theod. Code, iii, tit. iii, I)."

That the enjoyment of their privileges, apostolic or royal, was one of the chief causes of the prosperity of the universities, is demonstrated by every page of their history. More than once the University of Paris, obliged to defend its threatened exemptions, has forcibly demonstrated, in its representations to the kings of France, that it could not be divested of them without risk of driving away its students, or at least sensibly diminishing their number. Who can tell the number of masters and of pupils whose desire for study has been encouraged by the prospect of enjoying the favors granted to members of the universities? This will be better understood by those who examine with me the nature and importance of those privileges.

[1] Laurie, *op. cit.*, p. 200. The Theodosian Code justified the privileges accorded to the universities by these words: "Quo facilius liberalibus studiis et artibus multos instituant."

II

The first example of the privileges granted to universities must be sought for in the imperial constitution, the *Habita*, promulgated in 1158, at the Diet of Roncaglia, by Frederick Barbarossa, to the masters and students of Bologna.[1] "We will," said the Emperor of Germany in this memorable document, "that the students, and above all, the professors of divine and sacred laws, may be able to establish themselves and dwell in entire security in the cities where the study of letters is practised. It is fitting that we should shelter them from all harm. Who would not have compassion on these men who exile themselves through love of learning, who expose themselves to a thousand dangers, and who, far from their kindred and their families, remain defenceless among persons who are sometimes of the vilest?" And, in consequence, Frederick I decreed in the first place that any person against whom a student had to bring a suit, whether it were to demand the punishment of an offence or to obtain the payment of a debt, this person, though he might dwell in a distant province, should be tried in the place where the student resided; that is to say, in Bologna. Afterwards — and this is the most important point, for it contains the principle of an internal or at any rate exceptional, jurisdiction granted to the members of the university — the Emperor said: "If any person, for any cause whatsoever, wishes to bring

[1] See the complete text of the *Habita* of Frederick I, in Coppi's work, already cited, p. 73.

an action against students, he must cite them, according to their own choice, before their Professor or before the Bishop of the city." Thus, on one hand, Frederick I granted Bolognese students, when they were plaintiffs, the right to summon their adversaries for judgment to the place of their university residence; and, on the other, when they were accused, he freed them from the ordinary jurisdiction by leaving them their choice between an ecclesiastic or a university tribunal.[1] These two privileges, with some variations, were successively granted, either by civil governments or pontifical authority, to the different universities, and, of course, to the professors as well as to the students.

It was thus that, about 1198, a decree of Pope Celestine III decided that, for clerics residing in Paris, all suits relative to money matters should be tried before ecclesiastical and not before secular judges. "Bishops and clerics," said the pope, "have their own judges in fact, and they have nothing in common with the laws of the state."[2] And before this, about 1170, Alexander III, because of material injuries and also of a sentence of excommunication of which the students of Rheims complained, hastened

---

[1] The Latin text says: "... *coram domino aut magistro suo, vel ipsius civitatis episcopo.*" The word *domino* may seem equivocal. It has been variously interpreted. Some have sought to translate it by *seigneur*, lord; but Crevier, Savigny, and the majority of commentators suppose with reason that *dominus* simply means professor, and that *magister* was added so as to mark more clearly the sense of *dominus*. At Bologna the professors were often styled *domini legum*.

[2] "... *nec quidquam est eis publicis commune cum legibus*" (*Chartularium Univ. Paris.*, t. i, p. 12).

to recognize the justice of their position "when they claim that no one has the right to use violence toward them, nor to dare pronounce against them an ecclesiastical sentence, until it shall please them to appear judicially before their professors."[1] The popes were simply taking the course natural to them when they sought to extend the jurisdiction of ecclesiastical tribunals. But, which is more remarkable, the kings themselves, confirming the decisions of the sovereign pontiffs in every point, did not hesitate to limit the secular authorities in everything that concerned the universities. In 1200, in consequence of a quarrel that arose between the students and the citizens, in which the Provost of Paris had put himself at the head of the armed populace, and a student had been slain, Philip Augustus took sides energetically with the students. In the first place, he granted them a signal reparation. The provost was condemned to perpetual imprisonment, unless he preferred to submit to the ordeal by water, with the condition that if he succumbed under it he should be hanged. But for the future, in his ordinance of 1200, which may be considered the first official charter of the University of Paris, the king decreed that the students should be tried only by the ecclesiastical tribunal, that is to say, by the Episcopal Court of Paris. No student, no matter who he might be, could be arrested by an ordinary judge, unless there were urgent necessity for it, and with the proviso that he should instantly be remitted into the hands of the ecclesiastical judge.

---

[1] " ... donec coram magistro suo velint justitia stare (*Ibid.*, p. 5, et seq.).

And as to the chief of the students (*capitale scho-larium*), "our courts," said the king, "cannot lay hands upon him for any crime whatever"; [1] this was to proclaim, before the ordinary court of the provost of Paris, the almost absolute inviolability of the members of the university.

At Padua, in 1262, a law provided that the Podesta could not interfere in the brawls that occurred among the students, unless, at the end of two days, the affair had not been settled by the rector and professors. [2] It is to be noted that in Italy the right of internal or university jurisdiction was the rule generally followed in granting privileges, while in France it was the right of ecclesiastical jurisdiction that was most often granted.

There were, moreover, in Italy, from one university to another, and especially from century to century, considerable alterations in the judicial power of the university officers. The professors and rectors grew weary of exercising the functions of a criminal court, in which their professorial authority might be weakened; they preferred to retain civil jurisdiction only. At Verceil, for example, criminal matters were exclusively remitted to the city magistrates. At Rome, foreign students might choose as their judges either the professors, the cardinal vicar, or the rector of the university. At Naples, the criminal jurisdic-

[1] *Chartularium Univ. Paris.*, t. i, p. 59, " ... *In capitale Parisiensium scholarium pro nullo forifacto justitia nostra manum mittet.*"

[2] Coppi, *op. cit.*, p. 171. The Podesta was an imperial magistrate who had been established in place of a consul by Frederick I, after his victories in Italy.

tion fell to a magistrate appointed by the king, who was styled the justice (*justitiarius*). Civil suits were brought either before the justice, the professor, or the archbishop, at the choice of the contending parties. At Turin, the rector took part in the decision, even in the criminal cases transferred to the communal magistrates.

Certain details are still necessary in order to clear up, in the midst of the confusion created in the Middle Ages by the multiplicity of jurisdictions of every sort, the obscure and complex question of the privileges of the universities in this matter. When Gregory IX, in 1233, confirmed the foundation of the University of Toulouse, he formally prohibited that "either masters or scholars, either clerics or their domestics (*servientes eorum*), if they became guilty of any misdeed, should be judged by a layman." [1] He decreed, moreover, that laymen should be bound to appear before the ecclesiastical judges in any suits whatever that might be brought against them by the students. Orleans, Poitiers, Caen, and Bordeaux, whose universities were founded on the model of that of Toulouse, obtained the same privileges from the popes.

In the statutes given to the Medical Faculty of Montpellier, in 1220, by the Legate of the Holy See (which statutes were confirmed in 1258 by Alexander IV), we read as follows: "The Bishop of Maguelonne, after associating with himself as auxiliaries one of the oldest masters, and two other masters chosen from among those who are most discreet and honorable (*discretiores et laudabiliores*) should, in concert

[1] M. Fournier, *op. cit.*, t. i, p. 441.

with these auxiliaries, elect a master, either from
among these three auxiliaries or from the other masters, who shall administer justice, both to the masters
and scholars and to those who shall bring suits against
másters and scholars." [1] These regulations applied
to civil suits only; the Bishop of Maguelonne alone
took cognizance of criminal matters.

As may be seen, there were numerous variations
and a real complication in the rules established for
the purpose of giving the universities an exceptional
position before the law. While at Montpellier the
members of the university were judged in civil questions by a university professor, at Paris similar matters came under the jurisdiction of the provost,
constituted as "guardian of privileges." While in
Italy criminal suits were usually referred to the
municipal magistrates, in France they were brought
before the ecclesiastical tribunals. So, too, trials
relating to benefices held by a member of the University of Paris were tried, at his choice, before
the Bishops of Beauvais, of Meaux, or of Senlis. [2]
While admitting that these exceptional jurisdictions
conferred an incontestable advantage on both masters
and scholars, it must also be recognized that the
Church profited by them, since she substituted her
own courts for the secular ones by imposing ecclesiastical jurisdiction even on laymen who brought suits
against the members of the universities. The rising
universities were not, to tell the truth, anything more

[1] M. Fournier, *op. cit.*, t. ii, p. 5.
[2] This was established by a bull of Clement V in 1358. See
Crevier, *op. cit.*, t. ii, p. 209.

than dismembered parts of the ecclesiastical body; and it was only very gradually that they broke the filial bonds which united them to the Church. At Paris, for example, Parliament little by little absorbed the ecclesiastical jurisdiction.[1]

But what the universities preserved to the end was the special right conceded by Frederick I to the Bolognese, which at Paris was called the right of *non trahi extra,* which the historians of the Parisian University name also the *committimus,* and which the kings of France designated in their letters-patent by the strange expression *du droit de garde gardienne.*[2] This consisted, as I have already said, in the right of the members of the university, whether as defendants or as plaintiffs, to have their cases tried at their place of residence. The University of Poitiers thus justified this privilege in 1674: "The masters and students could not attend to their suits or prosecute them, not, at any rate, without abandoning their employments, functions, and studies, if they were obliged to bring them anywhere except before the judges of the aforesaid Poitiers."[3]

An example will make the importance of this privilege better understood. In 1358, the valets of the Bishop of Lisieux had stolen a horse from some of the students of the University of Paris. The

---

[1] In 1446 Charles VII gave the Parliament of Paris the right of judging the *causes, quarrels, and business matters of the university and its members.*

[2] By these words, *garde gardienne,* the king signified that he took the universities under his special protection. *Gardienne* is merely a superfluous word used to intensify the sense of *garde.*

[3] *Privilèges de l'Université de Poitiers,* p. 27.

University determined to cite the said bishop before the Provost of Paris in his châtelet (formerly the name of a court of justice in Paris). The bishop at first refused to come; but the University having decided to make a direct appeal to the king, the bishop, "in spite of a serious infirmity by which he was afflicted," complied with the injunction to repair to Paris.[1]

By the right of *garde gardienne*, therefore, the universities could withdraw an adverse party from his natural judges. This was assuredly a privilege which had its inequitable side, since, for example, it made it possible that a person living at the extremity of the kingdom might be summoned to Paris. Hence, in order to prevent abuses, it became necessary to limit the right, and to determine the distance beyond which one was no longer amenable to the courts of Paris, to two, or four, or six days' journey on horseback.[2] It must be admitted, on the other hand, that if this was a very considerable prerogative for the universities, it was partly justified in a time when local justice, administered in the name of the seigneur by the provost or the bailiff, was ignorant and often arbitrary, and that there was every advantage in substituting for it the regularly administered justice of great cities.

[1] Bimbenet, *op. cit.*, p. 131.
[2] An edict of 1722 again confirmed the privilege I speak of, to the University of Paris.

III

Taxes in the Middle Ages were laid on none but commoners and peasants. The nobility and the clergy were exempt from them. Hence, to free masters and students from all dues to the State and all municipal taxes, was simply to extend to them the privileges of the nobility and the clergy. In Italy, as in France and Spain, the exemption from fiscal charges was complete. All the statutes of the Italian universities formally recognized this privilege, says Coppi.[1] "The privileges of the University of Poitiers said that all members of the University must be held free, acquitted, exempt from all tollage, taxes, duties, loans, subsidies, and other assessments." The universities, in fact, were not merely dispensed from the regular imposts; they were so likewise from the extraordinary assessments which the depletion of the treasury frequently obliged the kings to lay upon the tax-payers. In 1440, King Charles VII, in order to meet the expenses of the war, had laid a tax on wine throughout the kingdom at the rate of twenty sous per cask; but on the complaint of the University of Orleans, he finally dispensed the students of that city from it, saying that would be "exempted from all tax on all the wine they had brought thither for drinking and other necessities."[2] Not long afterwards we see Louis XII, and a little later Francis I, exempting the masters and students of the University of Poitiers from any participation in the impost of four thousand livres, which he had inflicted upon the in-

[1] Coppi, *op. cit.*, p. 176.   [2] Bimbenet, *op. cit.*, p. 84.

habitants of the city of Poitiers, and also from a contribution established for the purpose of paying the hire of three hundred men of war.

What are nowadays called town dues (*octroi*) did not exist for the members of universities; they had the right to bring into the cities which they inhabited all sorts of provisions both for themselves and for their families. At Padua, in 1551, they were granted exemption from all duties on wine — an event which the students celebrated, the chroniclers say, by magnificent banquets in honor of Bacchus. At Orleans the members of the University claimed exemption for all articles of consumption in their possession, even for those which they sold again. In 1295, Philip the Fair decreed that the goods of the members of universities could not be taken or their revenues attached under any pretext.[1] In a word, the fiscal privileges of the universities were absolute, and justified this article of the statutes of the University of Padua: " Students must be considered as citizens in what concerns the advantages, but not in that which concerns the burdens of citizens." [2]

Exempt from taxes, the university was also exempt from military service. And this exemption extended not merely to war, but to the obligation of serving in the city militia as town guards. It was manifestly desired, through a high estimate of the superior importance of study, which was possibly not exaggerated, to free both students and professors from

[1] M. Fournier, t. i, p. 8.
[2] " *Scolares computentur cives quantum ad comoda et non ad incomoda.*"

all duties that could distract them from intellectual
labor. The letters-patent of the kings of France
constantly reproduce the same formula: they ordain
that all members of the university shall be exempt
from all patrolling or sentry duties, except in case of
imminent peril. As this somewhat vague expression
of "imminent peril" might give rise to different interpretations, it was defined. In 1577, Henry III specified for Poitiers that there would be imminent peril
"when the enemy's army should be within five leagues
of the city"; and before this, in 1448, Charles VI
decreed for Orleans that the members of the university were not to take up arms until the enemy was
ten leagues from the city.

Similar privileges existed in Italy, but, as it seems,
they were less extensive there. Exemption from military service was accorded only to the highest members
of the university. In 1264, an article in the statutes
of the University of Ferrara, whose title was "*De his
qui non tenentur ire in exercitum*," specified that the
dispensation was granted only to doctors in law,
medicine, and the liberal arts.

Like all university privileges, this one was frequently contested. In 1467, Louis XI resolved to
enlist all able-bodied men in Paris, between sixteen
and sixty years of age, including the members of the
university. The rector resisted, by calling attention
to the fact that the profession of arms was incompatible with that of study, and that the laws of the
Church exempted the university from military service, and left it no weapon but prayer. He added
another reason of a more practical kind: namely, that

parents would thereafter refuse to send their children to Paris if the obligation to bear arms was imposed upon them. The representations of the rector were effectual, and Louis XI contented himself with requiring that the university should cause a mass to be celebrated weekly for the king.[1] It must be said, however, to the honor of the universities, that they volunteered many times to perform military duties. In 1356, Paris being hard pressed by the English, the university decided that its members should take up arms for the defence of the city at the order of the rector. So at Poitiers in the fifteenth century, insurrections having broken out in the environs, the students called upon the chief municipal officers and declared that five hundred or a thousand of them were ready to arm in defence of order.

IV

One of the most astonishing privileges of the ancient universities was the power they had to suspend their courses, to go on strike, as we say nowadays, if for any reason, they were dissatisfied. This is what was called the right of *cessatio*, which was used and abused frequently. Things went so far that a university was sometimes seen to take flight, and change its place of residence on its own exclusive authority: thus, about 1320 the University of Orleans, vexed at the annoyances to which it had been subjected by the citizens of the town, thought it well to move to Nevers, where, for that matter, it was very ill received. The

[1] Crevier, t. iv, p. 316.

inhabitants of Nevers threw the rector's chair into the Loire, expressing the hope that, borne by the waters of the stream, and "with the assistance of the devil," it might return to the city whence it came.[1]

But, without proceeding to these extremities, other universities were accustomed to suspend at a moment's notice all their exercises until satisfaction had been afforded them. In a bull of 1231, Gregory IX thus formulated this privilege: "If an injustice is committed towards any one of you," he wrote to the masters and students of Paris, "if a serious injury like a murder or a wound is inflicted, unless justice is rendered you within fifteen days, you are permitted to suspend your lectures until you have obtained complete satisfaction."[2] The same authorization was given in case a member of the university were arrested and unjustly imprisoned.

I will recall briefly the circumstances under which this extraordinary right was granted to the University of Paris by the pope. A students' riot had occurred during the Carnival of 1229. Bands of half-intoxicated young men had sacked the house of an innkeeper and wounded several persons. The queen-regent, Blanche, ordered the Provost of Paris to punish the guilty : two students were put to death, "one of whom," says Crevier, "was a Norman and the other a Fleming, while those who had caused the disorder were all natives of Picardy." The university took

[1] Bimbenet, *op. cit.*, p. 88.
[2] *Chartularium Univ. Paris.*, t. i, p. 138, " . . . *liceat vobis usque ad satisfactionem condignam suspendere lectiones.*"

sides with its pupils and suspended all exercise of its functions. But as the queen was in no haste to allow the justice of its remonstrances, a great number of the professors dispersed, some to other parts of France, and others to foreign countries, until not a single famous master remained in Paris. The bishop launched excommunications against the deserters in vain. The pope was obliged to intervene and revoke the ecclesiastical censures and penalties, and the king made a formal apology in reparation for the wrong inflicted on the students, before order was re-established, and the university, victorious at all points, decided to resume its courses after an interruption of two years.[1]

The right to strike thus recognized as belonging to the universities entailed such troublesome consequences that Pope Alexander IV sought to modify it by his bull of 1255, by which he required that no suspension of courses should take place unless each of the Faculties consented to it by a two-thirds vote.[2] But the university pointed out with much vigor that the right of *cessatio* was its principal defence, " the buckler of the university," and it continued to make use of it.

In 1267, in fact, lectures were again suspended for three months, on account of the blows and wounds received by three students. It was not merely the scholastic exercises that were intermitted, but the sermons also. " In 1407," says Crevier, " Advent and Lent went by without there being either lectures or sermons in Paris, not even on Christmas or Easter,

[1] Crevier, t. i, p. 341.   [2] *Chartularium Univ. Paris.*, t. i, p. 273.

because the provost had caused two ill-conducted
students to be hanged."[1] The university threatened
to leave the kingdom and establish its chairs in a
foreign country. The provost was obliged to go in
person and take down the two students from the
gibbet, kissing them on the mouth, and conducting
their obsequies with great pomp.

In 1453, forty students were imprisoned in the
Châtelet; they were released, but during the tri-
umphal procession which followed their deliverance,
a collision with the police took place. A master of
arts was killed and some students wounded. The
rector nearly lost his life. The next day the *cessatio*
was decreed; and in order to bring it to a close, Parliament was obliged to ordain that eight archers, or
ushers, should make the *amende honorable* to the
university, wearing nothing but their shirts, and carrying lighted torches. The man who had threatened
the rector had his hand cut off.[2]

The history of the University of Paris is full of
these peaceful revolts, which ended by tiring out both
the royal and the pontifical authorities. In 1499,
the university took offence because Louis XII wished
to correct certain abuses. Placards were posted
throughout Paris, announcing a new *cessatio*, but it
was a failure. The king, in fact, conceded nothing.
He went through Paris at the head of his military
household, armed from head to foot, lance in rest;
and the university had to give way. This was the
last cessation.[3]

---

[1] Crevier, t. iii, p. 298.   [2] Crevier, t. iv, pp. 197–219.
[3] In 1432, Pope Pius II had already issued a bull interdicting the
cessations.

V

ı have by no means exhausted the list of immunities granted to the universities of the Middle Ages
by the favor of princes and of popes.   Besides the
important rights I have already enumerated, there
were numerous petty privileges, some of which I
shall indicate, in order to complete the picture.

Of the University of Turin, founded in 1412, historians relate the following usages : The troops of
comedians who gave representations in that city were
obliged to send eight free tickets of admission to the
syndic of the students.[1]   Every liquor-dealer was
likewise obliged to offer a bottle of brandy and a
pound of preserves, and every pastry cook a cake, on
the feast of the Epiphany.   At Orleans, the students
of the university, divided into four "Nations," had
the right to send twelve of their number — that is,
three from each Nation — gratuitously to the theatre.[2]
The laws of the period protected even the pleasures
of the students, and Savigny relates that at Bologna
the Jews were compelled to offer one hundred and
four livres and a half to the University of Law, and
seventy livres to the University of Arts, for the fêtes
of the Carnival.

Sometimes the privileges were conceded to a frac-
tion only of the university !   Thus, a general prohibition forbade the students to carry weapons.   The
brawls and riots which the ebullition of juvenile
spirits often gave rise to, justified this policy only too
well.   The popes declared in their bulls that students

[1] Coppi, *op. cit.*, p. 185.   [2] Bimbenet. *op. cit.*, p. 111.

who should violate this rule were excommunicated *ipso facto*.[1] And yet we see that at Orleans students belonging to the German Nation were authorized by Henry IV, in 1600, "to carry sword, dagger, and pistols, which is," added the King of France, "the true mark of noble birth." It is to be remarked, moreover, that the universities of the Middle Ages, both in Italy and in France, students of German extraction were nearly always treated with particular favor.[2]

Further, the members of the universities enjoyed a certain number of immunities of a specially ecclesiastical character. Both masters and students had a right to receive the revenues accruing from their benefices during seven years, and sometimes during ten years, of non-residence. In 1331, John XXII permitted any ecclesiastic who desired to follow the courses of theology and of canon law at Cahors to abandon his cure or his benefice if he provided a substitute accepted by his bishop. On several occasions the popes proclaimed that no excommunication could affect the heads of universities without a special edict from the Holy See.[3]

It remains to be noted that the privileges of the universities were not conferred on masters and students only: they pertained equally to all those who participated in any degree in the service of the university; to the inferior agents who were then styled

[1] Crevier, t. i, p. 353.

[2] "At the University of Bologna," says Coppi (*op. cit.*, p. 158), "the German 'Nation' was the most privileged of all."

[3] Crevier, t. i, pp. 290, 361, etc.

supposita, to subordinates, beadles, scribes, registrars;
to the messengers who played such a great part in
the universities of the Middle Ages; and, finally, to
the servants and domestics (*famulanti*) of masters
and students. The enjoyment of privileges extended
even to the tradesmen who furnished books and paper
to the students, to parchment makers, librarians,
etc. At the outset all librarians enjoyed the various
immunities of the university: librarians were rare
in the thirteenth and fourteenth centuries. Later,
when the profession increased in number, the privileged librarians were reduced to one or two for each
university. At Orleans things went so far that in
1521 a demand was made, though in vain, that the
clock-maker and the bell-ringer of the university
should be exempted from all taxes and other charges,
as well as the rector and the professors. Naturally,
there were abuses. Many called themselves students
who were not such, seeking to usurp a title which
conferred such great advantages.

Each university, then, sheltered under its protection
a considerable number of persons, and it need not be
wondered at that privileges so important in themselves, and so widely distributed, should have been
frequently contested. The universities had to struggle
with the municipal authorities, who could not but
regard with jealousy the independence of these scholastic societies, autonomous and all-powerful. They
had to contend also with the inhabitants, who, although
in general well-disposed toward the universities from
which they derived honor and profit, sometimes beheld with displeasure a large number of young for-

eigners [1] freed from all those financial obligations which weighed upon themselves all the more heavily because they were not shared by every one.

But notwithstanding the complaints arising from private interests or corporate jealousies, the universities maintained their privileged position to the end; and it must be acknowledged that in guarding it for them, the public authorities of the Middle Ages honored themselves and testified their zeal for intellectual labor. There was, on the part of kings as well as on that of popes, a sort of conspiracy in favor of the universities. On every page of the *Chartularium* of each of them may be found documents which bear witness to an unceasing solicitude for their welfare. It is Philip the Fair who decrees that the student, if arrested, shall be treated with every mark of respect while in prison, and even released on bail. It is Innocent III who enjoins the Bishop of Toulouse to receive poor students in the hospitals of the city, and who takes the trouble to write to the count, the consul, and the people of Toulouse to thank them for their good will toward the university. It is Philip the Fair, once more, who orders the inhabitants and merchants of the city of Orleans to sell provisions and let houses to the students at the most just price. It is St. Louis who, going to church at daybreak, and receiving on his head the contents of a pot which an early-rising student was emptying out of a window,

---

[1] It appears that, especially at the outset, the privileges of certain universities were chiefly reserved for foreigners, whom it was necessary to protect against the possible vexations proceeding from the citizens, the inhabitants of the city.

instead of being angered, conferred a prebendaryship on the student as a reward for getting up at such an early hour to study.

The student of the Middle Ages somewhat resembled the Roman citizen of former times, who made himself respected by all with the simple words : *Civis Romanus sum*. Strong by reason of the concessions made individually to each of its members, the university found another source of power in the fact that it was an organized body, administering itself. From this point of view, and in all matters which concerned its general interests, the University of Paris claimed to depend on no one but the king or the pope, according as the violations it had to complain of arose from the civil or the ecclesiastical power. So, too, the University of Padua called on the Venetian Senate. Everywhere, in a word, the universities were freed from the control of the local authorities, and recognized no other sovereigns than the head of the Church and the head of the State, and not always yielding even to them. And it may be permissible to conclude that possibly they maintained their prosperity more on account of their privileges than by the attraction of their teaching.

CHAPTER II

NATIONS AND FACULTIES

I. The Nations — Public character of lessons in the university schools — Great gatherings of students — Natural tendency to union between the students of the same country — Constitution of the Nations as free self-governing societies — The Nations in the University of Paris — They constitute the Faculty of Arts alone — Other methods of organization — Advantages and disadvantages of the distribution into Nations — II. The Faculties — Original meaning of the word — Specialization of studies — Growth of the four traditional Faculties in the University of Paris — Faculty of Arts, the first constituted — The superior Faculties: theology, civil and canon law, medicine — The "colleges" of Bologna — The four Faculties did not exist at all universities.

AMONG the characteristics which distinguish a university of the Middle Ages, making it something new in the world and truly original, there are two particularly important ones, which will form the subject of this chapter. These are, on the one hand, the fact that the university courses are public;[1] that the

---

[1] It was only in the sixteenth century that the public courses of philosophy, given in the famous Rue du Fouarre at Paris, finally ceased, and that the colleges, that is to say, private schools, completely absorbed the instruction of the Faculty of Arts. Ramus, the reformer of the University of Paris, complains strongly of it; he says with regret that instruction in philosophy is henceforth to be given privately, in each college; "it is not long ago," he adds, "that the last public lecturer in philosophy died." — *Avertissements sur la reformation de l'Université de Paris.*

lectures are not given behind closed doors, in a private school; that admittance is given freely to all classes, to men of mature years as well as to youths, to foreigners as well as natives. And, on the other hand, the fact that the different branches of human knowledge are already divided, separated one from another, and confided to special professors. To the state of educational chaos, so to speak, whose previous existence in the episcopal or monastic schools is testified to by the confused mingling of the seven liberal arts, the *trivium* and *quadrivium*, has succeeded the orderly distribution of the different matters to be taught and studied, the differentiation of theology and law, of medicine and of arts. It is true, that under arts was still included a confused medley of studies which were afterwards to constitute the independent categories of science and literature; and no line was drawn between secondary and superior instruction, which were not distinguished into two grades until a later time.

"Publicity" and "specialization," then, are two characteristic traits of early university organization; and with each of them essential facts are connected, — the establishment of *Nations* with the first, and the institution of *Faculties* with the second.

I

In essaying to delineate university life at Salamanca during the Middle Ages, a French writer thus expresses himself: "The students form a population apart in the city, having its customs, manners, its dis-

trict and even its courts, completely distinct from
those of the *bourgeois* and the merchants.   On a summer evening you see the students going about in
bands, wearing gowns of the same pattern; those belonging to the same kingdoms make groups together.
These are the haughty Castilians passing by; young
as they are, they hardly know what it is to laugh.
But what a contrast yonder! The Andalusians are
singing at the top of their voices as they walk.   They
carry guitars and tambourines, and are followed by a
crowd of urchins who fill the street with their cries.
See what handsome fellows they are! What an alert
bearing! And what a costume! They have torn
their gowns on purpose, as well as the long, black
cloaks which they wear with an impudent air.   They
have fixed three plumes in their hats." [1]

What the imagination of this author has seen from
afar in the streets of Salamanca in the Middle Ages,
might have been seen everywhere at that epoch.   In
every place the students, thanks to the university
privileges, formed a separate caste, as it were a scholastic city thrown into the permanent city and often
more populous than it was.   But everywhere, also,
they separated into distinct groups according to their
nationalities, and preserved the manners and customs
of their countries, as happens still in the universities
of Germany and Switzerland.

The "Nations," therefore, had their *raison d'être* in
the universities of the thirteenth century, in the
diverse origins of the students who were attracted to

[1] *Revue internationale de l'enseignement*, Paris, 1883, article de
M. Graux: L'Université de Salamanque in 1875.

the same city, not only from all provinces of one country, but from foreign lands as well, by the reputation of the schools established there. Assuredly there were not to be found in all the university cities groups of pupils as large as those brought together at Paris or Bologna by the renown of Abelard or Irnerius. Italian historians speak of ten thousand students in the thirteenth century, and of fifteen thousand in the fifteenth.[1] We have seen what an extraordinary number of auditors thronged the lectures of Abelard at Paris. "The number of clerics," says a chronicler of the time, "had come to surpass that of the laity," that is to say, of the ordinary citizens.[2] But even in the least important cities the scholastic population was considerable; and no one will be surprised at it who reflects that studies were at this time almost exclusively concentrated in the universities. Nowadays young men who study are scattered throughout all parts of their country; each city has its colleges and schools. In the thirteenth century they were obliged to meet each other in the comparatively few cities which possessed universities. For want of books they could not study at home, but were obliged to go to a distance to follow the lectures of one or another renowned professor. Their ardor for knowledge made them willingly expatriate themselves, in spite of all difficulties and obstacles. Felix Plater, a German who studied at Montpellier in the sixteenth century, relates that, starting from Basel, it took him twenty days to reach the end of his journey; that his

[1] Coppi, *op. cit.*, p. 117.
[2] *Chartularium Univ. Paris.*, t. i, p. 20.

companions and himself escaped the dangers that
threatened them only by chance.[1] At Montpellier the
average number of students was at least a thousand.[2]
Bimbenet reminds us that the chroniclers of the time
speak of five thousand students at Orleans in the
fourteenth century. At Poitiers, in the days of its
greatest prosperity, in the sixteenth century, some
estimate the number of students at two thousand,
others at four thousand. In 1554, four thousand
auditors followed the lectures in law given by Coras
in Toulouse.

Some exaggeration may doubtless be suspected in
these somewhat fabulous figures. It is none the
less true that, at least in the great universities, enormous numbers were assembled, comprising scholars
of all ages, conditions, and nationalities. And that
in these scholastic multitudes the students from each
province and country should have felt naturally drawn
together, and sought to live in greater intimacy, to
associate with each other, and to install themselves
in the same houses (*hospitia*), can be readily understood. It must not be forgotten that a part of these
youths, self-exiled through their love of knowledge,
were poor, and that they were often confronted with
the difficulties of making a living. Moreover, when
the police, even in great cities, were not as strictly
regulated as they are to-day, and when the majority
of the students were more or less foreigners, sepa-

[1] Felix Plater, a celebrated physician (1536–1614); he taught
for fifty-four years at Basel.

[2] See the *Fêtes du VIème Centenaire de l'université de Montpellier*,
1891. Discours de M. Croiset, p. 62.

rated from their families, and isolated by the difficulty of communication as well as by distance, it was entirely natural that each nationality should seek by an intimate union a sort of leverage, a material and moral force, which might enable it to protect itself.

These were precisely the reasons by which the kings justified the privileges granted to the universities. "We believe," said Philip the Fair in 1312, "that it is right to have a great respect for the labors, the vigils, the drudgery, the deprivations, the pains and perils encountered by the students in order to acquire the precious pearl of science, and that it is just to consider how they have left their friends, their relatives, and their country, how they have abandoned their goods and their fortunes. . . ." [1] But these were also the reasons which, within the precincts of the privileged universities, determined the special associations known as "Nations." "We are here," said the professors and students of the University of Paris in 1231, "we are here as foreigners, without the support of relatives or friends, exposed each day to atrocious insults which touch even our persons." [2]

Let us now examine, in the history of the University of Paris, under what form the "Nations," which had at first been nothing more than colonies of masters and students of similar origin, organized themselves into veritable corporations, each with its relative autonomy and its distinct leaders, "constituting," as Laurie says, "free self-governing societies within the universities."

[1] Crevier, t. ii, p. 140.   [2] Crevier, t. i, p. 420.

The precise date of the organization at Paris of the four Nations which maintained themselves there until the latest days of the university escapes the most minute research. Neither for the Nations nor for the Faculties was there any sudden blossoming, but rather a slow evolution, an insensible preparation for a definite condition. Already at the close of the twelfth century there is mention in contemporary documents of the various *provinces* of the school of Paris. The Nations are mentioned in the bulls of Gregory IX (1231) and of Innocent IV (1245). In 1245, they already elect their attendants, the beadles. In 1249, the existence of the four Nations — France, Picardy, Normandy, and England — is proved by their quarrels over the election of a rector.[1] In 1255, a letter addressed to the pope by the masters and students is stamped with the seal of the four Nations. In 1266 there were new discords, a new university schism, which, like the ecclesiastical schism resulting in two popes, ended in the election of two rectors, one for the French Nation, and one for the other three.[2]

Without quoting further from important documents, it appears from those I have cited that the four Nations, with their claims and prerogatives and pri-

[1] The English "Nation" comprised all the countries of the north and east which were actually foreign to France. In the fifteenth century, the name "English" having become odious, the English Nation was rechristened and became the German Nation.

[2] According to Denifle, the four Nations were constituted between 1215 and 1222, at the period when the university, then in process of formation, had most to contend with from the chancellor and chapter of Notre Dame.

vate seals, were constituted in the first half of the twelfth century. In 1250, the Faculties of Theology, Law, and Medicine were not yet organized bodies; they were not detached from the rest of the university to live a life of their own. At this epoch, therefore, the four Nations made up the entire university. Each of them had its chief, elected from among themselves, who was called the procurator. This title, which appears for the first time in 1218, in a bull of Honorius III, was preserved during the whole existence of the universities; and there were procurators of Nations almost everywhere, in Italy, Spain, and Germany. The four Nations joined, each casting an equal vote, in the election of the rector, who was at first merely the chief of the four Nations. Each of them deliberated separately, and was represented by its procurator only in the General Assembly; each made its own regulations, and collected and expended its own revenues. It was on this last account that each Nation, although it counted only as a single voice in the common deliberations and in the election of the rector, desired to be as large as possible; and there is proof that there was wrangling and pettifogging between Nation and Nation, and unfair advantage taken of cases of doubtful nationalities in order to lay claim to a particular student.[1]

Until the definitive constitution of the Faculties, that is, until 1270 or 1280, the four Nations included

---

[1] The Nations were subdivided, moreover, into smaller groups, the *tribes*. At Paris, for example, the French Nation was composed of five tribes or provinces: Paris, Sens, Rheims, Tours, and Bourges.

the totality of students and masters. After the formation of the Faculties, the four Nations comprised
only the members of the Faculty of Arts and those
students of other Faculties who had not yet obtained
the grade of Bachelor of Arts. The three superior
Faculties, Theology, Medicine, and Law, had nothing
in common thenceforward with the Nations. In spite
of some uncertainties at the beginning — it seems, in
fact, that the Faculty of Arts had had an existence in-
dependently of the four Nations in the second half of
the thirteenth century — from the commencement of
the fourteenth century and until the end, the Nations
were the four distinct companies which constituted
the Faculty of Arts. It was in this way that the University of Paris, in its complete form, was composed
of seven companies : the three Superior Faculties and
the four Nations, each having a deliberative voice in
the general assemblies, and in their totality appointing seven delegates whenever a deputation was to be
sent to the pope or to the king.[1]

What is peculiar to the University of Paris in the
picture that I have just drawn, is the distinction between the four Nations (composing the Faculty of
Arts) and the three other Faculties. In the other
universities of the Middle Ages, all the Faculties,
both masters and students, were distributed among
the different Nations, the number of which, moreover, was extremely variable. And, in fact, this second method of organization was the more rational.

[1] In 1509, for example, the University Assembly was composed of
the three deans of the Superior Faculties and the four procurators
of the Nations, presided over by the rector.

That it was not followed at Paris was chiefly because of the preponderance always held in this university by the Faculty of Arts, whether by reason of the importance of the studies it controlled, or by the number of its masters and students.

At Bologna, as at Paris, the Nations were constituted in the early years of the thirteenth century, but under a slightly different form. There the students were grouped in two distinct associations, the *Ultramontanes* and the *Citramontanes,* the foreigners and the Italians, who formed two universities, the Transalpine and the Cisalpine, each with its chiefs, who were not styled procurators but counsellors; the first was composed of eighteen Nations and the second of seventeen.[1] At Padua twenty-two Nations were enumerated. Montpellier had only three in 1339, — the Catalans, the Burgundians, the Provençals; each subdivided, however, into numerous groups. Orleans had ten : France, Germany, Lorraine, Burgundy, Champagne, Picardy, Normandy, Touraine, Guyanne, and Scotland; Poitiers had four : France, Aquitaine, Touraine, and Berry; Prague had four also, in imitation of Paris ; Lerida had twelve, in imitation of Bologna, etc.[2]

But, whether more or less numerous, and whatever their special organization, the Nations in all the universities bore witness to that need of association which

[1] At Bologna the students who belonged *to the town of Bologna* were not included in the Nations.

[2] In the English universities of Oxford and Cambridge the division into "Nations" was to some extent represented by that of North and South. See Mullinger, *op. cit.*, p. 135.

is one of the characteristics of the Middle Ages, and
which manifested itself at the same epoch in so many
ways, in the establishment of trade-guilds as well as
in the foundation of religious orders. By setting natural boundaries to the army of students, they exercised
a great influence on the development of the universities : they regulated their action. They were, to a certain degree, lay communities, assuring. to their members all the benefits and advantages of association.
They had all the qualities which belong to party
spirit; they had its defects likewise. And since the
evil must be told as well as the good, one of the consequences of their organization was to prevent the
blending and fusion of races, and to maintain the distinction of provinces and nationalities among the
pupils of the same university. Each Nation, in fact,
jealously preserved the customs and the language of
its province or country. Each had its special patron.
At Paris, the Nation of France invoked St. Thomas
of Canterbury, and later, St. William of Bourges, a
former student of the university. St. Romanus, Archbishop of Rouen, was the patron of the Nation of
Normandy. St. Charlemagne, after others, became patron of the Nation of Germany. But if the different
patrons of the Nations, all borrowed from the cata-
logue of Saints, were in harmony among themselves,
it was far different with the Nations, for they barely
understood each other. Rivalries and antipathies between one people and another were carried to the
very benches of their common school and engendered
a thousand quarrels there. To prove this it is sufficient to recall the ungracious epithets bandied between

the Nations, at a time when the English were called "drunkards and cowards," the French "proud and effeminate," the Germans "choleric, gluttonous, and dirty"; when the Normans were accused of being "charlatans and boasters," the Burgundians "brutal and stupid," the Flemings "bloody and incendiary men"; or when with less violence as to form, but with the same tendency to particularism, people spoke of the "dancers of Orleans," the "tennis players of Poitiers," the "dirty fellows of Paris," or the "lovers from Turin."

II

In its present signification, a "Faculty" (Faculty of Law, Medicine, etc.) is a scientific or literary body charged with a special branch of instruction in a university. As a matter of fact, it was much in this same sense that the Middle Ages understood Faculties. Duboulay thus defines the word: "A body, an association (*sodalitium*) of members devoted to special studies (*certœ alicui disciplinœ*)." But in the earliest times "Faculty" seems to have been merely a synonym of science and of art. Thus, in the statutes of the University of Naples, Frederic II speaks, in 1224, of those who *chirurgiœ facultatem instruunt;* that is, of those who practise the art of surgery. So too at Paris, in the first half of the thirteenth century, Crevier establishes by authentic texts that "faculty" was the equivalent of "class of studies." For example, in 1251, in a regulation of the university, after the enumeration of the arts and sciences taught there "theology, canon law, medicine, arts and grammar,"

it is said: "those who study in the aforesaid faculties." Now, grammar never having constituted a fifth
Faculty in the later sense of the word, it is evident
that the expression was here employed in its wide
signification of "knowledge," of "special science."[1]

At what epoch the four Faculties of the Middle
Ages were constituted as so many societies, bodies
independent of each other, although reunited under
the common laws of each university, it is difficult to
say with precision. The University of Paris, for
example, was already in existence; the general association of masters and scholars had been an accomplished fact since 1200; in 1208, Innocent III had
addressed instructions "to all the doctors of theology,
canon law, and liberal arts established at Paris, *universis doctoribus sacræ paginæ*, etc.; the university
had acted as a single person in 1221 by a formal dona-
tion to a religious order, styling itself *Universitas
magistrorum et scholarium;*[2] in a word, it had been
constituted for many years as a centre of studies;
and yet, in the middle of the thirteenth century,
there is still no sign of anything which resembles a
regular and formal distribution of students and professors into separate Faculties.

The formation of Faculties was the work of time.
Studies developed in different directions; the number
of scholars and masters in each specialty multiplied
before the scientific species which we call a Faculty
assumed its later form. Brought together by the
similarity of their labors, the professors of each

[1] Crevier, t. i, p. 375.
[2] *Chartularium Univ. Paris.*, t. i, p. 99.

branch of study at first grouped themselves spontaneously, in order to regulate all that related to
their special science and their own students. Different statutes for the masters in theology and the masters of arts were established in 1215 by the papal
legate, Robert de Courçon.[1] But the distinction of
Faculties does not clearly appear, notwithstanding,
until much later, in the second half of the thirteenth
century. The Faculty of Law did not have its own
seal until 1271. The seal of the Faculty of Medicine
is mentioned for the first time in 1274; and the same
Faculty did not have its first dean until 1265 or 1268.

It is from the confused mass of studies called
the "liberal arts" that, like several branches from
one stem, the Faculties gradually sprang forth: the
Faculty of Theology first of all, towards 1260. This,
if we may credit Duboulay and Crevier,[2] on the
occasion of the bull of Alexander III (1257) which
had opened the university to all the religious orders,
to the Carmelites and Augustinians as well as to the
Dominicans and Franciscans. Naturally, it was as
theologians, and in order to obtain the doctorate in
theology, that these monks had forced the door of
the university. Those of the university professors
who already made a special branch of theology were
the only ones who received them favorably, while
the masters of arts displayed the most lively repug-
nance at admitting the members of religious orders,
whom they looked upon as intruders. The theologians were in consequence led to form a separate

[1] *Chartularium Univ. Paris.*, t. i, p. 78.
[2] Crevier, t. i, p. 460.

group, and, without separating from the university, to constitute themselves a distinct Faculty.

During the years which succeeded, between 1260 and 1280, the Faculties of Canon Law or Decrees, and of Medicine, likewise organized themselves. In 1271 or 1272, as we have said already, the Faculty of Law, in spite of the opposition of the Chancellor of Notre Dame, at last possessed a seal of its own.[1] It must be noted that in the statutes of Robert de Courçon, in 1215, no mention is made either of law or medicine. So far as medicine is concerned there is nothing surprising in this omission, when one reflects that the Church had more than once forbidden not merely monks, but priests also — though unsuccessfully — to study or to teach medicine. The first public act of the Paris Faculty of Medicine dates from 1270; it is a decision rendered by the masters against a student who had been guilty of a fraud in order to obtain the licentiate's degree;[2] this document also makes mention of the Dean of the Faculty of Medicine.

It is thus that, towards 1275, the University of Paris is found constituted with its already long-established four Nations and its four Faculties.[3] Certain ambi-

[1] *Chartularium Univ. Paris.*, t. i, p. 503 : Agreement between the Chancellor of Paris and the Faculty of Decrees upon the usage of the seal of the said Faculty.

[2] *Chartularium Univ. Paris.*, t. i, p. 488.

[3] The question whether the regular organization of the Faculties preceded or followed that of the Nations has been much disputed by the historians of the University of Paris. It seems to me indubitable that the Nations are more ancient than the Faculties. This is the conclusion from all the facts I have cited. Moreover, it is more natural, more logical, that scholars and masters should have grouped themselves according to their natural affinities of race at first, rather than according to the similarity of their studies.

guities still remained, however; thus, in 1274, the Faculty of Arts styled itself *universitas artistarum*. But in 1277, the distinction of the Faculties was formally recognized by the assembled university; and in 1281, the university promised to defend each of its Faculties.[1]

From this time on the traditional four Faculties constantly perform autonomous and personal acts; they publish ordinances; they regulate the order of their lectures; they have their private assemblies and their leaders; they confer degrees on their own students. The three Faculties of Theology (*sacra Facultas*), of Law (*consultissima Facultas*), of Medicine (*saluberrima Facultas*), were denominated Superior Faculties because, in order to be admitted to them, it was necessary to have already received the degrees of the Faculty of Arts (*subtilissima Facultas*).

The separation of the Faculties is a feature common to all the universities of the Middle Ages. It does not appear, however, that it was everywhere made with the same precision as at Paris. At Bologna even the word "faculty" seems to have been unknown: the Faculties were represented there by "colleges," — college of jurists, college of physicians. It is known, moreover, that in Italy the distinct corporations of a single university themselves took the title of university, — university of arts, university of law.[2] It might be said that in papal bulls

---

[1] *"Declarat universitas facta facultatum esse facta universitatis"* (*Chartularium*, t. i, p. 590).

[2] The same was true at Montpellier, which imitated Bologna rather than Paris.

the primitive sense of the word "faculty" persists
even to the fifteenth century. In 1450, Nicholas V,
conceding to the University of Barcelona the privileges of that of Toulouse, enumerates in what
branches of instruction the *studium generale* might
operate : *in Theologia, Jure canonico et civili, Artibus
et Medicina:* and he adds, using a formula which
occurs in a great many pontifical acts, *in qualibet alia
licita facultate;* which cannot be translated but by
these words : "in any other permitted science." [1]
Nearly always the sovereigns pontiffs neglect to
notice the Faculties properly so called, and content
themselves with drawing up the list of sciences
taught. Thus, in a privilege relating to the University of Salamanca, in 1313, Clement V enumerates
as subjects taught: decrees, decretals, laws, medicine,
logic, grammar, and music.[2]

Remember, moreover, that the four classic Faculties did not exist in all the universities even when
the primitive number had been increased in them.
Complete universities were in the minority. On the
other hand, certain ones, Louvain for example, had
five Faculties, civil law being separated from canon
law. Possibly it was the same at Salamanca, where,
in any case, accessory chairs existed called *extrava-
gantes,* — astrology and the languages.

These peculiarities, however, are of small importance. What it is interesting to verify is that in the
majority of the great centres of instruction the
Faculties were established by the thirteenth century;

[1] Vicente de la Fuente, *op. cit.*, t. i, p. 336.
[2] Vicente de la Fuente, *op. cit.*, p. 313.

NATIONS AND FACULTIES   113

that at this epoch human knowledge, through a
natural division of labor and thought, through un-
noted progress in classical antiquity, had been divided
into several categories, a condition indispensable to
the development of higher studies. Assuredly, there
is nothing definitive, nothing necessary, in the scholastic division of the four Faculties; and it is possible
to imagine as many special Faculties in a university
as there are separate departments comprehended
under science itself. In our own century the Faculty
of Arts has been dismembered in order to give birth
to the Faculty of Sciences and the Faculty of Letters.
And doubtless the future will see new dismemberments
which will correspond to a more exact determination
of the various departments of science and to the extension of the field of thought. But the honor of
having begun the movement to divide the branches
of human knowledge, and thus prepare the way for
modern science, belongs to the men of the Middle
Ages.

CHAPTER III

GOVERNMENT OF UNIVERSITIES

I. Republican and democratic character of the universities — The election a general rule in the choice of the officers — Short terms of office — The special privileges conceded to university officers, nominal rather than real — II. The Chancellor: his functions — His authority decreased with the development of the privileges of the universities — Rivalry of the chancellor with the Rector of Paris — III. The Rector: his powers — Conditions of eligibility — Mode of election — Installation of the rector in the University of Bologna — IV. Other university officers — Procurators — Syndics — Beadles— The messengers —V. Self-government of universities — General council of the University of Paris — Separate meetings of nations and faculties — The deans.

I

THE universities of the Middle Ages were veritable republics,[1] almost independent, slightly subordinated to the State and the Church, with the peculiarity that, in the first centuries of their existence their subordination to the ecclesiastical power was the more pronounced, while, toward the end, the control of the civil power increased.

Moreover, they were federal republics which included a more or less extensive number of associations

---

[1] "The system of a republican régime has always been that of the University of Paris" (Crevier, *op. cit.*, t. ii, p. 295). This republican character was still more marked in the Italian universities.

and distinct companies: Faculties and Nations, independent themselves although incorporated with the
universities, having their separate deliberations and
regulating their own affairs.

The character of *self-government* which distinguished
the universities of the Middle Ages shows itself in
various ways: in the first place, in the principle of
election generally employed in the choice of officers;
again, in the brief duration of the powers conferred
on these officers; and finally in the eminently honorary
nature of these powers, the real spring of action re-
maining either in the hands of the particular assemblies of each Nation or Faculty, or in those of the
general assembly of the university.   In fact, not only
were the dignitaries elected, under varying conditions
and complex forms of which I do not pretend to give
all the details here, but, in addition, these elective
functions did not last long.   There was a perpetual
mobility, an incessant renewing of persons, in the
administrative posts of the university.   At Paris, up
to 1266, the rector was elected for a month or six
weeks only: it was thought that a great thing had
been done in establishing the rule that three months
should be the extent of his incumbency.   As time
went on it was a year, or two years, at most.   Like
all democratic societies which, jealous of their rights,
are averse to long concessions of their sovereignty,
and unwilling that the powers they delegate shall
remain long in the same hands, the universities, desirous to maintain "*la liberté du corps*," as Crevier says,
looked with suspicion on long terms of office without
disturbing themselves about the inconveniences that

might be occasioned by the too frequent change of persons. Indeed, it is incontestable that the authority of the officers elected by the universities was more honorary and decorative than real. These officers were hardly more than agents charged with executing the will of their constituents, or rather, like the rector, the *rector magnificus* of certain universities, spectacular personages whose chief duty is to parade in the front rank at ceremonies, and who, in a word, reign rather than govern.

II

There was only one exception to this democratic organization of the universities : that constituted by the existence of the chancellor, a personage apart, the only one whose power did not emanate directly from the universities themselves, representing the Church and, as Crevier says, "foreign to the body." This supremacy, however, was very often impatiently borne, and the history of the disputes between the University of Paris and its chancellors has more than once justified the proverb : " Our enemy is our master."

Before the foundation of the Paris University, it was only the Chancellor of Notre Dame who, according to the common ecclesiastical law, could confer the "license" at Paris, the right to teach (*licentia docendi*). From him emanated the power which elsewhere, at Angers and at Orleans, for example, was exercised by the ecclesiastic who taught philosophy and belles-lettres, and was called the *écolâtre*. "The keys of science," they said in the thirteenth century, "have been placed in the hands of masters by the sovereign pontiff, or by the Chancellor of Paris by delegation from the pope, in order to open the treasury of wisdom." [1] It was the chancellor's duty to draw up, seal, and forward to their destination, the acts passed by the Chapter of Notre Dame. By degrees his power over the professors and students became very great; he granted or refused arbitrarily the right to teach; he could excommunicate the rebels or confine them in his prison.[2]

But these extraordinary powers of the chancellor were bound to decline as fast as the universities attained a definite organization. The popes themselves aided the University of Paris to throw them off and to gain its independence. In 1219, Pope Honorius III decreed that the students should enjoy the right to teach, *licentia docendi,* if they were worthy of it, whether the chancellor were willing or not (*etiam invito cancellario*). At the same, he forbade the chancellor to excommunicate any member of the university without the authority of the Holy See.[3] In 1231, in the famous bull *Parens scientiarum* . . . , Gregory IX again restricted the authority of the chancellor within the narrowest limits.[4] Finally, in 1252, the university obtained from Innocent IV the right to have a seal of its own: "a right," says Thurot, "which was the sign and guarantee of complete independence." [5]

The Church itself, then, labored to reduce the power

[1] *Chartularium Univ. Paris.: Introductio,* p. xi.

[2] It was in 1231 only that the Chancellor of Paris ceased to have a prison of his own.

[3] *Chartularium Univ. Paris.,* p. 102. [4] *Ibid.,* p. 136.

[5] Thurot, *op. cit.,* p. 12. In 1221 the university had tried to have a seal; but Honorius III ordered it to be broken.

of its own delegate.   Thurot is in error, however, when
he affirms that the powers granted by the popes to the
University of Paris deprived the chancellor of all
his authority.   Père Denifle, relying upon the texts,
has demonstrated in an unanswerable manner, that
throughout the whole of the thirteenth century the
Chancellor of Notre Dame retained more power in
the university than any one else.   Jean de Garlande
said of him in 1250: *Parisius studii directas ducit
habenas.*

Boniface VIII, in 1301, declared that the government of the university belonged to the chancellor.
It is probable that the provincial universities, less
ambitious than the University of Paris and not so
independent, submitted to the supremacy of their
chancellors much longer.

All, or nearly all, the universities had a chancellor
appointed under slightly different conditions.   Sometimes this personage was appointed directly by the
pope: thus at Prague the Archbishop of the city was
invested by Pope Clement VI with these functions from
1347.   In 1219, Pope Honorius III issued the following
decree for Bologna: "Considering that the promotion
to degrees is granted to unworthy individuals, none
can be granted in future without the consent of the
Archdeacon of Bologna and a preliminary examination." [1]   From this period the popes addressed themselves to the Archdeacon of Bologna as the head of
the university.   The Bishop of Turin and the
Archbishop of Pisa were chancellors of these two
universities.   At Montpellier it was the Bishop of

[1] Savigny, *op. cit.*, t. iii, p. 165.

Maguelonne who acted as chancellor. In the imperial
University of Naples, which was constructed on an
entirely different plan and was closely dependent on
the State, the chancellor was appointed by the emperor. At Padua, the university became a party in
the selection of the chancellor; the professors elected
him and the pope confined himself to confirming his
powers.

The chancellor, therefore, notwithstanding the increasing autonomy of the universities, continued to be
an important personage. He was, it might be said,
the living symbol of the ecclesiastical origin of the
universities, and of the authority the Church still
claimed to exercise over them. It suffices, however,
to recall the names of some of the chancellors of
Paris, and notably that of Gerson (1392), to understand the importance of the rôle that devolved upon
men who were occasionally the most illustrious of
their age.

In the long struggle, lasting throughout the thirteenth century, to decide whether the chancellor or
the rector was to be the supreme head of the University of Paris, the rector finally triumphed; but the
chancellor continued, none the less, to exercise powers
and discharge functions of importance. There were
two chancellors at Paris, moreover, of whom the most
ancient belonged to Notre Dame, and the other to the
Abbey of Ste. Geneviève.[1] The following extract from

[1] Mention is made of the Chancellor of Ste. Geneviève for the first
time about 1255. There had been schools on the heights of Ste.
Geneviève in the time of Abelard; but it was about 1219 that masters and scholars first emigrated in great numbers from the city

Crevier fixes clearly the prerogatives they retained
up to the eighteenth century: " The Chancellor of
Notre Dame confers the license on those who are to
profess theology and medicine.   He formerly enjoyed
the same authority in the Faculty of Law, which
shook it off in 1679, but he still continues to receive
a fee from each licentiate.   He still confers the
license on half of those who annually present themselves to take the degree of Master of Arts.   The
Chancellor of Ste. Geneviève has for his share only
the other half of the Faculty of Arts." [1]

III

In nearly all the universities the rector either was
from the beginning, or gradually became, the first
scholastic magistrate.

The title of rector, with the prerogatives appertain-
ing to it, does not appear definitely until 1245.[2]   Before this period, the same word, which is sometimes
used in papal bulls, seems to have been synonymous
with "master regent."

It is probable, however, that in the University of
Paris the rector existed before 1245,[3] and we have

to the left bank of the Seine.   It was this which rendered the
appointment of a chancellor of Ste. Geneviève necessary.

[1] Crevier, t. vii, p. 137.

[2] Crevier claims, however, to find mention of it in the privilege
of Philip Augustus, of 1200, in which he speaks of the *capitale
scholarium Parisiensium;* which in a contemporary French ver-
sion is translated by *le chevetaine,* "the captain," of the scholars.
But this officer evidently had not as yet the character of a true
rector.

[3] From 1245 to 1252, says Denifle, *nihil aliud quam Facultatem*

every ground for supposing that the first rector was elected at the time when the four Nations, of which he was the chief, were organized: that is, as I have said already, from 1215 to 1225.

At first rector of the Nations, and, before the Faculties were formally constituted, rector of the still confused mass of the entire university, it seems that, at the time of the organization of the separate Faculties, he remained for some time longer the chief of the Faculty of Arts only, the other Faculties being subordinate at the outset merely to their respective deans. It was towards the close of the thirteenth century that the rector insensibly extended his authority over the Faculties of Law and Medicine, and still later, over that of Theology, though not without meeting strenuous resistance from their deans, and especially from the dean of the Faculty of Theology.[1]

Let me sum up in a few words the principal prerogatives of the rectors. At Paris it was the rector who convoked both general and special assemblies by means of beadles and presided over them. In these reunions it was he who proposed the affairs to be deliberated on and who decided them. It appears that he did not take part in the discussions. According to the statute of 1275, he had the additional right in the intervals between the assemblies of the Faculty of Arts, which, nevertheless, occurred once a week, to regulate pressing affairs with the assistance of the

Artium Rectori incumbentem videmus. And this lasted for several years longer.

[1] In 1291 the dean of the Faculty of Theology protested against the attempt of the rector to convoke it by means of the beadle; and this struggle was prolonged until 1341.

procurators of the nations. He thus constituted a sort of tribunal before which matters of discipline were, so to speak, judged in the first instance, though with the right of a final appeal to the assembly of the university. In the fourteenth century this tribunal met three times a week. The rector had also the disposal of a part of the dues collected from the students for the common expenses of the Faculty of Arts. Lastly he exercised a right over the sale of parchment, which was seldom authorized except at the annual Lendit fair.[1]

In other universities, and notably in Italy, the rector had still more extensive privileges. At Bologna, he exercised not only civil but criminal jurisdiction over the students and all members of the university. He condemned the delinquents either to fines or to exclusion from the university.[2] With the assistance of the *consiliarii,* who replaced at Bologna the procurators of the nations in the French universities, he constituted a sort of senate which took cognizance of a great number of affairs. He presided at the examinations and at the ceremonies at

[1] The Lendit (probable etymology, *Indictus,* the day fixed), a name which has just been revived at Paris to designate the annual competition in physical exercises in which the pupils of the lycées take part, was in the Middle Ages a fair which opened yearly, on June 12, in the plain of St. Denis, and which was also called the fête of the parchment. The university went thither in procession, headed by the rector. Arrived on the fair ground, the rector, before any other buyer, laid aside the quantity of parchment needed by the university, and received a gratuity from the merchants, which amounted in the sixteenth century to 2500 francs.

[2] At Padua, the rector of the " artists " took cognizance of all crimes save those in which condemnation entailed death or mutilation.

which degrees were conferred. It was he who in the public disputes between professors as well as students, received the petitions and formulated the questions. It was he, too, who, after having examined the respective merit of each professor, drew up every year what was called the roll, or *rotula*. And this variety of important prerogatives conferred upon the Italian rectors seems still more astonishing when it is remembered that in Italy the rector was usually a student, elected by his comrades, and that at times he was not more than twenty-five years old.

The different universities present, moreover, numerous peculiarities bearing on the election and conditions of eligibility of their rectors. At Paris the rector was originally elected by the procurators of the four nations, and later by four delegates who were called *intrants*, and who were themselves elected by the nations. No condition with regard to age was fixed for the rector; but his electors must be thirty years old. He must be taken from among the ruling masters of the Faculty of Arts. He might be a layman, but he must be a celibate.

At Bologna, the rector elected by the students must be himself a student,[1] be twenty-five years of age (the same limit was fixed at Montpellier; at Padua they contented themselves with twenty-two years), and not a member of any religious order. He was placed each year. As a rule he was chosen from among the wealthier students. The statutes of the University

---

[1] At Padua, where there were several rectors, the rector of the "artists" must be a physician. At Bologna, though by an exception, rectors might be chosen from among the professors.

of Louvain required that the rector should be *satis
dives et locuples;* it was desired that he should be
able to do honor to functions which admitted of considerable display.   At Dôle the rector could be neither
a monk, a member of a religious order, a native of
Dôle, a husband, nor a doctor.[1] Celibacy was ordinarily required.   At Caen, for example, whenever a
talented young professor obtained a chair of law or
medicine, haste was made to elevate him to the rectorship lest, by a speedy marriage, he might render
himself incapable of an honor of which he seemed
worthy.[2]   At Naples the position of rector was a permanent one and was filled by the civil authorities;
but in all the other universities, as I have said, the
function was elective.   At Oxford, in the earliest
times, the rector, who was afterwards replaced by the
chancellor as head of the university, was elected by
the graduates and his election confirmed by the Bishop
of Lincoln.[3]   At Salamanca the professors had at
their head a rector elected by the *cathedraticos,* or
regents of theology of the first rank.   He was always

---

[1] Doctor, that is to say, professor; it was held that the rectorial
functions could not be associated with the duties of instruction.   In
general, the rectors did not teach, except, as it appears, in some of
the Italian universities.

[2] J. Cauvet, *L'ancienne Université de Caen,* 1873.   The married
rector was an exception.   One example is cited at Padua in 1508.

[3] " At Cambridge there was no rector, but a chancellor, who possessed many of the powers of the Parisian and Bononian rectors.
Though elected by the two houses of regents and non-regents, he
had powers independent of the regents.   His powers were ecclesiastical, both in their nature and origin.   He was constituted, says
Dean Peacock, a distinct estate in the academical commonwealth."
—Laurie, *op. cit.,* p. 243.

chosen from some great family. He had very great privileges, and was always seated under a canopy at the public assemblies.

It was usual to have but one rector, except in the Italian universities, where there were several rectors at a time. At Bologna, at Padua, and at Verceil there were at first four rectors, one for the Citramontanes, three for the Ultramontanes. Later on, there were but two; one for the University of Law, and the other for the University of Arts.

The true reason which prevented the rectors of the Middle Ages from playing a really important part in the universities, was the temporary character of their functions. How could they acquire great moral authority in a few months? The mediocrity of their rôle is sufficiently proved by little facts like these: In 1373 and in 1374, two rectors of Paris inform us, one that he has had the rector's book rebound in red leather and provided with new clasps; the other, that he has had a silver chain affixed to the rectorial seal. University officers who relate things so insignificant can have had very few important ones to do.

It was above all by the display, the external show of his position, that the rector was a notable person. He walked in the first rank, not merely in the university ceremonies, but on public occasions. At Bologna he took precedence over the archdeacon (the chancellor), the bishops and the archbishops, him of Bologna alone excepted. The rector of Paris took precedence even of the archbishop; more than once he sat in the Royal Councils with the prelates, the princes and the nobles. In an age when outward show impressed the popular imagination still more forcibly than in our own day, the rector was distinguished by the splendor of his costume, and the long procession which thronged after him wherever he went. And this prestige of the rectorial dignity lasted to the very end. In the eighteenth century, during the long quarrel that they entered into for the sake of maintaining their right of precedence against the claims of the bishop, the rectors of Poitiers said: " The rectors of universities are vested in purple and ermine like the kings, and, in consequence, they retain the function of sovereignty and of royal majesty." And they complacently recall how Ferdinand, King of Spain, caused the Rector of the University of Alcala to be seated between Cardinal Ximenes and himself.

The election of the rector, also, was surrounded everywhere by a great number of precautions and formalities. The heads of the universities were chosen with very nearly the same forms as were the popes; the duration of the conclave which was to elect them was even determined by that of the flame of a candle of fixed weight. The installation of the new rector gave rise to one of the most brilliant and imposing ceremonies of the Middle Ages. Consider, for instance, how the thing was done in a little university, that of Dôle: " Convoked the previous day, by its general beadle and by placards posted on the doors of the churches, the university assembles in the Hall of Laws, or some other suitable place, under the presidency of the acting rector, who opens the session by a discourse on the importance of the choice to be made, and the necessity of electing an honorable candidate whose merit shall be obvious to all. Afterwards he administers the oath to the electors on the Gospels, designates those who are to count the votes, and requests the former to repair, without going out, to a special hall which is called the conclave. From the moment when they cross its threshold they are prohibited from leaving it until after having made an election, under penalty of being excluded from the university for a month. If there is a tie, the acting rector takes part in the voting and ends the deadlock. But he alone can enter the chamber where the deliberations are going on, and which cannot, in any case, last more than an hour. During this time the general assembly remains in session, anxiously awaiting the announcement of the person elected, and whose choice they are to ratify. Introduced with pomp into the assembly, he swears to maintain the honor, the discipline, the peace, and the privileges of the body, to cause the statutes to be observed, and to make no decision without the advice of the council." [1]

At Bologna the assumption of the rectorial power was accompanied with the greatest pomp. The cathedral was the place ordinarily chosen for the ceremony. Drums and trumpets opened the march; then followed the students bearing gilded fasces, in memory of the Roman magistrates; then the keepers of the seal and the statutes of the university, who carried the gown of the rector; a beadle followed with a silver sceptre. The rector advanced in the midst of the procession, vested in a red robe with golden ornaments, sur-

[1] *Les Universités de la Franche Comté*, par H. Beaune et d'Arbaumont, p. xlviii.

rounded by all the dignitaries of the university, and
followed by all the students. All the magistrates of
the city and the dignitaries of the clergy were assembled in the church. There the discourses were delivered; the rector was formally invested with his gown;
and the crowd afterwards accompanied the newly
elected to his dwelling, through streets adorned and
decked in holiday attire. The remainder of the day
was devoted to games and public rejoicings.[1]

The services of the rector were not rendered gratuitously, but neither were they richly rewarded. At
Paris the rector had what was called the right of the
chappe,[2] a payment made by the new Masters of Arts,[3]
besides the tax on the parchment levied at the Lendit
fair, and certain other revenues. At Padua the salary
of the rector was at first fifty ducats, afterwards one
hundred; at Pisa, in 1473, forty florins, afterwards
sixty or one hundred. But what proves that the rector
was not highly paid by the university — although he
carried a large violet purse at his belt, " in which,"
says Duboulay,[4] " the common people believed that
there were always one hundred gold crowns, I know
not on what foundation " — is that candidates for rectorial functions were usually sought for among those
who possessed private fortunes; still another proof
is found in the gratuities solicited occasionally by the
rectors and granted by the Nations. In 1347, the

[1] Coppi, *op. cit.*, p. 147.

[2] The *chappe*, that is, the habit, the rectorial costume.

[3] Crevier, t. iii, p. 391.

[4] Duboulay, *Remarques sur la dignité, puissance, authorité et
jurisdiction du Recteur de l'Université de Paris.* Paris, 1668,
p. 24.

rector was allowed four livres; in 1410, thirty gold crowns, "to assist him, no doubt," says Crevier, "in defraying the cost of his dignity." [1] The smallness of these sums would cause a smile if one did not take into consideration the value of money in an age when King Charles V thought he had paid Erasmus generously for his translation of the Ethics of Aristotle, by giving him one hundred francs.

In spite of its short duration and its meagre rewards, the office of rector was sought for none the less, and much intriguing was done to obtain it. This was because it assured, in the first place, several months of supremacy and universal respect to him who exercised it; whenever a member of the university addressed the rector, in Paris at all events, he said to him, *Vestra amplitudo*. . . . It was also because, after having attained the rectorship, there remained to the rectors throughout their lives something of that prestige which attached in Rome to men of consular rank; the rector of Paris was inscribed first in the list which the university annually submitted to the pope for the conferring of benefices.

IV

I shall not dwell upon the other university dignitaries, and shall limit myself to little more than enumerating them. The Nations had their chiefs everywhere, the procurators at Paris, the counsellors (*consigliarii*) at Bologna. [2] The procurators of Cam-

[1] Crevier, t. ii, p. 372.
[2] At Bologna there were as many counsellors as Nations, namely,

bridge were called vice-rectors. The procurator kept
a register of his administration; there was a *liber pro-
curatoris* as there was a *liber rectoris*.

Here are a few details concerning the rôle of the
procurators of the medical students at Montpellier in
the sixteenth century. This dignitary was elected annually by his comrades, and might be taken indifferently from the ordinary students or the bachelors.
"As the common welfare," said the statutes of 1534,
"depends upon those who administer the public functions, special care should be taken to select a faithful
and zealous procurator, who will show himself jealous
for the honor and the interests of the university; any
one who leads a dishonest life, who is addicted to gaming or debauchery, is unworthy of this office and should
be excluded from it." The procurator of Montpellier
had the right to remonstrate with professors who
were not punctual in giving their lectures : " At the
request of the students in medicine, I, the procurator,
accompanied by counsellors [1] and assisted by a notary
and witnesses, have presented myself to the doctors
who through unwillingness do not deliver their lectures, and have requested them to fulfil their duties."
The badge of office of the procurator at Montpellier
was a baton of honor, which he carried in the public
ceremonies.[2]   At Paris the procurators of the Nations
wore red robes.

The procurator, therefore, was the agent, the *chargé*

eighteen for the Ultramontanes and seventeen for the Citramontanes.

[1] The procurator of Montpellier was assisted by counsellors.

[2] La Valabrègne, *La Vie Universitaire à Montpellier*, 1890, p. 9
et seq.

d'affaires, as one might say, of the students. Sometimes he represented a Nation, sometimes a Faculty, according to the customs of different universities. At Paris the procurator of the Nation of France had special privileges; in case of a vacancy in the rectorate, he was considered the head of the Faculty of Arts. At first the powers of the office did not regularly last longer than a month, but they were afterwards extended to a year.

Another university magistrate who did not exist everywhere, but whom we find at Paris and at Bologna, was the *syndic*, who was also called the "fiscal procurator." At Paris, the syndic, according to Duboulay and Crevier, must have been instituted by 1203.[1] But he seems to have played a sufficiently unimportant part. At Bologna, and at Padua and Pisa as well, the syndic, who sometimes took the title of vice-rector, was elected every year by the students. He replaced the absent rector. Normally, he represented the university before the tribunals.[2]

Other offices were rendered necessary by the administration of the university revenues, — at Louvain the *receptores*, simple stewards or cashiers; in Italy, the treasurer, who was sometimes chosen from among the professors and again from the students.

In like manner the drawing up of acts and registers was confided in Paris to a registrar (*greffier*), and in Italy to a notary, to archivists, etc.

The universities had subaltern agents also, the

[1] Crevier, t. i, p. 284.

[2] Among the dignitaries of the university must also be reckoned the conservator of royal privileges (at Paris the provost) and the conservator of apostolic privileges (usually a bishop).

beadles, whose business it was to announce the days and hours of lectures, to publish the decisions of the university councils, to transmit the summons of the rector, to assist the professors during their courses, and to maintain good order in the schools; and who, moreover, with their silver maces, preceded the rector in the public ceremonies. At Paris there were fourteen beadles, two for each Nation and Faculty. In certain universities the beadles seem to have been something more than mere agents for material services. In Italy, according to Coppi, one of their duties was to exercise "a secret surveillance over the private conduct of the professors."[1]

The university personnel was numerous, as may be seen. It comprehended also, among those entitled to the privileges of the university, all whose industry was necessary to the carrying on of the studies: booksellers, paper makers, bookbinders, parchment makers, illuminators, copyists, etc. In Italy the *stationarii* were required to furnish the students with all the books and manuscripts they needed. The trade in books was a university monopoly. The trade of the copyists, who put the lectures of the professors into circulation among the students, was very lucrative and gave employment to many persons. The booksellers sometimes abused the favorable conditions created for them by the scarcity of books, and in 1275 the University of Paris intervened to tax at four deniers the book, their right of brokerage.[2]

Finally, a word must be said concerning the messen-

[1] Coppi, *op. cit.*, p. 161.

[2] " When printing came to transform and renew the industry of the book trade, it remained none the less under the protection of the

gers, who, at the beginning, formed a part of the
membership (*suppôts*) of the university. There is
mention of the *nuntii* as early as the edict of Frederick Barbarossa, in 1158.[1] From the earliest times
the University of Paris appointed messengers, whose
duty it was to carry the letters of the students to the
provinces or to foreign parts, and to bring back the
answers and the money, clothing, and other things
which parents wished to send to their children.
"But the insecurity of the roads at the time often
caused interruptions in the journeys of the messengers.
The students were more than once obliged to have
recourse to the citizens of Paris in order to procure
what they needed. The citizens profited by the occasion to claim the privileges of messengers. The
university agreed to take them under its protection,
and thereupon a distinction arose between the great
and the petty messengers of the university.[2] The
university messengers did not confine their labors to
the service of the masters and students, moreover.
They gradually extended it to the transportation of
letters and packages for private persons; and this was
the origin of the establishment of stage coaches, which
formed one of the most important sources of the
university revenues.[3]

university; and up to the French Revolution the *libraires jurés* of
the university received their investiture from the rector, and the
Faculty of Theology had the right of censorship over all writings
which might touch upon the faith." — Vallet de Viriville, *Histoire
de l'Instruction publique*, p. 128.

[1] Frederick accorded the privileges granted by this charter, "*tam
ipsis scholaribus quam eorum nunciis.*"

[2] Caillet, *de l'Administration en France sous Richelieu*, 1857, p.
443.

[3] At the outset the taxes paid by the petty messengers, that is,

V

The real power, in the universities of the Middle Ages, as I have said, was not in the hands of the dignitaries I have just enumerated. It remained either in the general assembly (*congregatio generalis*) of the university or in the individual assemblies of each Faculty and Nation. The universities were essentially federated republics, the government of which pertained either to the whole body of the masters, as in the University of Paris, which was a university of professors, or to the whole body of the students, as in the democratic University of Bologna, which was a university of students. The rector and the procurators were mere delegates, charged with the execution of the wishes of the corporation. "They had no inclination," says Crevier, "to transfer the rights of the body to its heads."

From the close of the thirteenth century, in 1289,[1] there sat in the general council of the University of Paris, the rector, who presided, the procurators of the Nations, and the deans of the Faculties.[2]

Only the Superior Faculties had each its dean, the rector being the special head of the Faculty of

by the letter carriers and couriers, accrued either to the procurator of the Nations, the rector, or to the deans of the Faculties. In the seventeenth century the stage coach service became a public one; but it was understood that a part of the proceeds of this service would remain at the disposition of the university, which used them to pay a salary to the professors of the colleges of the Faculty of Arts. This prepared the way for the reform of 1719, the year when gratuitous instruction was established.

[1] Crevier, t. ii, p. 118.

[2] At Bologna the deans were called "the priors."

Arts. In 1267 or 1268 there occurs for the first time in the acts of the University of Paris, mention of the deans of the Faculty of Decrees and the Faculty of Medicine; in 1290, of the dean of Theology, who seems, in the earliest times, to have been the same person as the Chancellor of Notre Dame. In the eighteenth century, when Crevier drew up the list of the dignitaries of the University of Paris, the deans were regulated thus: the dean of the Faculty of Theology was the eldest of its secular professors; the Faculty of Law chose its dean yearly from its professors, following the order of seniority; the Faculty of Medicine alone, since 1338, had had an elected dean whose official term lasted two years.

The deans held a very important office. They were the real administrators of their respective Faculties. They presided in the assemblies of their company, and were members of the council of the University.

At Paris, the professors alone composed the assemblies of the Faculties. It was necessary to be a Master of Arts to be a member of the Faculty of Arts; and a professor, to take part in the deliberations of the other Faculties. "All powers," says Thurot, "were concentrated in the assemblies of the companies; they passed the regulations, examined particular requests, and nominated directly to all the offices. . . . Ordinarily their chiefs could decide nothing without having taken the orders of the company."[1] It was, therefore, the special councils of each Superior Faculty, and of the four Nations assembled in the Faculty of Arts, which regulated all that concerned

[1] Thurot, *op. cit.*, p. 20.

discipline, the collection and employment of revenues, the character of the courses and discussions. In the Superior Faculties votes were cast by persons; in the Faculty of Arts, by Nations.

One divines the part reserved to the general assembly of the university, a sort of supreme and regulating council, which for the most part contented itself with confirming the decisions of the companies when they were submitted to it. The rector, as president, proposed the subject of discussion; then each of the companies deliberated separately; after which the procurators and the deans reported to the council, which deliberated on them, the opinions of the Nations and the Faculties; and the rector summed up. Here are some examples of the decisions arrived at by the Assembly of the University: in 1333, abolition of the provinces of the Nation of England; in 1356, determination of the limits of the Nation of England and the Nation of Picardy; in 1389, obligation imposed on bachelors in theology to sojourn in Paris until their licentiate. In all of these matters the university did hardly more than intervene to give additional weight to the separate resolutions of each company. A certain number of questions, however, were in the exclusive jurisdiction of the great council of the University: all those which related to the common privileges of the University, and to the violation or abuse of these privileges; those, also, which concerned the industries placed under its protection, such as book and parchment making.

In the other universities we shall find, with certain variations, the same system of self-government. At

Prague there was at first a *congregatio universitatis*, in which masters and students had equal votes. This was the primary assembly. Above this sat a special university council (*concilium universitatis*) composed of eight members, two from each Nation. The supreme council, under the authority of the rector, became the directing power of the University of Prague. At Cambridge, the internal regulation of the education and of the degree system rested practically with the voting masters, in spite of the considerable prerogatives conferred on the Chancellor.

It is permissible to say, then, that in the heart of the Middle Ages, when all the nations, from the political point of view, knew as yet nothing but the régime of a more or less absolute monarchy, the universities had already made trial of liberty in their internal life: they were republics of letters and of scientific men in a world still bowed down under the domination of emperors and kings. Undoubtedly they depended on the pontifical authority for the general regulation of discipline and the programme of studies. It was the papal legates who presided at all the reforms of the University of Paris, in 1366 and 1452, before the civil authority had laid hands upon it, under Henry IV, in 1600. But in the election of their officers, in the details of their organization, in the daily management of their affairs and their interests, the universities had nevertheless a vast field of independent action before them. They were the first bodies, since ancient times, to exercise self-government, and thus to give an example to the statesmen of the future. I do not deny that the liberty they enjoyed had its excesses, its abuses, and also its weaknesses,[1] that their régime was sometimes anarchic; in spite of all, they lived, they prospered. They applied successfully a system of government which modern peoples are more and more tending to extend, not simply to studies and scholastic matters, but to the whole body of their affairs and interests of every kind. Before the free English monarchy, the University of Paris had been, under a nominal chief, the rector, an example of representative and parliamentary government. Before the modern republics of the old world and the new, the University of Bologna had made trial of democratic government.

[1] It is a strange thing that the assemblies of Paris, after having been only too tumultuous and disturbed by shouts and quarrelling, became almost deserted. In 1417 it was asserted that while not more than five or six were present in the cloister of the Mathurius (the place of the gatherings of the Faculty of Arts), not fewer than thirty scholars were counted at the same moment in a wine shop, *in tabernis*.

CHAPTER IV

SYSTEM OF GRADUATION

I. Examinations and grades wholly unknown to antiquity — Graduation is an invention of the Mediæval Universities — Analogy with the apprenticeship and mastership of the commercial guilds — Origin of university degrees — Time of their institution — The *licentia docendi* — The right of conferring degrees assumed by the ecclesiastical power — II. The three university degrees: bachelorship, licentiateship, mastership or doctorship — The bachelor — Various meanings of this word — The "determinance"; first trial in the Faculty of Arts — The bachelor of arts, of theology, of medicine, of law — The bachelorship an apprenticeship for the license — III. The licentiateship — Masters or doctors — Various procedures of the faculties of arts, of theology, etc. — The conferring of the mastership a ceremony rather than an examination — Forms of promotion in Bologna, in Montpellier — Considerable expense attending the promotions — Defects and abuses.

I

IF it be true that there is good ground of complaint at present against the multiplicity of examinations; if the objections made by those who protest against the unreasonableness of competitions and the infinite variety of diplomas are well founded, it is the Middle Ages which must be held responsible, for they were the first culprits; it is the universities of the Middle Ages which must be blamed, for they were the inventors of examinations and degrees. In Greek and

Roman antiquity there is no trace of any test of capacity, nor even of any conditions whatsoever, being imposed on any one who desired to teach. Neither the sophists nor the philosophers of the school of Socrates were graduated. Theirs was the age of absolute liberty of instruction. It is true that Quintilian, the celebrated professor of rhetoric, was pensioned at Rome by Vespasian,[1] but he had no greater need than his contemporaries of a degree of any sort to justify him in keeping school.

It is in an edict of the Emperor Valentinian, in 329, that a distinction, though still a vague one, is drawn for the first time between the sophists of that age, wandering and worthless professors, who, it was said, having no right to teach, ought to be dismissed and requested to vacate the premises, and the masters who, on the contrary, being held in esteem by competent men, ought to be distinguished from their rivals and authorized to teach.[2] It is none the less true that it was the Middle Ages that really inaugurated a system of graduation, conferring the right to teach after a certain term of studies and appropriate examinations.

Mr. Laurie has made the clever remark that, in instituting their degrees, the universities were merely imitating customs already established in the industrial and commercial corporations.[3] "The members of a guild corporation were divided into three distinct classes — *apprentices, assistants* or *companions,* and

---

[1] ". . . *e fisco salarium accepit.*" See my *Histoire des doctrines de l'Éducation,* t. i, p. 33.

[2] ". . . *exceptis his qui a probatissimis approbati ab hac debuerunt colluvione secerni.*"   [3] Laurie, *op. cit.,* p. 215.

masters. These assistants were in France frequently called *garçons* or *compagnons du devoir.* The assistants were not admitted to the grade of 'master' until they had performed some special task assigned to them. . . . It was only if this *chef-d'œuvre* was found satisfactory that they were installed as masters —a ceremony which was generally followed by a banquet. The *garçon* who obtained his mastership obtained thereby for the first time freedom to exercise his trade, or craft, and all the rights of a member of the guild."

Is not this a very exact image of what took place in the university corporations when it was understood that in order to become a master of arts, and have the right to follow the profession of teaching, one must have spent a certain number of years on the benches of a school and have passed a successful examination before competent judges ?

It is manifest that the universities borrowed from the industrial corporations their "companionships," their "masterships," and even their banquets; a great repast being the ordinary sequel of the reception of the baccalaureate or doctorate.[1]

The comparison will seem even more just when one reflects that the grades were not what the baccalaureate, for example, is in France at present, — a mere evidence of successful studies, a passport granted to those who, after passing regularly through

[1] " The trial for the mastership, by public disputation against all comers in presence of the other masters, was analogous to the *chef-d'œuvre* that the aspirant to the mastership of a craft had to submit to the judgment of the jurors of his craft." Laurie, *op. cit.*, p. 218.

the classes of a college, seek to make some sort of place for themselves in society. The grades, the "degrees," were then professional titles, something like the different orders which must be received by an ecclesiastic before arriving at the priesthood. They conferred the right to exercise an exclusive profession ; like the *licentia docendi*, granted very early at Paris, without examination, moreover,* and without much care, by the Chancellor of Notre Dame ; or like the *licentia medendi*, accorded to the physicians of Salerno from the twelfth century.

It is impossible to fix precisely the period at which the system of degrees began to be organized. Things were done slowly. At the outset, and until towards the end of the twelfth century, there existed nothing resembling a real conferring of degrees in the rising universities. In order to teach, it was sufficient to have a respondent, a master authorized by age and knowledge. Abelard was not reproached for teaching without a degree, but for teaching without a master, *sine magistro*. So, too, at Bologna, Irnerius does not seem to have been the pupil of any one, or to derive his eminent and indisputable learning from any one except himself. This was the time when a pope, Alexander III, opposed the pretensions of the bishops who wished to have the right of conferring the license to teach reserved exclusively to them or their delegates, and seemed to believe that the teaching faculty was a gift of God. At any rate, he formally forbade that any sum of money should be required from the candidates as the price of the right to teach, which was granted them, and he required that "any capable and instructed man" (*idoneus et litteratus*) should be authorized to keep school.[1]

The "license to teach," nevertheless, became by slow degrees, as masters and pupils multiplied, a preliminary condition of teaching, a sort of diploma more and more requisite, and of which the bishops or their representatives, chancellors or *écolâtres*,[2] were the dispensers. Up to the fourteenth century there was hardly any other clearly defined university title: the license to teach law or medicine at Bologna or Salerno, where law and medicine were still the only studies in vogue; the license to teach the arts and theology at Paris, where the arts and theology were still in ascendency.

Originally, the license was conferred without an examination on whomever was held to possess the necessary aptitude. By degrees greater severity was introduced, principally in what concerned theology, the popes being specially interested in the teaching of it. In his bull of 1231, Gregory IX recommended the Chancellor of Paris to make a serious investigation of the capacity and the morals of aspirants for professorships: "Future chancellors," said he, "shall swear not to receive as professors of theology and canon law any but worthy men, able to do honor to their precepts, and they shall reject all who are unworthy, without respect either to persons or to nations. Before conferring the license, the chancellor

[1] *Chartularium Univ. Paris.*, t. i, p. 5. So, also, in the Lateran Council of 1179, the same pope said: *Nullus quemquam, qui sit idoneus, petita licentia interdicat (Ibid.*, p. 10).

[2] Ecclesiastical professors who taught philosophy and belles-lettres in each cathedral school.

shall allow three months to elapse, dating from the day when the license was asked for, and during these three months he shall make inquiries of the professors of theology and other serious and instructed persons, in order to become acquainted with the life and manners, the knowledge, capacity, love of study, perfectibility, and other qualities needful in those who aspire to teach; and, these inquiries finished, he shall grant or refuse the license according to his conscience." [1]

Gradual progress was thus being made toward a regulation, toward a system of examinations. Conditions were imposed already. Acting professors were consulted as to the merits of their pupils. Later on, these professors will examine the candidates, and subject their knowledge and their abilities to established tests. It was required that the inquiry intrusted to the chancellor should extend over three months. Later, it will be from the candidates themselves that a scholastic probation, and evidence of a certain number of years devoted to study, will be required.

At the beginning, then, the "license to teach" was neither a degree, nor an examination. In any case it was the sole degree. [2] True, bachelors [3] and doctors, that is, as it seems, students and professors, were already much spoken of; but there was neither a bachelorship nor a doctorship. "Doctor" or "master" meant then any one who taught. "Originally,"

[1] *Chartularium Univ. Paris.*, t. i, p. 237.

[2] "A *degree*, originally, was a license to teach." Malden, *On the Origin of Universities*, London, 1849, p. 112.

[3] In the bull of Gregory IX (1231), there is already question of bachelors: "... *qui et qua hora et quid legere debeant bachellarii.*"

says Crevier, "the terms *doctor* and *professor* were synonymous."[1] There were *doctores juris*[2] at Bologna from the twelfth century, and from the thirteenth *doctores medicinæ, philosophiæ,* etc., but all these before the examinations which afterwards gave a right to these titles had been instituted. In other words, "doctor" and "master" were expressions employed at first in a general sense before taking a definite signification in order to designate the degrees, the particular grades of the university hierarchy.[3] It was altogether natural, in fact, that he who had obtained the license to teach (*licentia docendi*) should be called *doctor*. So, too, there were "bachelors," that is, apprentices, beginners, although there was as yet no thought of establishing an examination corresponding to the first grade of studies, and although there was nothing that resembled what, in the fourteenth century, was called the *déterminance*, or the bachelorship.

Another peculiarity of these somewhat obscure and confused beginnings of the graduation system is that the professors, who were not as yet formed into a regular corporation, a Faculty, exerted a merely secondary influence, and played but a minor part in the granting of licenses. The time had not yet come

[1] Crevier, t. v, p. 149.

[2] Irnerius, however, is styled *magister* and *dominus*, but not *doctor*.

[3] "In the early days of the school of Bologna," says Savigny, "the expressions, *doctor, magister,* and *dominus* had the signification of *professor*. These titles could not designate an office or a degree, since at that time nothing of the sort existed."

when, in this matter, the principle would prevail that
responsibility ought to be allied to competence; and
that academic degrees could not legitimately be conferred except by academic bodies. Originally it is
the Church, the teaching Church, which believes that
it alone has the power and the right to appoint professors. And when, later on, assailed by the incessant
progress of university autonomy, the Church will be
obliged to concede this right, at least in so far as it is
real and positive, to the members of the university,
the chancellor retaining a merely nominal authority,
and having nothing to do except to countersign the
diplomas granted by the Faculties — it will not abdi-
cate all claims upon it. In 1522, and in 1547, we
shall see the popes giving to their legates, by formal
bulls, the right to create bachelors, licentiates, and
doctors, with all the privileges attached to these
titles.[1] Likewise, in 1550, we shall find Julius III
granting to the Society of Jesus the right to confer degrees upon all the pupils in its colleges. But in these
latter cases, the Church will at least content itself with
claiming for its delegates, or for a favorite and especially loved congregation, a participation in a privilege
which it no longer dares to contest with the enfranchised and all-powerful universities. Originally, on
the contrary, it was not merely a part but the totality
of the academic investitures which the Church claimed
the right to exercise, and which, in fact, it did exer-

---

[1] Crevier, t. v, pp. 204, 475. The University of Paris protested
energetically moreover against these bulls, which protest, it appears,
remained ineffectual.

cise. " In the thirteenth century," says M. Germain, "at Montpellier, as at Paris and Bologna and everywhere else, degrees were conferred under the auspices of the ecclesiastical authority." [1]

II

When the different Faculties had been constituted in the midst of the university, each with its regular course of studies and its special corps of professors, the system of degrees followed naturally from the necessity of controlling the work of the pupils, of closing by examinations and by private or public acts, and of celebrating by ceremonies, the successive periods of study. Already, in preceding centuries, the old distinction of *trivium* and of *quadrivium* had displayed a tendency to mark out two stages in the study of the liberal arts. This tendency became general. Thenceforward there were several degrees in each Faculty, and nearly the same degrees, with the same names, in all the Faculties. The professors became the judges of their pupils, and recommended to the chancellor, who no longer had anything to do except to record their decisions, the candidates whom they deemed worthy to be graduated.

[1] Germain, *Étude historique sur l'école de droit de Montpellier*, 1877, p. 10. M. Germain cites the following fact in corroboration: " In 1268, the King of Aragon, James I, conceived the notion of appointing a professor of civil law, in his capacity as seigneur of Montpellier, and without the concurrence of the Bishop of Maguelonne. The latter protested, and the pope, Clement IV, gave judgment in his favor, by citing a canon of Eugenius IV, who had invested the bishops with the privilege of appointing the professors to their chairs."

At Paris — and the usages established at Paris, except in the case of certain peculiarities which I shall point out in the other universities, became during the course of the fourteenth century the general rule — three degrees were distinguished, the bachelorship, the licentiateship, the mastership or doctorship.[1] To be exact, the mastership did not constitute a special degree, — the mastership was merely a title, the consequence of the license and its formal consecration. "The assumption of the title of master by the licentiate," says Laurie justly, "was a merely ceremonial introduction into the magistral body."

Let us begin by examining the first of these three academic degrees, the baccalaureate, to discover its origin : neither the word nor the thing is as clear as it might be.

Littré sets forth as follows the various significations of the word bachelor : "In its primitive sense, the *baccalarius* was a countryman who managed a certain number of 'manses,' that is, of estates. The name was also given to a young warrior who was not yet a knight. Then there were bachelors of the Church who were ecclesiastics of an inferior degree. In the trade corporations there were bachelors called *juniores* who managed the minor affairs of the corporation. Finally, and from the same current of thought, sprang the bachelors of the Faculties." [2]

---

[1] "The grades, steps, or degrees were nominally four, actually three, viz., bachelor, licentiate or master, finally doctor." (Laurie, *op. cit.*, p. 228.) It would be more exact to say : bachelor, licentiate, finally master or doctor.

[2] Littré, *Dictionnaire de la langue française*, on the word *Bachelier*.

"Bachelor," then, was a very general term, whose different uses were justified by the fact that it was always applied to an inferior, a beginner, an apprentice. It was thus that the word, in growing still more common, became the synonym for a young man who was serving his apprenticeship in life.[1] So, too, a "bachelette" was a young girl.

Introduced into scholastic language, the word "bachelor" was at first employed only to designate the youngest students, those aspiring to the licentiate. Even when a real examination, the *déterminance*, had been instituted as the preliminary test imposed on students of the Faculty of Arts, it did not at once become customary to give this examination the name of *baccalaureate*,[2] and not until the fifteenth century do we find the word "bachelor" plainly used to designate a student who had successfully undergone the trial of the *déterminance*.

The *déterminance* was, then, the first form of the bachelorship of arts. It was regularly established at Paris from 1275. In what did it consist? *Determinare*, in the barbarous Latin of the Middle Ages, was to posit a thesis, to argue a question,[3] to explain a logical term or proposition, and to reply to objec-

[1] Finally, all celibates came to be called bachelors, . . . " *qui non habent uxorem.*" In English the word still retains this signification.

[2] "The determinants or bachelors were not granted regular diplomas. The Nation merely sent them certificates of their degree " (Thurot, *op. cit.*, p. 48).

[3] The complete expression was *determinare quæstionem*. Crevier defines the " determinance " as a public act in which the candidates for bachelorship explained in a consecutive discourse some question of logic (Crevier, t. i, p. 398).

tions. There was as yet no question of written exercises, of essays, to be composed on a given subject. The teaching of the Middle Ages was altogether oral; the great scholastic exercise was debate, discussion. And notwithstanding the modifications it underwent during the course of centuries, the *déterminance*, or test for the bachelorship, remained, after the pattern of the studies which it assumed, an argumentation, a *disputatio* more formal than the others. It took place under the superintendence of one or more professors and in presence of the other students. It was, moreover, an internal examination, so to speak, and the title to which it gave a right did not need to be sanctioned by the chancellor.

Certain conditions were imposed upon the candidates who desired to sustain the *déterminance:* they must be at least fourteen years of age; have pursued a course of logic during two years, etc. We shall see, moreover, over what books this course of logic ranged.[1] M. Thurot maintains that this semi-domestic test of the *déterminance* was "of easy access." I do not absolutely deny this. It is, nevertheless, certain that a youth of fourteen or fifteen needed a good deal of strength of mind to undertake a public argumentation, prolonged through several days, before an audience which was sometimes imposing, the professors of the Superior Faculties and ecclesiastical dignitaries being invited to be present at it. "The determinant," says Thurot, "was obliged to argue every day during Lent, or, when for the Lenten discussions were substituted

[1] See Part III, chap. i.

those of Christmas, during an entire month." [1] The *déterminance*, properly so called, was followed, moreover, by a real examination; that is, by interrogatories bearing on logic again, and on grammar, and which was conducted by examiners who had been graduated at least three years, and were elected by the Nations. The minor university title, the bachelorship, was not, after all, such an easy thing to win; and I should be disposed to agree on this point with Mr. Laurie: "If we keep in mind," he says, "the youth of the candidates, the want of books, and the method of teaching, we shall be satisfied that even this minor degree marked the conclusion of a period of hard and sustained work. There was no food for the mind, but there was a great deal of severe discipline of the memory and intellect." [2]

Originally established in the Faculty of Arts, the baccalaureate was afterwards extended to the other Faculties under special forms and conditions. Thus, the baccalaureate in theology implied three series of examinations. To enter the first, it was needful to be twenty-five years old, to have studied for ten years, and to be neither a bastard nor deformed. The candidates were examined on the principles of theology, and restricted, besides, to lectures on the Bible and to

[1] The details of the regulations of the test of the *déterminance* were frequently modified. Toward the close of the thirteenth century, it was preceded by a private examination intended to serve as a first selection and elimination from the formal trial of candidates esteemed incapable. The time of the public dispute, which at first took place during Lent, was in the fifteenth century fixed between St. Martin's Feast, Nov. 11, and Christmas.

[2] Laurie, *op. cit.*, p. 274.

argumentations. They were called *biblici ordinarii et cursores*. The conditions for the second part of the baccalaureate were that one must have studied nine years, have given two courses on the Bible, and two conferences, or a sermon and a conference, in order to make proofs of a talent for preaching, and, finally, to sustain an argumentation called *tentative;* after which the candidate was authorized to read Peter Lombard's *Book of the Sentences;* finally, the bachelors of this second category, who were called the *Sententiarii,* when they had finished their course on the *Sentences,* became *baccalarii formati,* which was the last step to be taken before presenting themselves for the license.[1]

The Faculties of Civil and of Canon Law, and the Faculties of Medicine had their bachelors also. At Bologna the "bachelor," of whom no mention is made until the end of the thirteenth century, was a law student who had followed the lectures of professors during several years, and who had been authorized to direct the extraordinary courses which were called *repetitions.* For bachelor of medicine, five years of preliminary studies were required at Paris. The examination was not public. For canon law, again at Paris, preliminary evidence of attainments in grammar and in logic was required ; but it was not necessary, as one might be tempted to suppose, to produce a diploma as bachelor of arts, which sufficiently proves that the various baccalaureates were internal examinations peculiar to each order of Faculties, and giving no rights in the others. Originally it was necessary to prove in addition that one had studied civil law for three years

[1] See Part III, chap. ii.

in another university (civil law not being taught at Paris). This condition, suppressed by Innocent VI, was replaced by the requirement that canon law should have been studied during forty-eight months within a period of six years. These proofs having been supplied, the candidate had to submit to an examination; and afterwards to accomplish two public acts called *propositum* and *harenga*. The *propositum* was a decision grounded on one or two juridical questions; the *harenga* was a discourse, an "harangue," in honor of canon law. The Faculties of Civil Law exacted similar proofs and conditions.

It results from the foregoing remarks, that in all the faculties there was a baccalaureate,[1] or first term of studies, sanctioned by appropriate examinations. This baccalaureate was really a degree, notwithstanding Thurot, who declares that it was simply "a state,

---

[1] I shall not run the risk of taking sides between the different explanations proposed for the etymology of the word "baccalaureate." Vallet de Viriville claims that it is derived from *baculum* (*bâton*) by an analogy drawn from the contests in which young soldiers were exercised. Littré also admits that its origin must be sought in the word *baculum*, but he traces the filiation differently. "It is not an altogether unlikely conjecture," says he, "to suppose that the word *bâton*, piece of wood, became a *bachelerie*, a sort of rural domain." We have already seen that to Littré the primitive signification of "bachelor" was the manager of a rural domain. Laurie suggests another explanation which to us appears wholly fantastic. "The original of the word seems to have been *baccalarius*, and this is said to be derived from the low Latin *bacca* (for *vacca*), a cow. Accordingly it originally meant a cowboy or herd serving a farmer." In any case, it is quite certain that we must reject as devised too late and devoid of serious foundation, that etymology by which the word *baccalarius*, become *baccalaureus*, was supposed to have connection with the laurel berry.

the apprenticeship of the mastership"; a grade, how-ever, which might be said to make one with the immediately superior degree, the license, a degree conferred by the faculties without the intervention of the chancellor. To-day, in France, at least, in the Faculties of Letters and Sciences, the bachelors usually consider the gaining of the diploma of the bac-calaureate as a definitive act which concludes their studies. The bachelor of the Middle Ages, on the contrary, was only an apprentice who aspired to the license and the mastership. It was said of the bach-elor of arts that *incipiebat in artibus.* The bachelors took part in the instruction given in their respec-tive faculties; they pursued courses then called *extraordinary,* now *complementary,* and which were added to the regular, or *ordinary,* courses taught by licentiates and doctors. The bachelors, then, did professional work; they already practised, under the direction of masters, the instruction they intended to give. "The bachelorship," says Laurie, "had a pro-spective rather than a retrospective significance; that is to say, it did not so much mark a course finished as 'inception in arts,' with a view to a mastership."[1]

---

[1] At Oxford and at Cambridge matters were regulated in much the same way, with possibly still greater precision. Four years' study was required before the *déterminance.* Moreover, there were special and sufficiently odd titles given to express the different degrees of the scholastic term; for example, the student who could present himself as a public disputant was called *sophister generalis.* The candidate for the baccalaureate who was called the *questionist,* before *determinare quæstionem,* must *respondere ad quæstionem.* See Mullinger for all these details, *op. cit.,* p. 354.

III

If, as we have seen, the licentiate was the first academic degree established in the order of time, it remained, even when the custom of preceding it by the baccalaureate had been confirmed, the degree *par excellence*, the most serious, the most important examination, and, in certain Faculties, the only serious and important one; the mastership and the doctorate were but its natural consequence and consecration.[1]

The masters of arts at Paris seem to have taken part for the first time, in 1213, in the conferring of the licentiate's degree. Six of them, three chosen by their colleagues and three by the chancellor, presented the candidates to the latter, attesting by an oath taken with their hands on the Gospels, that the aspirants merited the degree. Evidently they could not make this declaration until they had ascertained the capacity of the candidates by a preliminary examination. The manner of this examination was often modified, and I cannot hope to describe its successive and varying forms. As in the case of the baccalaureate, there were antecedent conditions, — to be twenty-one years of age, unmarried, to have passed the *déterminance*, either at Paris or some university which possessed a determinate number of regents, etc. There was some wisdom in these precautions taken by the Middle Ages in order to prove that the aspirants

---

[1] "The mastership," says Thurot, "was to the licentiateship what the wedding party is to the nuptial benediction; a ceremony celebrated in honor, and on occasion of, the Sacrament that has just been received."

for degrees had pursued a regular course of studies; but the rules too often remained a dead letter. The examination itself took place in the presence of the chancellor, assisted by various examiners chosen by him.[1] It was not public, but what was then called an examination *in cameris*. Nevertheless, at certain periods, the candidate was obliged to give a public lecture. The examination was on grammar, logic, Aristotle's physics and morals, and also, as it appears, on the elements of mathematics and astronomy.[2] It must not be forgotten, either, that the bachelors, as real apprentices, must at once practise teaching and give lessons to those of their younger comrades who were aspiring to the baccalaureate.

In his opuscule entitled *De Conscientia*, Robert de Sorbon[3] has given the most precise details concerning the examinations undergone by the candidates for the licentiate. The candidate, already a bachelor, sought the chancellor, and received from him a book upon which he was to be interrogated; he carried it away with him, read it over, and then "noted and studied the questions wherein difficulties might be encountered." Thus prepared, he returned to ask for a day on which he might be examined. He then made his appearance before a jury composed of the chancellor and several doctors, who made him debate the sub-

[1] There were differences, moreover, between the examinations held before the Chancellor of Notre Dame and those that passed in presence of the Chancellor of Ste. Geneviève. See Thurot, p. 53.

[2] The rules enacted at the time of the reforms of 1366 and of 1452 added metaphysics also.

[3] On Robert de Sorbon, see Part III, chap. ii.

ject; they admitted him if he succeeded; if not, they put him back for a year.

The licentiate was conferred in nearly the same way in the other Faculties. But the licentiates were less numerous; in the Faculty of Theology, for instance, the conferring of the licentiate's degree took place every two years, in the year called the *Jubilé*. It was the same in the Faculties of Decrees and of Medicine.

After the chancellor had conferred the licentiate-ship in arts, adding to it the apostolic benediction, the new licentiate had to be accepted by the masters in arts, in a sort of ceremony which properly consti-tuted the act of conferring the mastership. He pre-sented himself in the first place before the rector, promising to respect the statutes of the university, taking, in a word, an oath of university loyalty. Then, on a fixed day, he went in great pomp to the schools of his nation, in the rue du Fouarre, and there received the master's cap, the doctor's cap, from the master under whose direction he had pre-pared and undergone his examination for the licen-tiate.

The mastership in arts was, in fact, equivalent to the doctorate. It was the highest title in this order of studies. It gave those invested with it the right to sit in professorial chairs. The appellation of doctor in arts was, it seems, never customary in Paris.

The title of master and that of doctor were never, for that matter, clearly distinguished throughout the Middle Ages, even in the superior Faculties. In the University of Paris as in that of Bologna, for the theologians, the jurists, and the physicians, there was a series of public examinations, or, at least, a series of ceremonies conducted with the most extreme formality, which followed the licentiate and terminated the student life in order to give access to the professorial career. This *ensemble* of acts was sometimes called the mastership and sometimes the doctorate.[1]

At Paris, mastership in the superior Faculties admitted of even more formality, and especially more solemnity, than mastership in arts; it pre-supposed three successive acts, called by different names according to the Faculties,[2] in which argumentations and discourses alternated with ceremonies and rites having an almost religious character. It does not appear that mastership, at Paris, gave occasion for awarding a special diploma. At Bologna it was otherwise; and Savigny affirms that diplomas were given there for the licentiate as well as for the doctorate. At Prague, the title of master was employed for the Faculties of Arts and of Theology; the title of doctor for law and medicine. At Bologna, in the fourteenth century the law students underwent two sorts of examinations which, moreover, succeeded each other very closely,[3] a private examination which resulted in the licentiate; and a public one which resulted in the doctorate. In

[1] The title of doctor was especially customary in the Faculties of Law. At Bologna the professors of law regarded it as their exclusive property.

[2] These acts for the mastership in theology were called *vesperies*, *aulique*, and *resompte;* for the mastership in medicine, *vesperies*, *principium*, and *pastillaire*.

[3] Savigny cites the example of a licentiate of Bologna who did not pass his examination for the doctorate until ten years after taking his license : it was a rare exception.

the first of these, two texts (or themes) of Roman law and two of Canon law were assigned to the candidate. The jury was composed of three doctors who questioned the candidate or argued against him. They were, said the regulations, to treat the candidate paternally, under penalty of a year's suspension. The second test, which was more solemn, was called the *conventus;* it most frequently took place in the cathedral, but sometimes within the school. There, the licentiate, a candidate for the doctorship, delivered a discourse and maintained a thesis in law. None but students argued against him. Then the archdeacon of Bologna or a doctor delegated by him, proclaimed the new doctor. He was given the insignia of his dignity, the book, the ring, and the doctor's cap, and was made to seat himself in a chair.[1] There were, besides, three categories of doctors: in Roman law, in Canon Law, or both Roman law and Canon law at the same time.

Things were conducted in much the same way at Montpellier. In the fourteenth century one became a doctor of law there in this wise: "The licentiate," says M. Germain, "according to the statutes of 1339, then led necessarily to the doctorate, and in some fashion made one thing with it; for it involved, in an express manner, the authorization to perform all the doctorial acts, *licentia omnes actus doctorales agendi.* The licentiate was the really serious degree. All be-

---

[1] Savigny, *op. cit.*, chap. xxi. At Bologna, as at Paris, the students were obliged to give evidence of a certain number of years passed in study. Ten years were necessary to become a canonist, and eight to become a civilian.

yond it was purely ceremonial. The prior of the doctors (the eldest, or the elected chief) convoked the entire university in the church of St. Firmin to confer the licentiate. The candidate, inquiries having been made concerning his morals, his birth, and his capacity, drew by lot, at daybreak, in a book of civil or of canon law, the subject of his theses, and that very day between Nones and Vespers, after but a few hours of preparation, he went to defend them in the bishop's hall, in the house or palace ordinarily inhabited at Montpellier by the Bishop of Maguelonne. The *soutenance* was an imposing affair. All the doctors of the faculty must be present and take an active part in it, in presence of the bishop or his delegate. When it was over they handed in their notes and pronounced a judgment in accordance with which the candidate was either admitted or adjourned. If he was adjourned for incapacity he was informed of it secretly in such a way as to spare him all confusion. If, on the contrary, he passed, he was publicly proclaimed doctor, and by virtue of this decision, he might take the doctor's cap when and where he chose, either at Montpellier or at any other university. If he immediately decided for Montpellier, the ceremony of his reception was at once proceeded with. The bell of the university summoned masters and students into the church of *Notre Dame des Tables* for that purpose. The recipient went thither escorted by his friends; and there, in the midst of a throng anxious to do him honor, he commented on the text of a law or a decree; after which the president again interrogated the doctors on his capacity, and admitted him to take the oath. The oath taken, he granted him the right to *read*, to teach, to instruct, in a word, to fulfil all the doctorial functions at Montpellier or elsewhere, conformably to the constitution of Pope Nicholas IV. Then the doctor whom the recipient had chosen as sponsor conferred on him the insignia of the doctorate, gave him investiture by the chair, the book, the cap, the kiss or the accolade, and the benediction.[1]

Complexity, as one sees, was not lacking in the form of the examinations of the Middle Ages. Never was beheld such a profusion of formalities, pompous ceremonials, solemn engagements and oaths, private and public argumentations, discourses and harangues. Never, moreover, did it cost more to obtain degrees, especially the higher degrees. To arrive at the doctorate, particularly, one needed to be actually rich, rich in money still more than in knowledge. At Salamanca, to intrigue for the honors of the doctorate, one of the formalities required from the candidate was to defray the expenses of a brilliant *corrida de toros*. Elsewhere, and almost everywhere, it was a question of paying for sumptuous banquets. At Bologna, the doctor-candidate had to furnish clothing for a large number of persons. Savigny relates that, in 1299, when the promotion was refused to Vianesius, whose fault was that of not being related to the doctors whose duty it was to receive him, he had already spent five hundred livres in buying scarlet cloth for pelisses. In 1311, Pope Clement V decreed that the candidate should swear not

[1] Germain, *Étude historique sur l'École de Droit de Montpellier*, 1877, p. 26.

to expend more than five hundred livres for his promotion.[1]

The baccalaureate and the licentiate were evidently not so costly as the doctorate, that *actus triumphalis* of graduation. But for these degrees also there was considerable expense for display. It has been said that in France everything ends in song; in the universities of the Middle Ages everything began and ended with banquets. A banquet before and after the *déterminance;* a banquet after the license; a banquet after each act of the mastership; banquets always and everywhere. And these banquets sometimes assembled the whole Faculty, all the masters in arts, all the licentiates. Ramus complained, in the sixteenth century, that of the nine hundred livres which medical studies cost, three hundred were devoted to banquets.

But, aside from the extraordinary expenses entailed by feasts and rejoicings, there was also a fixed tariff for the examinations. The Nations were paid, the Faculties, the beadles, the examiners, even the Chancellor himself was paid. Sometimes wine and spices were distributed to the examiners. There were plenty of regulations declaring that the licentiate's degree must be conferred gratuitously; it was forbidden, for example, to receive anything from the candidate but four sous for the grass or straw strewn over the floors of the examination halls by the beadles, — straw in winter, grass in summer. But these prohibitions were constantly violated. In 1424, in the Nation of

[1] "To arrive at the title of master," says Thurot, "a man expended his patrimony and exhausted the purse of his friends; he often remained in debt and needy for the rest of his life."

England, at Paris, it was customary to give half a franc for the *déterminance;* for the baccalaureate, when one repaired to the schools of the rue de Fonarre, four sous; for the examination itself, two sous; for the license, one franc, etc. The Faculties of decrees and of medicine in the Paris University seem to have been those in which the expenses of examination were greatest; the student in canon law gave four sous to each doctor-regent on the day of the harangue; the licentiate offered repasts to the doctors, and paid for their wine while the examination lasted. So, too, the medical student, at the time he received the mastership, paid ten gold crowns to the president, and gave caps and gowns to all the master-regents.

But it was not alone these fiscal abuses, these exorbitant expenses which vitiated the system of examinations in the universities of the Middle Ages. What is to be said of the absence of publicity which was the common trait of most of the trials, except those which sinned in the other direction by excessive display and external pomp? The examiners showed extreme indulgence. They were sometimes obliged to reverse their decisions.[1] Not a single case of a candidate who failed is found on the register of the Paris Medical Faculty from 1395 to 1500. The examinations were often mere formalities. Even this might be excused if attendance at the courses had been rigorously required. But dispensations were frequently granted; and to pay for it was sometimes all that was necessary to obtain the certificate of attendance

[1] It must not be forgotten that the degrees were one of the principal sources of revenue to the professors.

during the scholastic term. Abuses were increased by the multiplication of universities; they became each other's rivals and sold diplomas at a discount. "Composed of a small number of masters and students," says Thurot, "the provincial universities were lax in their examinations and even sold their degrees. Students bought their bachelor's degree there and went at once to Paris to obtain their license." But even at Paris trickery and corruption insinuated themselves even into the solemn decisions pronounced when degrees were conferred. The examiners willingly displayed a certain partiality toward the nobles and the great.

To sum up, in all that concerns the conferring of degrees, the universities of the Middle Ages seem to have drawn up admirable regulations on paper, much better ones than they succeeded in enforcing. It is in the system of examinations that their laxity is perhaps most evident — it appears also in the lack of discipline of the students, in the lack of regularity on the part of the professors — in the vices inseparable from a democratic government, where the chiefs, usually elected, were not always sufficiently independent to resist solicitations and offers of money, and where some anarchy was mixed with a great deal of liberty.

Part III

THE COURSE OF STUDY AND THE METHODS OF TEACHING

CHAPTER I

THE FACULTIES OF ARTS

I

LET us transport ourselves in thought to Paris, in any year you please of the thirteenth or fourteenth century, and in any day of autumn or winter, from the morrow of St. Denis (October 10) to the first Sunday of Lent. The bells of the cathedral of Notre Dame, which are heard in all the quarters where the students reside, on the river banks, and on the heights

167

of Ste. Genevieve, almost as clearly as in the streets adjoining the city[1] — the bells of Notre Dame have just announced with a great clamor that the hour has struck for the re-assembling of the classes in all the schools.

It is very early in the morning; dawn has not yet broken. The customs of a rude and vigorous society which has no fear of overdriving, do not permit young men "to spend in slumber the time most precious for study." At five o'clock,[2] or six o'clock at latest, at the moment when the Carmelites of the Place Maubert ring the bell for their first mass, the Regents of the Faculty of Arts resume their customary lessons. From every direction great numbers of students quitting the private houses, hotels, or colleges, where they live, turn toward the *Rue du Fouarre*,[3] where most of the schools are established. The street is closed: a barrier prevents the entrance of pedestrians or of carriages, the noise of which might disturb the scholastic exercises; a turnkey opens the door to students and closes it behind them.[4] Other students, but in

[1] It is known that the City, that is to say, the little island on which Notre Dame is built, had been originally the centre of studies; but gradually the schools and scholars crossed the bridges and established themselves on the left bank of the Seine, in what is still known as the Latin Quarter.

[2] In some verses entitled: *Of the Unhappy Condition of those who Study at Paris*, Buchanan complains, about 1526, that in his time the bells still rang at five in the morning.

[3] The *Rue du Fouarre* got its name from an old word signifying "straw," on account of the straw spread on the ground in the classrooms.

[4] In reality, the *Rue du Fouarre* was not closed until 1403, by authority of the Provost of Paris.

smaller numbers, present themselves in the Clos-Bruneau.[1] With the latter mingle youths of a more advanced age, and even mature men; these are students of the Faculty of Decretal, which also has its exercises in the Clos-Bruneau. All of them are decently and modestly clad, as is enjoined by the rules. Their robes are long, closed in front, and floating; about the neck they have a short scarf, and on the head a sort of skull-cap, and they wear short shoes. It is in spite of constantly renewed regulations that some of them, under pretext of being noblemen, are carrying small-arms, daggers or poniards; and that others, in imitation of the dandies of the period, have short, close-fitting coats, caps trimmed with diverse ornaments, and long shoes, pointed and turned up at the toes. But in general the dress is simple, almost poor; and these students, nearly all of whom wear the same black uniform, resemble the young ecclesiastics of our modern seminaries.

Their scholastic equipment is small; almost nothing beyond what is necessary for writing. They carry a copy-book for the purpose of taking notes during the professor's lecture, and also, when they are able, a manuscript copy of the work which is to be the subject of the lecture, a Priscian's grammar, or a translation of Aristotle: manuscripts which they have borrowed or bought, often at a high price, from the

---

[1] Now the Rue St. Jean de Beauvais. Until 1202, the Clos-Bruneau was a vineyard belonging to the Bishop of Paris, who ceded it in order that houses might be built there. As a great number of students could find no room in the *Rue du Fouarre*, the Faculty of Arts spread into the Rue Bruneau.

librarian, or the *Stationarius*, who, as his name implies, stations himself close to the schools so as to provide the scholars with paper and books.

Let us enter at hazard a class-room in a school. There are plenty of them, but they are all much alike, and in each a master assembles the pupils who have registered themselves to follow his course, for instruction which is everywhere the same. The student has not, in fact, the right to go to one school on this day and another on that. There must not be a single student at Paris without his determinate master (*qui certum magistrum non habeat*).[1]

The class-room is in nowise luxurious, or even comfortable.[2] The school furniture is of the simplest, being composed of nothing but a platform chair and desk for the master. The pupils sit on the ground, which the beadle has taken care to cover with a little straw, as a preventive against dampness or dust. That there are no seats for the students, is due in the first place, assuredly, to economy, because there is no money to buy any; but it seems that a moral notion also underlies the fact; as late as 1451 the students will still be enjoined to sit on the ground, and not on chairs or benches, in order, they will be told, that they may escape all temptation to pride.

The professor mounts his platform; he is a master-regent of the Faculty of Arts. He is very young, for

[1] *Chartularium Univ. Paris.*, t. i, p. 79.

[2] In the thirteenth century, each master hired a class-room on his own account. Later on, toward the close of the same century, the Nations bought the schools of the *Rue du Fouarre* and allotted them among the masters.

he is just beginning; he was not promoted to the mastership until a few months ago, and he was then only twenty-one years old. He wears a black gown with a furred cowl, conformably to the statutes of 1215, wherein Robert de Courçon had prescribed that "no master, reading in arts, shall wear anything but a *chape*, or cope, round and black, and reaching to the heels, at least when he is a new beginner."[1]

The lessons commence as soon as the prayers of thanksgiving have been recited. The professor has a text-book, or, perhaps, several text-books, before him; for it is still customary in the Faculty of Arts to explain several books during the same lesson, both in grammar and logic.[2] He reads slowly, and in a low voice, *voce submissa*, each sentence of the text; then he comments on it and paraphrases it while the silent and attentive students diligently transfer the words of their master to their copy-books.[3] In the school we have entered, the master has written down beforehand all he has to say; in the neighboring school, they say, the professor extemporizes; but the majority of the masters find it more convenient to dictate their courses from a manuscript, and the students themselves prefer this method of instruction. There are even schools, or so it is alleged, where the master contents himself

[1] *Nullus . . . habeat capam nisi rotundam, nigram et talarem, saltem dum nova est* (*Chartularium Univ. Paris.*, t. i, p. 73).

[2] "In the thirteenth century," says Thurot, "several different books were explained during the same lesson."

[3] The students, however, sometimes departed from their habitual calmness. When the Faculty, in 1355, wished to prohibit dictated courses, there was almost a riot in the Rue du Fouarre: the students hooted, hissed, stamped, and threw stones.

with handing over his manuscript to a student, who reads it in his place.[1]

Beginning at about six in the morning, the ordinary lessons are protracted with no haste on the part of the master. In fact, it is not until nine o'clock that somewhat different exercises, the *extraordinary* courses, must begin.

The extraordinary courses are still given in the *Rue du Fouarre*, but other courses of the same kind are taught almost anywhere, at the option of the professors.[2] They may give extraordinary lessons even in their chambers. These are the same students whom we shall presently meet again at the extraordinary course, but neither the same master, nor the same books of instruction will be there. The professor is still more youthful than he who gave the ordinary lesson in the morning. Although the masters of arts also give extraordinary courses, it is a simple bachelor who is now about to teach. He is barely seventeen or eighteen years old; and he might be younger still, since they go up for the baccalaureate at fourteen or fifteen. Nor is the costume the same; both masters and bachelors, when they teach *extraordinary*, may wear gowns

[1] In 1355, and again in 1366, the practice of dictating lessons was forbidden. The lectures were to be delivered in "a continuous discourse." But these rules were not observed, although each new master was obliged to swear that he would conform to them. The indolence of professors, and of students likewise, carried the day, and the use of dictation prevailed.

[2] In 1355, nevertheless, the Faculty forbade extraordinary courses to be given anywhere except in the schools of the Nations; that is to say, in those of the Rue du Fouarre.

of any material they please. As to the books which
form the subject of the lesson, they are no longer the
classic works of grammar and logic which constitūte
fundamental instruction, but Aristotle's treatises on
ethics, which have always been authorized; and, when
the prohibition of earlier days shall have been re-
moved, they will be the works of the same author on
metaphysics and physics. Again, they may be some
elementary book on rhetoric, or a treatise relating to
the sciences comprised in the *quadrivium*, — arithmetic, geometry, or astronomy.

The students whose day's work we are following are
not merely present at a single extraordinary *course*.[1]
Since 1254, the Faculty of Arts has authorized two extraordinary courses on days when the ordinary lessons
are given, and three on holidays, when the latter are

---

[1] I italicize the word *course* because the extraordinary lecture
was given *ad cursum, cursoriè*. The meaning of these expressions
has been much disputed. Some authors have thought they must be
understood to indicate a somewhat different method of explication,
the lectures given *cursoriè* or *extraordinariè* not admitting so exhaustive an interpretation as those given *ordinariè*. To illustrate
this view the fact has been cited that at the University of Prague
the bachelors had to abide by the reading of the text in these extraordinary courses, and had no right to comment on it. But in
opposition to this opinion it must be observed that both Masters in
Arts and titular professors gave extraordinary lessons, and that it
is improbable that these masters changed their usual simple style
when speaking at different hours and on other books. I think
that a cursory lecture meant a course distinct from the regular
elementary lessons; what we call nowadays, in our French Faculties, complementary courses or conferences, in contradistinction
to the authoritative professional lectures. This opinion has been
strongly stated and maintained by Mullinger (*op. cit.*, appendix E.).

omitted, but which are not, for all that, days of complete repose. The student of the Middle Ages is accustomed to spend the greater part of the day, or about seven hours, in class with his masters.[1] Buchanan will say, in the sixteenth century: "A short interval is grudgingly allowed for dinner." It is not until evening, after the diversions at the meadow of St. Gervais, the "field of sports" of the university of the Middle Ages, and perhaps after a halt in some wineshop, that the student, re-entering his chamber,[2] at last has time for his personal tasks — tasks, moreover, of the most restricted and mechanical sort, since, for want of books, they are usually limited to copying, recopying, and revising the notes taken at the courses, or learning them by heart.

Lessons upon lessons, in one form or another, are, then, the habitual exercises daily offered to its pupils by the Faculty. Once a week, however, the usual monotony of instruction and of studies is interrupted by the hebdomadal disputation. The masters assemble together every Saturday, and hold a discussion on some given subject in the presence of the students. True, it is merely a spectacle as yet, at which the youngest students may be present without participat-

[1] I cannot agree with the judgment formed by a writer of our day (M. Lecoy de la Marche, in his interesting work, *La Chaire Française au moyen âge*, Paris, 1886, p. 456), who claims that "the methods of the Middle Ages left a great deal to the initiative of the student . . . and permitted him to work alone." The contrary is true.

[2] In the earliest times "each scholar inhabited, alone or with a comrade, some modest tavern chamber, with his little collection of volumes or rolls of parchment" (Lecoy de la Marche, *op. cit.*, p. 461).

ing; nevertheless, they are already learning, in these dialectical tournaments and passages at arms, to develop an enthusiasm for the art of discussion. They take sides for the *respondens* or for the *opponens*,[1] and are thus preparing to become subtle and daring disputants, on the day when, promoted to the baccalaureate, their turn will come to be admitted to the honor and the risk of disputing publicly.

II

The sketch I have just made, incomplete as it may be, has already given a general idea of the studies in the Faculty of Arts at Paris; and also — Paris being the great model for this kind of instruction — in the other universities. Arts signified in the first place the ancient *trivium* and the ancient *quadrivium*, with a marked emphasis on dialectic; it also meant philosophy, which, with the works of Aristotle on psychology, ethics, the natural and physical sciences, and metaphysics, gradually made its way into the schools, so successfully that the Faculty of Arts became a Faculty of Philosophy. Let us see, now, in order to get a complete notion, what were the classic books of instruction in arts.

The most ancient rule of studies in the University of Paris dates from 1215; it was drawn up by the Cardinal-Legate, Robert de Courçon.[2]

---

[1] The *respondens* defended a thesis (*respondebat de questione*), while the *opponens* attacked it.

[2] *Chartularium Univ. Paris.*, t. i, p. 781.

The works which, according to these first statutes, must be read in the ordinary lessons, were the following: 1. Aristotle's treatises on logic; 2. Priscian's grammar. The text of the rule says: *libros Aristotelis de dialectica tam de veteri quam de nova; et duos Priscianos.* These words require some explanation. Ancient dialectic, as we learn from the later regulations of 1252 and 1255,[1] comprised various portions of the *Organon,* either interpreted by Porphyry[2] or translated by Boethius;[3] and in addition, several special works by Boethius: — 1. what was called the *liber Porphyrii,* that is, his *Introduction to the Categories of Aristotle,* translated from the Greek in the fourth century by the Latin writer Victorinus and annotated by Boethius; 2. the *Predicaments (predicamenta),* which also are the categories of Aristotle, doubtless in the translation made by Boethius; 3. the *Interpretatio* or *Hermeneia*[4] (*periarmenias,* in the barbarous text of the statute of 1255); 4. finally, the Divisions and Topics of Boethius (with the exception of the fourth book of the Topics). The new logic, doubtless so called because it was not known by Abelard and his contemporaries, was, nevertheless,

[1] *Chartularium Univ. Paris.,* t. i, pp. 228, 278.

[2] Porphyry, an Alexandrian philosopher (233–305 A.D.).

[3] Boethius, a Latin philosopher, born in 470 or 475, died in 524. He had a great influence on the studies of the Middle Ages. Besides his other works, original and translated, which I cite in this chapter, his treatise *De Consolatione* was studied in the schools.

[4] The *Hermeneia* was already as in the time of Abelard, who has written " Aristotelis duos tantum, ' Prædicamentorum ' scilicet et ' Peri Ermenias,' libros usus adhuc Latinorum cognovit."

the old dialectic of Aristotle, Latinized by Boethius. It comprised the other portions of the *Organon:* the *Prior Analytics,* the book *par excellence,* since it contained the theory of the syllogism; the *Posterior Analytics,* or the theory of demonstration; the *Topics;* and lastly the *Elenchi,* or the Arguments of the Sophists.

To these works on pure, deductive, and formal logic, it is somewhat surprising to find the programme adding Priscian's grammar on the same scheme of studies, or, to be more exact, the two Priscians. The first Priscian, *Priscianus major,* comprised the first sixteen chapters of the *Institutio grammatica* of the celebrated Latin grammarian;[1] the other, *Priscianus minor,* the last two chapters of the same work. On one side the abstract rules of reasoning; on the other, the abstract rules of language; such was, naturally enough, the substratum of instruction at a period when men neglected the study of things, realities, in order to occupy themselves solely with logical and grammatical forms.

Let us see now what were the texts reserved for the extraordinary courses, "for the feast days" (*festivis diebus*), as the statutes of 1215 call them; which shows that extraordinary courses were originally given on holidays only. It must not be forgotten, however, that there were nearly one hundred annual holidays. Among these books, only half classic, as we may say, and which in any case ranked as merely secondary in

[1] Priscian (fifth century) had kept a famous school at Constantinople.

the estimation of both masters and scholars, several
again related to grammar or to logic. Among this
number were the fourth book of *Topics* by Boethius,
eliminated, no one knows why, from the ordinary
lessons; and the *Barbarism*, a now nearly forgotten
work by Donatus,[1] the grammarian of the fourth century, which treated of grammatical figures.[2] But this
second list of the plan of studies of 1215 includes
also works of quite a different range, since it com-
prises the *Ethics* of Aristotle; that is to say, the
Nicomachean Ethics. True, this was an elective
study; one read it *si placet*. The extraordinary
courses, also, gave a good deal of attention to rhetoric,
and to what was summed up in a single word as the
quadrivialia, or works relating to the arts of the
quadrivium.

But the works of Aristotle, in spite of the superstitious veneration with which the name of the philosopher was already honored, were far from being
acceptable as a whole to the suspicious orthodoxy
of the Church, then sovereign mistress of studies.
"Let no one," said Robert de Courçon, "read either
the *Metaphysics* or the *Natural Philosophy* of Aristotle,
or the abridgments (*summæ*) of these works; nor" he
added, linking Aristotle with the heretics of the

---

[1] Donatus was the master of St. Jerome. The *Barbarism* was the
third book of his *Ars major*.

[2] In the statutes of 1252 and 1255 another modern work appears,
the *Sex principia* of Gilbert de la Porrée, Bishop of Poitiers, born
in 1070, died in 1154. He had taught theology at Paris. The *Six
principles* were on the *Categories* of Aristotle. (See Hauréau, *de la
Philosophie Scholastique*, t. i, p. 298.)

period, "the writings of David of Dinant,[1] the heretic Amauri,[2] or the Spaniard Mauricius."[3]

Time was necessary before the prohibited portions of Aristotle's works should obtain right of entrance into the schools of the Faculty of Arts. The Bull of Gregory IX, in 1231,[4] regulating instruction in arts, again insisted on the needful exclusion of his books on natural philosophy, at least "until they shall have been examined and expurgated." It was in 1255 that Aristotle's *Physics*, interdicted until then under pain of excommunication, was officially authorized at Paris, simultaneously with his metaphysics, the work *de Animalibus*, and the treatise on the Soul: in a word, all of the greater and lesser works of the Greek philosopher, which thenceforward entered, in their totality and triumphantly, into the university schools, to exercise there for several centuries an intellectual domination whose equal it would be impossible to find in the history of human thought. Certain other universities had preceded

[1] David of Dinant had taught at Paris in the twelfth century; he maintained the pantheistic proposition that "every creature is God."

[2] Amauri of Bena had been a professor at Paris in the twelfth century; he was considered one of the promoters of the sect of the Albigenses. Persecuted and condemned during his life, he was so even after his death in 1204. "*Corpus magistri Amaurici extrahatur a cemeterio et projiciatur in terram non benedictam,*" said the decrees of the Provincial Council of Paris in 1210.

[3] Mauricius is unknown, and M. Renan has claimed (*Averroës et l'Averroisme*) that Averroës should be read here instead of *Mauricius*. But it is plain from a passage of Albertus Magnus, cited by Père Denifle (*Chartularium*, etc., t. i, p. 80), that Mauricius was a philosopher quite distinct from Averroës.

[4] *Chartularium*, etc., t. i, p. 138.

Paris in this wholesale adoption of Aristotle. Thus, in 1229, the professors of Toulouse, in a letter addressed to the other universities, boasted among other advantages possessed by their university, that students might there study "the *libri naturales* prohibited at Paris," and thus penetrate to their depths, even to their marrow, the secrets of nature (*naturæ sinum medullitus perscrutari*).[1]

It must not be forgotten, however, as I have already remarked, that everything in the works of Aristotle which displayed the spirit of observation and the experimental researches of Plato's great rival, — all that was called at Toulouse the *physica realis*, — was relegated to the second place, and almost ranked among what we call nowadays optional studies. The statutes of 1255 determine the number of weeks, especially in the latter half of the year, that may be devoted to these lectures, which had not as yet the honor of a regular and continuous course, and which could only be treated superficially. Logic manifestly held the first place. To reason well had become the whole duty of the studious man. There was no thought of knowing the history of humanity, still less of observing the phenomena of nature. If rhetoric was occasionally taken up, it was in order to draw from it certain rules of pure form, not to seek insight into the beauties of literature. The masterpieces of classic antiquity were unknown. Dialectic had invaded all things; the syllogism was of universal application. "Logic," says Thurot, "was regarded as the art of arts, the science of sciences."

[1] *Chartularium*, etc., t. i, p. 131.

The successive reforms in the University of Paris made very little modification in the plan of studies that I have outlined. The reform of Cardinale St. Marc and Montaigu, in 1366, merely replaced Priscian's grammar by Alexandre de la Villedieu's [1] famous book, the *Doctrinale puerorum*, written in leonine verse, which remained the grammatical text-book until it was in turn dethroned by the grammar of Despautère in the sixteenth century. The reform of Cardinal d'Estouteville, in 1452, on the eve of the Renaissance, left things pretty much as they were. "Aristotle," says Crevier,[2] "was still in possession of all his glory." And he adds, "As yet there was no question of rhetoric."

I have spoken of the Faculty of Arts at Paris only; but the programmes were the same everywhere. I have before me, for example, the statutes of the Faculty of Toulouse in 1309,[3] in which are found the same books, but with the difference that Aristotle's *Ethics* and *Physics* occupy a more important place. Thus, the ten books of Nicomachean Ethics had to be read in two years, and read from one end to the other (*legantur completè*). Another distribution of subjects is made, and a different order proposed for the succession of lectures; but it is always, as one may say, the same game of cards, though played in another style. Aristotle reigns as sovereign master at Oxford, and

[1] Crevier, t. ii, p. 450. Alexandre de la Villedieu, born in Normandy, composed his *Doctrinale* in 1209.

[2] Crevier, t. iv, p. 190. The greatest novelty of the reform of 1452, with reference to the studies in the Faculty of Arts, was the introduction of the study of Latin versification.

[3] M. Fournier, t. i, p. 465.

Cambridge also. But it seems that he is less directly approached, and that logic is studied chiefly in abridgments and epitomes. "The most popular text-book of logic," says Laurie, "was for centuries the *Summulæ* of Petrus Hispanus."[1] So likewise Mullinger: "For two centuries and a half the *Summulæ logicales* reigned supreme in the schools."[2] A part of this work, entitled *Parva Logicalia*, was the standard book at Leipsic and Prague.[3]

It remains to be shown in what manner the standard works, of which I have drawn up a list, were distributed throughout the two periods of study; one of which constituted the preparation for the baccalaureate, and the other for the licentiateship. The candidate for the determinance, at the end of the thirteenth and during the fourteenth century, must have studied, either in ordinary or extraordinary courses, all of Aristotle's works on logic, Priscian's grammar, Boethius's *Divisions* and *Topics*, Donatus's *Barbarism*, and the *Six Principles* of Gilbert de la Porrée. Aspirants to the licentiate's degree must have studied the same books, and, further, must have heard Aristotle's treatises on physics, psychology, and ethics. They must also have attended a hundred lectures on mathematics and astronomy. The statutes of the University of Vienna, in 1389, required the study of five books of Euclid,[4] and

---

[1] Petrus Hispanus was none other than Pope John XXI, who occupied the pontifical throne from 1276 to 1277.

[2] Mullinger, *op. cit.*, p. 178.

[3] The *Parva Logicalia* (the seventh treatise of the *Summulæ*) were also studied at Paris. See Thurot, p. 47.

[4] There was a translation of Euclid due to Boethius.

also of the book on the sphere, doubtless the *Sphera mundi* of the English computer, John of Holywood, better known under the Latinized name of Sacrobosco, and whose works remained classic down to the sixteenth century. Another work mentioned in the programme of the University of Vienna was the *Theory of the Planets*, a treatise by the Italian mathematician, Campano of Novara.[1] In 1427, the same work was taught at Paris. Little by little the Middle Ages threw off the yoke of pure scholasticism, and acquired a taste for the sciences; at the same time, toward the close of the fourteenth century, and more especially in the fifteenth, literary studies, such as rhetoric and poetry, dependencies of grammar, began to be cultivated with ardor, in spite of the resistance offered by the old scholasticism, whose motto was: "Good grammarian, bad logician."

III

We know now what were the texts and the authors upon which the attention of those who were called *artists* was concentrated during three or four centuries, and which sufficed for the intellectual education of a long series of generations, — the arts then constituting the general instruction received by all students, even those who were later on to pursue special courses in the Faculties of Theology, Law, or

[1] Music, the fourth art of the *quadrivium*, was not altogether neglected; it was studied at Vienna, and notably at Salamanca. At Paris it was but little cultivated; it appears occasionally in connection with the chants of the Church.

Medicine. We have yet to examine the methods followed in the explanation of these authors.

Thurot, and Mullinger after Thurot, have described
very exactly the two essential processes of the professors of the Middle Ages. The first consisted in
examining the text (*expositio*) ; the second, in discussing it (*quæstiones*). "The method pursued," says
Mullinger, "appears to have been of two kinds, of
which Aquinas's Commentary on Aristotle and the
Quæstiones of Buridanus on the *Ethics* may be taken
as fair specimens." [1]

The first step was a work of subtle analysis,
wherein the commentator twisted in every way possible the text to be examined, and, indeed, dissected
it. "The lecturer," says Thurot, translated by Mullinger, "commenced by discussing a few general
questions, having reference to the treatise which he
was called upon to explain, and, in the customary
Aristotelian fashion, treated of its material, formal,
final, and efficient causes. He pointed out the principal divisions ; took the first division and subdivided
it ; divided again the subdivision, and repeated the
process until he had subdivided to the first chapter.
He then again divided, until he had reached a subdivision which included only a single sentence or
complete idea. He finally took this sentence, and
expressed it in other terms which might serve to
make the conception more clear. He never passed
from one part of the work to another, from one chapter to another, or even from one sentence to another,

[1] Mullinger, *op. cit.*, p. 359. Thurot had said the same thing
before Mullinger, and in the same terms (*op. cit.*, p. 74, in note).

with a minute analysis of the reasons for which each division, chapter, or sentence was placed after that by which it was immediately preceded." [1] Each day this painful and tedious labor was renewed, and it could have no other result but to give the auditors as exact a knowledge as possible of a text indefinitely analyzed and paraphrased.

The other method, which was no longer a servile commentary on the text, and in which the spirit of liberty already manifested itself to a certain degree, consisted in applying to all doubtful questions, susceptible of being discussed in various senses, the proceeding that had been adopted by Abelard in the *Sic et Non*. "Whenever a passage presented itself that admitted of a twofold interpretation, the one or the other interpretation was thrown into the form of a *quæstio*, and then discussed *pro* and *contra*, the arguments on either side being drawn up in the usual formal way. . . . Finally the lecturer brought forward his own interpretation, and defended it against every objection to which it might appear liable; each solution being formulated in the ordinary syllogistic fashion, with major, minor, and conclusion."

The defects of such instruction are evident. Either one was bound by the text which he was simply endeavoring to comprehend, and which was appreciated only from the standpoint of order and method, and the logical value of propositions; or, using the same text, he gave himself over to a purely dialectical argument, circumscribed strictly by the limits of the given subject. No appeal to the imagination, still

[1] Mullinger, p. 360, and Thurot, p. 73.

less to observation, experience, or fruitful induction, was made. Nothing but a vain and empty verbiage, endless distinctions, and a sterile tramping over a single spot.

In studying the pedagogic methods of any period in which they were developed, allowance must be made for the environment; it must be remembered that they were not always the effect of an *a priori* system or reasoned-out conception, but were often the necessary result of circumstances; in a word, that they were employed not as the best that could be thought of, but as the only ones possible at a given period in history and with the resources at one's disposal. So in the Middle Ages it was the multitude of pupils to be taught, on one hand, and the scarcity of books on the other, rather than a preconceived pedagogic theory, which was the chief reason why the methods then in use were adopted. Students being unable to possess their own text-books, as at present, how was it possible to make them acquainted with the classic author, unless by a complete reading and most detailed, laborious, monotonous, and yet necessary explanations? So, too, the pupil, having no means, as in our days, with which to supplement the master's lessons by private study with the aid of books treating of the same subjects, the lecture could not be a rapid exposition, which merely allowed certain brief notes to be taken. Finally, was it not from the same causes that another defect proceeded, — the abuse of memory by learning things by heart? It was necessary to engrave literally on the mind what it was not possible to find again in books, because one had no books.

It was necessary to make up for the absence of libraries. . . . What, for that matter, is a mind ornamented and enriched by souvenirs retained word for word, if not a miniature living library?

Yet there were at least two things in the pedagogic errors of the Middle Ages for which the excuse of circumstances cannot be pleaded, and in which the real genius, the evil genius of this period of human education, so inferior on many sides, is plainly marked: on one hand the superstitious reverence for texts, and on the other, the abuse of dialectic and discussion.

That the men of the sixteenth century, crushed, one might say, under the avalanche of books which the newly invented art of printing threw down upon them should remain in general humanists rather than realists, readers rather than observers of nature, may readily be conceived. But that, in the Middle Ages, so many successive generations of laborious and studious men should have consented for centuries to grow pale over a small number of texts, always the same, re-read and commented on to satiety, gnawing, as it were, the same bone forever, is a thing that can only be explained by supposing a special cast of mind, an extraordinary intellectual passivity, a complete absence of initiative and spontaneity. Since there were hardly any books, it seems as if it would have been so simple to turn to another side and study things in themselves; to open, in fine, the great book of nature. But no; men preferred to keep on repeating, mechanically and laboriously, paraphrases scrutinized a hundred times already; to close their eyes to the realities of the world, in order to concentrate,

and at the same time to squander, on certain pages of
marvellously bad Latin, prodigious efforts of attention. It would not have been so bad had they clung to
the spirit of an author in studying him. But no; it
was the letter, the literal form, which they scrutinized.

"The distinctive character of instruction in the
Middle Ages," Thurot[1] has justly said, "is that
science was not taught directly and in itself, but
by the explanation of books which derived their
authority solely from their writers." This principle
was acted on in all the Faculties, and Roger Bacon
thus formulates it: "When one knows the text, one
knows all that concerns the science which is the
object of that text."[2] They did not speak in the
Middle Ages of "taking a course of logic or of
ethics," but of "*reading* a book on logic or ethics."
Instead of "following a course," "hearing a book"
was always the phrase used (*legere* or *audire librum*).
Such methods were evidently a mere extension to
human studies of the habits contracted in the study
of theology. Just as there were sacred books con-
taining all truths from the religious point of view,
and needing only to be commented on and learned
by heart, so, from the scientific point of view, there
must be traditional books whose substance it was
sufficient to extract by perpetual deductions in order
to acquire all permitted knowledge. Although, in a
word, the school might be said to be distinct from

---

[1] Thurot, *op. cit.*, p. 65.

[2] *Scito textu, sciuntur omnia quæ pertinent ad facultatem prop-
ter quam textus sunt facti.* R. Bacon, *Opus Majus.*

the Church, nevertheless the methods of the Church reigned in the school, and the professors taught just as the preachers exhorted.

The other characteristic of the pedagogy of the Middle Ages, its mania, was the taste or rather passion for disputation. Really independent researches being forbidden, discussion, by bringing two different and contrary interpretations into opposition, gave both scholars and masters at least the shadow of liberty of thought. Never has there been such an abuse of argumentation; when the sixteenth century brought into the world another spirit and better methods, it found all the educational institutions transformed into fencing schools of dialectics. "They dispute before dinner," said Vivés,[1] in 1531; "they dispute during dinner; they dispute after dinner; they dispute in private and in public, at all times and in every place." And the same author has given a satirical description of these interminable disputes: "Their self-esteem," he says, "bound them to get up questions on the simplest propositions. On the mere words, *Scribe mihi*, they put questions of grammar, physics, and metaphysics. They gave their adversary no time to explain himself. If he entered into any developments, they cried, 'To the point! to the point! reply categorically!' They had no concern for truth, but sought merely to defend their opinions. Is a man too hardpressed? He eludes the objection by force of obstinacy; he denies insolently; he blindly strikes down all opposition in despite of evidence. To the most convincing objections, which drive him to the most

[1] Vivés, *De causis corruptarem artium*, t. i, p. 345.

absurd consequences, he contents himself with reply-
ing: 'I admit it, because it results from my thesis.' . . .
Provided one can defend himself logically, he passes
for an able man. The character, not less than the
intelligence, is ruined by disputation. Men shout
until they are hoarse; they make use of insulting
speeches and threats. They even come to blows,
bites, and buffetings. Discussions degenerate into
quarrels, and quarrelling into fighting."

Perhaps there is some exaggeration in the details of
this picture, but the background is exact. "What are
the contests of our *savants*," said a Chancellor of
Paris, "if not real cock-fights? . . . One cock struts
up to another, and bristles his feathers. Our people
do the same. They have not beaks and spurs like the
cocks, but their self-conceit is armed with a redoubta-
ble *ergot*." [1] The most frequent result of the discussions was not the elucidation of the questions in dispute, but the embittering and exasperation of minds.
Insults, if not blows, were the conclusion of many a
disputation. At Poitiers, in the eighteenth century,
there were two professors of physics at the College of
St. Martha, one of whom, following Descartes, taught
the theory of the *plenum*, and the other that of the
vacuum, after Newton. One day their quarrel became
so furious that the Cartesian, driven to extremes, cried
out: "The vacuum has no existence except in your
head!" (*non datur vacuum nisi in capite tuo*).

[1] Lecoy de la Marche, *op. cit.*, p. 452. According to some authors,
the French verb *ergoter* (to cavil) is derived from the *ergot* (spurs)
of cocks. But it is more probable that the etymology of this word
is from the conjunction *ergo*, with which the disputants prefaced
the conclusion of their arguments.

IV

The Faculties of Arts evidently had a mixed character. As schools of high dialectic and philosophy, they belonged to what we now call superior instruction; but, as schools of grammar and elementary acquirements in rhetoric and mathematics, they were the doubtful equivalent of that special order of instruction which has been distinguished from all others under the title of secondary. It is clear that very young students in arts, who being not yet fourteen — the minimum age for the determinance — were preparing for the baccalaureate, could not be considered as students of superior instruction. The mixed character of the Faculty of Arts, and the resemblance between its schools and modern colleges of secondary instruction, gradually became more accentuated in the later centuries of the Middle Ages, when the Faculty was obliged to bring together and unite not only the houses of study called colleges, but especially the boarding-houses called *pedagogies*,[1] both of them dependencies of the university, and in which the majority of the students became boarders.

" In the fifteenth century," says Thurot, "an important revolution was effected in the discipline of the Faculty of Arts. The majority of the students, even those whose home was in the city, lived in college dor-

[1] We distinguish between the *pedagogies* and the colleges, because the former were originally grammar schools, while the colleges were religious houses intended especially for students in theology; but the distinction soon vanishes, and the word "college" is applied to every school where young men were instructed.

mitories."[1] The revolution signalized by Thurot began long before the fifteenth century, since the *pedagogies* were very numerous at Paris at the close of the
fourteenth century, while on the other hand, the college of the Sorbonne, the first of several similar
colleges, dates from 1257.[2]

A question of discipline was certainly the chief
determining cause of this considerable change in the
primitive regulations of the Faculty of Arts. Given
the extreme youth of the greater number of students
in arts, and it is plain enough that it was dangerous
to leave them uncontrolled in the street of Paris,
lodging where they could in the houses of citizens or
in hotels. To guard them against the perils of liberty,
put an end to their disorder, and quiet their turbulence, they were gathered together in boarding-houses
under the authority of a pedagogue. On the other
hand, certain colleges owed their origin to generous
founders, who, to aid poor students, established free
boarding-houses where they might find food and shelter. "In the twelfth century, and for a long time
after," says Crevier, "the colleges were not schools
where lessons were given to those desirous of learning. . . . Their only purpose was to serve as a residence for young students under a master who conducted them to the public schools."[3]

It now remains to be explained how the *pedagogies*
and colleges, which were at first mere boarding-houses
or asylums, became veritable schools with special mas-

[1] Thurot, *op. cit.*, p. 92.

[2] See next chapter concerning the foundation of the college of the
Sorbonne.   [3] Crevier, t. i, p. 271.

ters, attracting, by degrees, nearly all the students of
the Faculty of Arts, and gradually engrossing instruction, until, in the sixteenth century, the schools in
the Rue du Fouarre were finally closed, and the colleges absorbed the entire Faculty of Arts.[1]

There were always grammar schools at Paris, and
grammar then embraced the elements of literature,
and included the study and explanation of the poets.
These schools gradually developed until logic was
almost the only subject left for exclusive treatment
by the Faculty of Arts. Grammar schools were necessary, moreover, to instruct children in reading, writing,
the elements of grammar, and ordinary rhetoric, that
is to say, the formulas to be employed in writing a letter to a bishop or a nobleman; and also the elements
of calculation, or what was then called algorism. They
soon began to teach the first principles of logic in
these schools, according to the *Summulæ* of Petrus
Hispanus,[2] and thus prepared the scholars, by the
time they were twelve or thirteen years old, to follow
the logic courses of the Faculty of Arts. In the
earliest times the pedagogues, or heads of boarding-
houses, led their pupils to the schools of the Rue du
Fouarre. After a while it was found more convenient to have them instructed inside the houses. The
pedagogy became a complete and enclosed college.
The Rue du Fouarre saw the number of its students

[1] At the end of the fifteenth century the colleges and pedagogies
contained nearly all the students in arts. In 1469 the Faculty of
Arts had decided not to give certificates of studies except to such
scholars as resided either in a *pedagogy*, a college, with their
parents, or with some member of the university, whom they served
gratuitously.   [2] See above, p. 178.

generally diminish, and ended by being entirely deserted. "In 1460," says Thurot, "the majority of the
regents of the Nation of France taught in the boarding-houses. . . . What gave the final blow to public
instruction was the obligation to reside in the *pedagogies* and colleges, which was imposed on the masters
about 1524. It was necessary thereafter to submit
to this obligation if one aspired to the functions of
Rector, Procurator of Nations, or Dean of Faculties."

It was thus that the Faculty of Arts gradually
became blended with the colleges, of which it was no
longer, one might say, anything more than the federation. These colleges had become very numerous:
there were some fifty of them in the fifteenth century,
among which, it is true, a certain number were theological colleges or religious houses, or else hospitable
houses opened to foreign students; for example, the
Scotch college, founded in 1326, and that of the
Lombards, in 1334. But many others, such as Har-
court College (1280) and the famous college of Montaigu (1314), seem to have been from the outset real
schools of secondary instruction.[1]

However this may be, the institution of colleges
at Paris rendered the greatest service to the Faculty
of Arts. And it is not uninteresting to dwell on the
meaning of this evolution imposed by the force of
circumstances on the university of the Middle Ages,
obliging it to pass from the almost absolute liberty of
early times to the régime of seclusion and dormitory

[1] See in Vallet de Viriville (*op. cit.*, p. 166) the enumeration of
the colleges established in Paris before the Revolution. This list
includes more than eighty establishments.

life and from the system of public courses to that of private classes taught within the colleges. It was a preliminary step toward the necessary distinction between the student in the school and the student in the university; between secondary and superior instruction, between what is suitable for children of from twelve to fifteen years, or even above that, and students of twenty. Thenceforward there was more labor and discipline on the part of the pupils, and more regularity and assiduity on the parts of the masters. Moreover, the university kept a close watch on these establishments incorporated with itself; it exacted guarantees from the headmasters or principals who directed them; it obliged its rectors to visit them once a year; and, in 1445, it declared solemnly that "it existed almost entirely in its colleges, and had been preserved by them alone from total destruction during the misfortunes of the wars that had afflicted France." [1]

Bologna also had its colleges; that is, says Savigny, its "corporations of poor students supported by a founder and living under a common surveillance." [2] But these colleges, which seem to have been nothing more than hospitable houses where foreign students installed themselves, had no importance and played no part in the constitution of the Italian universities.

It was otherwise in England, where "the collegiate system," says Laurie, "so soon dwarfed the univer-

[1] Crevier, t. iv, p. 134.

[2] Savigny, ch. xxi, 71: for example, the *collegium Avenionense*, founded in 1263, and the *Collegium Hispanicum*, founded by the Popes in 1364.

sity."[1] Laurie attributes the foundation of colleges
to the same causes that I have indicated: on one
hand, the difficulty of lodging a great number of students conveniently in private houses, and on the
other, the inconvenience of leaving very young persons
exposed to the myriad temptations of city life, without restraint.   At first there were "halls," "hostels"
(*hospitia*), regulated lodging-houses, where the students resided at their own cost, under the supervision
of a principal appointed by the chancellor.[2] At Cambridge there were the *Hospitia artistarum* and *Hospitia
juristarum*. To the *hospitia* succeeded the colleges;
that is to say, endowed halls, where the students
had free quarters, but where they had, in return, to
submit to the obligations imposed by the college
statutes.

"The most important of the early college foundations of England," says Laurie, "was that of Walter
de Merton, chancellor of the kingdom, in 1264, called
'*Domus scholarium de Merton*.' Merton himself must
have had his eye on the Sorbonne. Merton's house
was substantially what we should now call a secular
college. No 'religious person,' that is, no monk or
friar, was to be admitted. His aim was to produce
a constant succession of scholars devoted to the
pursuits of literature."[3]

---

[1] Laurie, *op. cit.*, p. 245.   [2] Mullinger, *op cit.*, p. 217.

[3] Laurie, *op. cit.*, p. 252. It was at Merton College that Duns
Scotius studied, "the subtle doctor" (1275–1305), who entered the
Franciscan order, and whose disciples were in controversy with the
Thomists, the Dominicans, disciples of Thomas Aquinas. William
of Occam, "the prince of Nominalists" (1280–1347), was educated
at the same college. He taught at Oxford and at Paris.

Other colleges of Oxford and Cambridge were established on the model of Merton: notably, at Oxford, University Hall (1280), Exeter College (1314), Queen's College (1340), etc.; at Cambridge, Clare Hall (1320), Pembroke Hall (1343), Trinity Hall (1350), etc.[1] In England as in France, the collegiate system replaced the régime of the day school, of free and independent life. The colleges of Oxford and Cambridge, like those of Paris, became essential elements of the university, true centres of education and instruction. Doubtless the establishment of colleges had been prepared for, from the beginning of the universities, by the two facts: 1st, that students often lodged at the houses of their professors; 2d, that in the Faculty of Arts at least (notably at Prague) the regents voluntarily gave lessons in their own houses; so that, from these small beginnings, the colleges and their classes followed by a natural evolution. It is none the less true that the face of things was changed. The universities had made a great experiment in the day school for students of all ages. And it must be thoroughly recognized that this experiment, which people seem to wish to renew in our day,[2] has failed, since the Middle Ages, as they were ending, turned into another path, and even replaced by the strictest sort of discipline the liberty of earlier days.

[1] See in Vallet de Viriville (*op. cit.*, pp. 136 and 187), the list of colleges at Oxford and Cambridge.

[2] " It is curious to note," says Laurie, " that in these latter days the non-collegiate or unattached system of the thirteenth and fourteenth centuries has been revived. Undergraduates may now live in licensed lodging-houses, and we may yet see restored, both in England and in Scotland, the hostels of the Middle Ages."

On the other hand, the transformation wrought in
the disciplinary and pedagogic regulations of the
Faculty of Arts had this necessary consequence :
that, at least in Paris, this Faculty, thenceforward
dismembered, as one might say, and whose very
numerous regents dispersed themselves among divers
colleges, had no longer more than a nominal unity.
Finally, its character as a school of preparatory, and,
to repeat the word, "secondary," instruction, gradually became more defined so that after the sixteenth
century the higher movement in literature and science
was developed apart from it.　It retains nothing but
elementary classical instruction, and that in such
measure as is permitted it by the constantly increasing activity of the religious orders, and particularly
of the Jesuits, thus leaving an open field, in the
modern universities, to the Faculties of Philosophy,
Science, and Letters.

CHAPTER II

THE FACULTIES OF THEOLOGY

I. The Superior Faculties — Primacy of the Faculty of Theology — The other arts and sciences assistants of the divine science — The Theological Faculty of Paris, the model of all similar Faculties — Its authority as a council in the questions of doctrine — Federation of convents and colleges — Dominicans and Franciscans — Foundation of the college of Sorbonne — II. Books and methods — The *Bible* and the *Book of Sentences* by Peter Lombard — Exposition and discussion — Subtilities and cavilling — The geometrical method applied to theological subjects — Aridity of this method of teaching — Criticisms of Gerson and of Clemengis — Examples of the questions debated in the theological schools — Relation of theological and philosophical studies.

I

HAD I followed what might be called the order of precedence, it is not with the Faculty of Arts that I should have begun my examination of the studies and methods of instruction in the universities. In reality the Faculty of Arts took the lowest rank, preceded, as it was, by the so-called superior Faculties of Theology, Law, and Medicine. But the arts serving as a general preparation and introduction to the special sciences, it was logical and necessary to study in the first place the organization of instruction in the Faculty of Arts.

Among the special sciences, that of theology occupied the first place, at least in the beginning. The

Sacra Facultas, as it was called, was considered superior to all the others.[1] It could not have been otherwise
at a time when the Church was still all-powerful,
when universities were founded under the patronage
of Popes and had a thoroughly ecclesiastical character,
and when study in general seemed to have no other
aim than that of serving religion.[2]

Theology was represented as the first of arts, as the
supreme science of which the others could not be more
than the respectful handmaidens.

"Logic is good," said Jacques de Vitry,[3] passing in
review the seven liberal arts, "for it teaches us to
distinguish truth from falsehood; grammar is good,
for it teaches how to speak and write correctly;
rhetoric is good, for it teaches how to speak elegantly
and to persuade. Good, too, are geometry, which
teaches how to measure the earth, the domain of our
bodies; arithmetic, or the art of computing, which
enables us to estimate the fewness of our days; music,
which reminds us of the sweet chant of the blessed;
astronomy, which causes us to consider the celestial
bodies and the stars shining resplendently before God.
But far better is theology, which alone can be truly
called a liberal art, since it alone delivers from its
woes the human soul." The seven arts were thus dis-
possessed, in favor of theology, of their beautiful

[1] . . . *Præest reliquis sicut superior,* said Alexander IV, in a
Bull of 1256. *Chartularium Univ. Paris.,* t. i, p. 343.

[2] . . . *Theologia imperat aliis scientiis, ut domina, et illæ sibi,
ut famulæ, obsequuntur. Ad hanc singulæ in viis suis levant et
habent intuitum. Chartularium,* etc., p. 343.

[3] Jacques de Vitry, a French preacher, died in 1244, cited by
M. Lecoy de la Marche, *op. cit.,* p. 458.

qualification of liberal; and were chiefly appreciated and lauded in view of their moral and religious bearing; that is to say, of the services they might render to religion.

It was at Paris, "the theological university *par excellence*," that theological studies were established soonest and most firmly. It was in the image of the Faculty of Paris that the Popes successively organized other Faculties, some instituted simultaneously with the university itself, as in the case of Toulouse, Prague, Vienna,[1] etc., and others superadded to universities that had long been flourishing, like the Faculty of Theology at Bologna, created in 1362. And if it is exact to say in general, yet without forgetting local differences, that instruction in all subjects was practically the same in all of the universities, this observation is specially applicable to instruction in theology, which being more directly watched over and regulated by the Church, and, by the very nature of its object allowing less latitude than other studies, necessarily presented more uniformity and repeated itself everywhere under identical conditions.

What, among other things, demonstrates the peculiar importance attached to theology, is the fact that the study of it was far more prolonged than was the case with any other branch of knowledge. One could be a master of arts at twenty-one; a doctor of law or of medicine at twenty-six or twenty-seven; but a doctorate of theology could not be obtained before

---

[1] The statutes of the Theological Faculty of Vienna, promulgated in 1389, establish a faithful reproduction of the customs followed in the Theological Faculty of Paris.

completing the thirty-fifth year.[1] Consequently this
doctorate was especially appreciated and honored.
"The qualification of doctor of theology," says Crevier, "was so highly esteemed at that period " (that
is to say, in the fourteenth century) "that Pope John
XXII, who did not possess it, feared that use might
be made of that fact to lessen his authority.[2]

The importance of the Theological Faculty of Paris
did not arise wholly from the fact that it was a teaching body, conferring degrees much sought after, and
making doctors such as Albertus Magnus and Thomas
Aquinas. In reality, it constituted for the Church
of Rome and for all Christendom a sort of consulting
committee in ecclesiastical matters; it was "the permanent council of the Gauls," whose right to give
doctrinal advice in matters of faith was recognized,
and which more than once permitted itself to differ in
opinion with the Popes.[3] King Charles VI, in a
formal declaration of 1414, set forth that "the members of the Paris Faculty of Theology hold the first
rank in the science of sacred letters."[4] And he
added: "The people recognize this fact, and the
Court of Rome has itself admitted it when, on sev-

---

[1] Robert de Courçon did not require more than eight years to be
devoted to theological studies; but the course was prolonged to
fourteen years at the beginning of the fourteenth century.

[2] Crevier, t. ii, p. 321.

[3] For example, when, in 1331, the Faculty refused to adopt the
opinions of John XXII, on "the beatific vision of the saints."
In sending the decision of the Faculty to the Pope, the King of
France adjoined to it this curious commentary: "Our doctors
know better what is to be believed in matters of faith than the
jurists and clerics who compose your Court, and who know little
or nothing of theology."   [4] Crevier, t. iii, p. 379.

eral occasions, both former and recent, ambiguity or doubt had arisen concerning the doctrines of the Christian religion, it has not disdained to address itself to the council of the faith residing in Paris in order to obtain a clear decision on these points."

What gave its peculiar force and original character to the Theological Faculty of Paris was the fact that it was not merely a body of professors: it was, as it has been very well defined by Thurot, "a federation of religious and secular communities." [1] Its roots penetrated not solely into the secular colleges, but also into the convents of the various religious orders. It benefited, in consequence, by whatever there was of vitality and power in these church corporations.

As a rule, both masters and students belonged either to the order of St. Dominic, or to one of the four mendicant orders — the Franciscans, the Augustinians, the Jacobins, and the Carmelites — or other communities. In the majority of the convents there were public chairs of theology, whose incumbents were members of the Faculty. In 1253, for instance, there were twelve professors of theology, [2] nine of whom taught in the convents. So, too, the great majority of students and aspirants to the baccalaureate and the doctorate were members of a religious order. Thus, in the fourteenth century, from 1373 to 1398, out of one hundred and ninety-two bachelors who received the license, one hundred and two belonged to mendicant orders.

[1] Thurot, *op. cit.*, p. 132.

[2] In 1207 Innocent III had limited the number of chairs in the Theological Faculty of Paris to eight; but the constantly increasing number of students rendered it necessary to establish four more.

The Dominicans had obtained authority to establish
a chair of theology in their convent in 1229; they
had a second one later on. And their example was
followed by the other communities. The two greatest
doctors of the Middle Ages, Albertus Magnus, "the
universal doctor,"[1] and his pupil, Thomas Aquinas,
"the angel of the schools,"[2] taught in the Dominican convent. In that of the Franciscans taught
Alexander of Hales,[3] "the irrefragable doctor," who
was the master of St. Bonaventure.

There is no doubt that this participation of the
religious orders in the teaching of theology called out
many complaints on the part of the university. "This
partition is harmful and unjust," said the masters of
the university about the year 1250; "unjust because
we are seculars by origin, and the regulars come to
deprive us of the heritage of our fathers."[4] But the
regulars, being aided by the pontifical power, gained
the day. The Faculty of Theology remained a collec-
tive body having its ramifications in all the convents.
Each newly founded religious order claimed to par-
ticipate, by means of some of its own members, in
the university teaching of theology; and when, in the
sixteenth century, Loyola created the famous society

[1] Albert the Great (1193–1280) taught at Paris about 1236. Concerning Albert the Great, see the already cited work of M.
d'Assailly.

[2] Thomas Aquinas (1227–1274) followed his master, Albertus
Magnus, to Paris, and there expounded the *Book of the Sentences*
and Holy Scripture. He was born in Italy. His works have
been reprinted many times, and comprise more than twenty folio
volumes.

[3] Alexander of Hales, born in England in 1245.

[4] Crevier, t. i, p. 397.

which was to take so eminent a place in the Catholic Church, there were Jesuit professors of theology, at least in certain Faculties.[1]

The Faculty of Theology, however, did not depend solely on the religious congregations, the solid studies pursued within the convents,[2] and the masters who taught there in the name of the university; it also included the theological colleges and secular establishments. The most celebrated of these is that which became famous under the name of " Sorbonne," organized in 1257 by Robert de Sorbon, chaplain to Louis IX. "Before Robert de Sorbon," says Crevier, "no college for secular students in theology had been established at Paris. He wished to procure for them this advantage, already enjoyed by several of the regulars, and he founded a house for sixteen poor students in theology, four from each of the Nations composing the university."[3] By his letters patent of 1257, Louis IX made formal cession to his chaplain of "a house situated at Paris in the rue Coupe Gueule, before the palace of the Hot Baths of Julian."[4] The foundation was confirmed in 1259 by a letter from Pope Alexander IV. Such were the modest beginnings, under the name of the "Congregation of poor masters of the Sorbonne," of a building which was to play such a

---

[1] At Poitiers, for example, in the sixteenth century, the Jesuits had two chairs of theology in their college of Ste. Marthe.

[2] On theological studies in the convents, see Thurot, p. 113 et seq.

[3] Crevier, t. i, p. 434.

[4] *Chartularium Univ. Paris.*, t. i, p. 247. The Sorbonne seems to have been the model of Merton College in England. So likewise the University Hall, founded at Oxford in 1280, and intended for four masters to live together and study theology.

brilliant part in the future career of the University
of Paris, and which absorbed the Faculty of Theology,
whose principal seat it became.[1] They were beginnings, moreover, at which it has never blushed, for
the Sorbonne was founded, as has been seen, in a
spirit of charity and benevolence toward the poorest
students, and to a certain extent, also, in a spirit of
liberty, by the secular clergy in order to contend
against the regulars. And might not these seculars
of the thirteenth century, opposed as they were to
the invading corporations, be considered as in a sense
the laity of that age?

However that may be, the college of the Sorbonne
soon had its own public courses in theology. Other
colleges, likewise composed exclusively of theologians,
were founded between 1250 and 1300.[2] Even those
which had been originally under the control of the
Faculty of Arts reserved a certain number of places
for students of theology: among these, the college of
Navarre, established on the heights of St. Geneviève
in 1304, took the first rank.[3] "The houses of Sorbonne and of Navarre," says Thurot, "were almost a
match, by themselves alone, for the religious orders.
They gave the Faculty of Theology the greater number
and the most distinguished of its secular masters."

It was in the convents and colleges, then, that the

[1] Even to-day "the Sorbonne" is a synonym for the group of
Faculties which are the heirs of the University of Paris.

[2] See Thurot, *des Communautés séculières ou collèges, op. cit.*,
p. 122 *et seq.*

[3] The college of Navarre, founded by Queen Jeanne of Navarre,
wife of Philip the Fair, was intended to receive seventy poor students, of whom twenty were to be theologians.

Faculty of Theology had its seat: it was there that masters and pupils exercised themselves, the one in disputations and in preaching, and the others in instruction. From the commencement of the fourteenth century, the special activity of the Faculty, aside from the studies undertaken and the instruction given in the communities, seems to have been visible chiefly in the public acts which preceded the baccalaureate and the mastership. "Superintendence of these acts became the principal occupation of the masters." Instruction was confided almost entirely to the bachelors: what proves this is that the reform of 1452 consisted in requiring the masters to give a lecture once a fortnight.

II

One can make short work of naming the books taught and studied in the Faculty of Theology: the Bible, quite naturally,[1] and Peter Lombard's book of Sentences. Thence arose the names of *Biblici* and of *Sententiarii* applied to bachelors in theology according as they were authorized to make their courses in the Bible or the Sentences. It is to be noted that one was a *Biblicus* before becoming, three years later, a *Sententiarius;* thus giving the impression that the Bible was easier to explain or of less importance than the compilation edited by Peter Lombard. The same conviction is evidenced by the fact that the ordinary lecture, which was reserved for the masters, and

[1] The Bible was probably read in the Latin translation made in the fourth century by St. Jerome, and called the Vulgate.

which according to usage in all the Faculties was
given before nine o'clock in the morning, also dealt
with the book of the Sentences.   Holy Scripture was
explained in the extraordinary courses.[1]

What then was this book by Peter Lombard which
occupied so lofty a position, and was placed on a
footing of equality, to say the least, with the Bible
itself ?   Simply a collection, a methodical arrange-
ment of extracts, constituting a complete treatise on
theology,[2] under the form of sentences and maxims;
or in other words, of thoughts borrowed either from
the Scriptures or the Fathers of the Church.   It was
divided into four parts.   The first treated of God and
the Trinity; the second, of the creation, and the relations between the visible and the invisible worlds;
the third, of the redemption, faith, hope, and charity, the virtues, and sin; the fourth, of the sacra-
ments.

It was to this theological manual that the ordinary
methods of scholastic teaching, exposition, and discussion were applied.   The regulations of the reform
of 1366 prescribed to both bachelors and *Sententiarii*
the reading of the very text of Peter Lombard, and
its exposition phrase by phrase.   But the method of
"questions" was chiefly employed: the opinions of
theologians of recognized authority were pitted against
each other; the *pros* and *cons* were urged in the form
of syllogisms.   But these premeditated discussions,
which were in fact mere monologues, since the pro-

[1] Thurot, p. 110.
[2] Crevier is of opinion, however, that Lombard "had omitted
certain very important matters."   Crevier, t. i, p. 204.

fessor did all the talking, — making both question and answer and defending in turn the two contrary opinions before concluding, — had nothing spontaneous about them: as a rule, they were read; although products of the same method as the lectures of Abelard, they had none of the life and animation which characterized the teaching of the great professor of the twelfth century. Though the reform of 1366 prohibited the bachelors, when making their courses, from having anything but a notebook to assist their memory in recalling the principal divisions, arguments, and quotations of their lectures, yet they none the less persisted in a custom which better suited the laziness or the intellectual mediocrity of the masters. The bachelors were often observed reading argumentations which they had not composed themselves.[1]

Crevier has defined theological instruction as a whole during the Middle Ages with sufficient clearness.[2] According to him, scholastic theology must have had three principal characteristics. First, It reunited in one body of doctrine, or one general system, all questions relating to religion; such is, in fact, the essential merit of the book of the Sentences. Second, It treated these questions not by authority alone, but in part by reasoning; on condition, be it understood, that the ever-docile reason should submit itself to the demonstration of traditional beliefs: as soon as one

[1] At the period of the reform of 1452 the bachelors were authorized to read their lectures, but they were recommended to take care that they were composed by themselves.

[2] Crevier, t. i, p. 100 *et seq.*

departed from tradition he was denounced as heretical and counted as naught. In 1248 propositions like the following were everywhere esteemed erroneous and heretical: "There are many eternal verities which are not God." "He whose natural dispositions are greater, will have a greater share of grace." Finally, it employed "the geometrical style," and proceeded by axioms, theorems, and corollaries. Founded on revealed truth, on dogmas whose authority nobody then dreamed of contesting, theology could, in fact, like geometry, which rests upon self-evident principles, be built up entirely by pure deduction and rest on syllogisms. No appeal was made to feeling in teaching religion; just as no appeal was made to experience in teaching philosophy. There being no criterion of truth but the agreement between consequences and principles admitted as beyond discussion, there resulted an apparently rigorous body of instruction, solid in proportion as the bases of its perpetual reasoning were solid, but desperately dry, and as cold as geometry.

Even contemporaries — for example, Gerson[1] — were under no illusions regarding the defects of such a method. They reproached it for insisting complacently on useless questions while neglecting essential points of doctrine; for plunging into vain curiosities, and, as Crevier says, "into dialectical bickerings and metaphysical abstractions." [2] Lost in the mirage of their subtile discussions, these logicians of theology forgot the art of preaching; they could no longer

---

[1] Gerson, *Contra vanam curiositatem in negotio fidei.*
[2] Crevier, t. iii, p. 182.

speak to the heart, move souls, or communicate faith; they knew nothing save how to argue, distinguish and conclude. On the other hand, they plunged into vain and sometimes ridiculous researches, and, Popes themselves, — as for instance, Clement VII, — treated them as "visionaries." [1] In theology as in philosophy, life drew further · and further apart from this tiresome accumulation of syllogisms; reality escaped from these refined abstractions; and the sterile effort of theological dialectic no more resulted in assuring the progress of faith and practical devotion, than the subtleties of philosophy assisted in arriving at a single new scientific fact. "The acute argumentation of our theologians," said Clemengis, [2] "have at first glance something shrewd and ingenious about them; but if you cast away the husk and envelope of the words and try to find the fruit, they vanish into smoke, because they are empty within."

Let me cite some examples of the theological problems to which grave doctors consecrated all the resources of their logic. "In order to convince the least instructed," says an author, who is nevertheless very catholic, M. d'Assailly, [3] "one must choose among a thousand such, certain of these inane questions which then had the run of the schools, and whose solution it is, I think, superfluous to indicate." — "What is the interior structure of Paradise?" — "Is the body of our Saviour Jesus Christ clothed in the Eucharist?" — "Is the water changed into wine before

[1] *Ibid.*, p. 186.

[2] *Ibid.*, p. 180. Clemengis died in 1435. He was rector of the University of Paris, and director of the College of Navarre.

[3] O. d'Assailly, *Albert le Grand*, Paris, 1870, p. 175.

suffering, with the wine, the eucharistic transformation?"—"Is it of the divine essence to engender or
to be engendered?"—"What do the angels do with
the bodies of which they have made use to fulfil a
mission upon earth?"—"What was the color of the
Virgin's skin?"—"*Utrum beatissima Virgo in concep-
tione habuerit dolorem vel aliquam delectationem? . . .*"
Observe that these follies are quoted, not from some
obscure theologian, but from the *Summa* of Albertus
Magnus.

The theology of the Middle Ages had, nevertheless,
one merit; namely, that it was always associated, at
least by its most famous representatives, with philosophic studies.[1] Was not Albertus Magnus nicknamed
"the ape of Aristotle" because, like his disciple,
Thomas Aquinas, he had ardently studied and paraphrased the Greek philosopher?[2] If the philosophy
of that age was generally religious, and could be defined as *intellectus quœrens fidem,* theology, on the
other hand, was thoroughly impregnated with philosophy and found its motto in the inverse formula, *fides
quœrens intellectum.* In the book of the Sentences
the portion commented on with the greatest care and
insistence was the first part, the most metaphysical,
the most philosophical division of the whole, since it
treated of God, the principle of all things.

But from this very tendency to philosophize, or, at

[1] "It was at that time impossible to study theology without
knowing logic thoroughly," says Thurot. "It ensued that the
students were prepared for theology by instruction in logic and
philosophy."

[2] "Albertus Magnus," Renan has said, "was a paraphrasist,
Thomas Aquinas, a commentator of Aristotle" (*Averroës,* p. 188).

any rate to reason, proceeded the incurable evil of this
prolix and babbling theology whose travail brought
forth all that litter of dissertations, that mass of
huge volumes now forgotten and hidden in the dust
of libraries.   Commentaries were piled on commentaries until in the end the sacred texts were lost sight
of; no one went back any longer to the source, and
when the sixteenth century arrived, the theologians of
the Reformation found the Bible again with the same
astonishment, the same enthusiasm, as the humanists
of the Renaissance rediscovered Homer and Vergil.
And it is permissible to agree with the judgment
passed on scholastic theology in the fourteenth century by the very irreverent Petrarch,— Petrarch, the
first of modern men, — when he wrote to a friend in
one of his familiar letters: "Look at these men who
spend their whole life in altercations, sophistical
subtleties, in incessantly turning their brains upside
down in order to solve empty little questions; and
accept as true my prophecy concerning their future:
their reputation will pass away with their existence,
and the same sepulchre will suffice to enshroud their
names and their bones " (*unum sepulchrum nominibus
ossibusque eorum sufficiet*).

CHAPTER III

THE FACULTIES OF CIVIL AND CANON LAW

I. The University of Bologna, the first centre of legal studies
— The civil and canon law — Success of these studies in spite of
ecclesiastical opposition — Reason and consequence of this success — The Popes themselves patronize the universities of law
— II. Irnerius and Abelard — The Pandects of Justinian —
Knowledge of the Roman law conserved by the clergy — The
disciples of Irnerius — Vacarius and Placentinus — Accursius
and Bartola — The method of Irnerius — The *glossæ* and the
summæ — III. Order of the lessons — Rules followed in Montpellier, in Toulouse — Enumeration of the books interpreted —
The *corpus juris* of Justinian — The common law — Minute
enumeration of obligatory tasks imposed — Ordinary and extraordinary books — Oral teaching — The repetitions — The disputations — Duration of the studies — IV. The canon law —
Faculties of *decretal* — The *Decretum* of Gratian — Other books
— Conclusion.

I

IF it is in the University of Paris that one should
study the teaching of arts and theology, because it
was especially in Paris that these branches were held
in honor, it is to the University of Bologna, and also
to the provincial universities of France, Orleans, Toulouse, and notably Montpellier, that one must go to
seek, in the Middle Ages, teaching of law that is
really important and flourishing.

Law, in those times, signified, on the one hand, civil
or secular law, inherited from the Romans, and chiefly

214

determined by the Justinian Code; and, on the other hand, canon or ecclesiastical law, as established by the decisions of councils and the decrees of Popes. Thence ensued two orders of instruction, two Faculties, often blended into one: the majority of the universities teaching canon law and civil law at the same time and constituting what might be called mixed Faculties, where one became, according to the expression then in use, *doctor in utroque jure*. We hardly find anywhere except at Paris, — where it had been established in consequence of the provision forbidding the teaching of civil law, pronounced by the Popes in the first years of the thirteenth century, — a special Faculty of Canon Law, or Faculty of *Decretal*. But everywhere else legal instruction was twofold in character, and in certain centres of study, Orleans for example, the university was nothing but a university of law: it had no other chairs.

There is nothing to surprise us in the fact that the studies which formed men of business, and prepared wise counsellors and skilful jurists for the service of kings and popes, were held in high regard thus early. Even then these were studies which, in a word, already seemed the most necessary from the utilitarian and practical point of view, since they afforded the means of regulating those material interests which the Middle Ages, in spite of the reputation they have gained for idealism, neither disdained nor neglected.[1] Thus M. Fournier is able to say, doubt-

---

[1] The members of the Faculties of Arts, however, did not at first evince much sympathy for the science of law, which they regarded as a trade rather than an art.

less with some exaggeration, that "all the vitality
of the ancient provincial universities depended on the
teaching of law and the Faculty of Law." [1] Although
this statement is not absolutely exact, since, to cite
no other instance, the considerable development of
medical studies at Montpellier gives it a formal con-
traction, it is certain that the study of law did not
merely flourish in the Middle Ages with a special
brilliancy, testified to by the celebrated names of
Irnerius, Accursius, and Bartola, but that, concur-
rently with theology, it was sometimes prejudicial to
other studies, and especially so to pure science and
letters. This is what Crevier affirms, when, in defin-
ing the condition of studies at the close of the fourteenth century, he says: "Theology and canon law
afforded a short and secure way of arriving at ecclesiastical dignities. Hence students, as soon as they
had acquired a moderate provision of grammar and
logic, devoted themselves to these sciences, so useful
to success; while the arts, which could merely adorn
the mind, were abandoned." [2]

Instruction in Roman law, however, did not succeed
in gaining and keeping a foothold in the schools and
universities of the twelfth and thirteenth centuries
without a struggle. It is indubitable that the Church
at first beheld with anxiety and suspicion the development of those studies in civil law which she was later
on to patronize and protect. There was a moment
when the civil lawyer was considered the enemy of
God; and John of Salisbury relates that several of
his contemporaries burned and destroyed such manu-

[1] Fournier, *op. cit.*, t. i, Préface, p. viii.   [2] Crevier, t. iii, p. 190.

scripts of civil law as fell into their hands. The same conservative and traditional spirit which opposed the introduction of Aristotle's works on physics in the Faculty of Arts, was still more bound to resist the progress of civil law, considered as the rival of ecclesiastical law. In the twelfth century the councils of Lateran (1139) and of Tours (1163) forbade members of religious orders to study civil law. St. Bernard complained bitterly of the ardor with which the clergy threw themselves into legal studies. In 1220, a Bull of Pope Honorius III prohibited the teaching of civil law at Paris and the neighboring cities.[1] In 1254, Innocent IV extended the same prohibition against Roman law for all France.[2]

It is interesting to note the reasons urged by the popes in justification of this prohibition. That to which they chiefly appealed was the fact that the study of civil law was prejudicial to the science which they naturally ranked above all others, namely, theology.[3] But they advanced other considerations: in the first place, the pretended inutility of this study. "Although Holy Church," said Honorius III, "does not reject the docile co-operation (*famulatum*) of the secular laws, yet, as in France and other provinces, the laity do not use the laws of the Roman Emperors;[4] and as, moreover, ecclesiastical suits are seldom met with which may not be settled by the rules of canon law alone, we forbid, under pain of excommunication, both at Paris and the neighboring towns and cities,

[1] *Chartularium Univ. Paris.*, t. i, p. 92.   [2] *Ibid.*, p. 261.

[3] "We desire," said the Pope, "*ut plenius et perfectius studio theologiæ insectatur vel saltem philosophiæ disciplinæ.*"

[4] Allusion to countries governed by common law.

any person to employ himself in teaching or learning
civil law."

It appears, moreover, that the Sovereign Pontiffs
had been shocked by the luxurious habits and osten-
tation of the professors of law, who were richer than
their colleagues of the other Faculties, in consequence
of the profits derived from their pleadings and con-
sultations.   Nothing can be more significant on this
head than the following passage from the bull of
Honorius III: "We have learned with sorrow that,
abandoning the study of philosophy, to say nothing
of that of theology, the majority of the clergy hasten
to the lectures on secular law; and that, in the majority of states, no one is chosen by the bishops to occupy
positions of dignity and honor, or ecclesiastical pre-
bends, unless he is either a professor of civil law or
an advocate. . . ."   Then follows a delineation of
the privations imposed on themselves, *per contra*, in
their modest way of life, by the nurslings of philosophy (*alumni philosophiæ*); "while our advocates, or
say rather our devils (*advocati nostri, immo diaboli*),
covered with purple, mounted on richly caparisoned
horses, in the glitter of gold, the whiteness of silver,
the splendor of precious stones, their royal vestments
reflecting the splendors of the astonished sun (*stu-
pentem reverberantes solem*), make ostentatious display
and give rise to scandal everywhere."   And the Pope
concludes by forbidding the bishops to consider the
title of professor of laws a sufficient recommendation
for ecclesiastical preferment, and by formally prohib-
iting "in France, England, Scotland, Flanders, Spain,
and Hungary" all teaching of civil law.   It is true

that, himself mistrusting the results of this prohibition, the Pope added, "If, however, the heads of the State permit" (*si tamen hoc de regum et principum processerit voluntate*).

Is it by reason of this restriction, which reserved the rights of emperors and kings, that civil law, in spite of the threats of excommunication, became common in all the universities? It is permissible to think so, since the study of law could alone guarantee to the temporal sovereigns capable ministers, such as that William of Nogaret, professor of law at Montpellier, who was of such great assistance to Philip the Fair in his quarrels with Boniface VIII. In any case, the organization in the vicinity of Paris of the University of Orleans is proof enough that the Popes were not obeyed.[1] It is manifest that the bishops themselves were not rigorous toward the jurists very long. In the middle of the thirteenth century, Roger Bacon points out the progress of civil law, and what he calls "the abuse of it that has been made in Italy."[2] And he adds: "The jurists have acquired such influence over the minds of prelates and princes that they monopolize all places and favors at their disposal, so much so that students of philosophy and theology remain empty handed, no longer having the wherewithal to live, to buy books, devote themselves to research, or experiment on the secrets of science. Even the jurists who study canon law only have not the necessary resources for life and study unless they have at

[1] "The Popes were greatly respected in the Middle Ages," says Thurot, "but their decisions were executed only in so far as people chose."

[2] Roger Bacon, *Compendium Philosophiæ*, ch. iv.

the same time acquired a knowledge of civil law. . . .
The civil lawyers alone are honored and enriched."[1]

Even the favor of Popes was not always refused to
civil law. Thus, Clement V, who had himself studied
law in the schools of Orleans, formally consecrated,
by his Bull of 1306, the legal instruction of that
university.[2] It is true that Clement V was no other
than that famous Bertrand de Goth who, having
become pope through the protection of Philip the
Fair, seems to have ascended the pontifical throne
only to make himself the tool of the King of France.
"Let none wonder," said he concerning the jurists of
Orleans, "that the sun glistens on their golden buck-
lers, for they are the defenders of the country; they
disentangle rights from the midst of the most hidden
facts; they re-establish the rights of every man and
come to the aid of the human race; thus meriting
by the results of their science as much as if they had
saved the country by wounds received in combat."
What a contrast with the language employed a hundred years earlier by the predecessors of Clement V!
All the Avignon Popes, moreover, followed the example of Clement V and showed themselves so favorable
to civil law that no further opposition was made to
the progress of legal study.

---

[1] Another writer of that age (cited by Mullinger, *op. cit.*, p. 211)
claims, on the contrary, that the study of canon law also led to riches
and preferment. But he agrees with Roger Bacon in affirming that
theology was abandoned and that the mass of students adhered to
the study of law.

[2] Fournier, t. i, p. 11. "The studies of canon and of civil law,"
said the Pope, "have always been held in honor at Orleans: they
shall flourish there anew by the help of God."

It will have been observed that, in the passage
already cited from the Bull of Honorius III, the Pope
alluded to the common law countries where Roman law
was not in use; for instance, the northern and central
provinces of France. There, assuredly, was a difficulty, a local obstacle to the development of the study
of Roman law. But attention has been drawn by
others to the fact that "in France had been carried on
a preservation of old customs which, though not less
varied than the feudal divisions, preserved the method
and frequently even the stipulations of the Roman
law. If the Popes, who protected their canons, made
opposition to Roman law, the kings of France were
favorable to the study of it. St. Louis caused the
works of Justinian to be translated."[1] The Roman
laws, then, were interesting things to know, even in
the common law regions; and elsewhere — for example, in the south of France — they were the common
law of the land.

I shall end these general considerations by pointing
out that the study of civil law was one of the forces
which contributed most toward the emancipation of
the universities, toward freeing them from ecclesiastical dependence, and preparing for and introducing
therein the lay spirit. This progress was chiefly due
to the very character of that instruction which, treating exclusively of human affairs and temporal interests, directed the thoughts of those who pursued it,

[1] V. Leclerc, *État des Lettres au XIIe Siècle*, p. 510. Compare
Montesquieu, *Esprit des Lois*, vol. xxviii, ch. xlii; "Philip the
Fair caused the laws of Justinian to be taught simply as *written
reason* in those regions of France which were governed by custom."

either as students or masters, toward the things of this world. But account must also be made of the special fact that the study of law made its adepts wealthy; so that the jurists gradually renounced the austere life imposed by their poverty on other members of the university. From the thirteenth century, according to the testimony of Roger Bacon, the professors of law at Bologna married, organized their households according to the fashions of the period, and adopted the same mode of life as the laity.

II

It was from Italy, and above all from Bologna, that great intellectual centre both of canon and of Roman law, that the first impulse to legal study came. Irnerius, who taught at Bologna in the first half of the twelfth century, was the renovator of legal study, and he is entitled by that fact to a place analogous to that we have assigned to Abelard among the founders of universities.[1]

He had himself studied in the schools of Constantinople, and this earliest Renaissance, like the Renaissance of the sixteenth century, seems to have been in part, at least, a ray from the science of the Orient, illumining Italy in the first place, and then stealing gradually over the other countries of Western Europe. An accident, a fortunate find, contributed to the restoration of Roman law. In 1135 or 1137, at the sacking of the little town of Amalfi, some one laid hands on

---

[1] Irnerius, whom Crevier styles "the German Irnerius," seems, nevertheless, to have been born in Italy, at Milan or Bologna.

a copy of the *Pandects* of Justinian. Irnerius was charged with the revision of the text, and it was probably at this period that he was commissioned by the Emperor Lothair II to teach law in the University of Bologna.

It must not be imagined, however, as has been mistakenly done by Montesquieu,[1] that the petty fact of discovering the lost text of the *Pandects* was like a resurrection, "a second birth," for Roman law, and that, swept away by the fall of the Western Empire, hidden for six hundred years, the Justinian law was picked up by chance in the twelfth century. As a matter of fact, the study of Roman law had never been completely abandoned, even during the darkest period of the ignorance of the Middle Ages. The learned had always known of the Theodosian Code. The Code and the Constitutions of Justinian were studied before the finding of the *Pandects*. And Savigny has forcibly demonstrated, in a chapter entitled "The Roman law preserved by the clergy," that there had never been a complete interruption in the study of it. Irnerius merely resumed the study of civil law, and gave it prominence by the public character of his lectures and the novelty of his method.

It was the pupils of Irnerius who spread a taste for the same studies throughout the other schools of Europe. As early as 1149, one of his disciples, Vacarius, carried the laws of Justinian to England and taught in the Oxford schools.[2] So, too, the law

---

[1] Montesquieu, *Esprit des Lois*, vol. xxviii, ch. xlii.

[2] It is interesting to note that in England, contrary to what

university of Montpellier sprang directly from the
University of Bologna.   The Italian Placentin, born
at Plaisance, after having taught at Bologna and
Mantua, established himself at Montpellier about
1160 or 1180.[1] He was, say the chronicles of the
time, the first who *read* at Montpellier.[2] Another
Bolognese professor, Azo, likewise emigrated to
Montpellier, and it is related that many Italian
students followed him thither.

Montpellier was not the only place in France to
profit by the intellectual movement which had its
starting-point at Bologna. "Our Frenchmen," says
Crevier, "went to Bologna to gain a knowledge of
Justinian law, and brought it back from there to
Angers, Orleans, and Paris."[3] The statutes drawn
up in 1306, by Pope Clement V, to regulate the order
of the lectures of the professors of law at the University of Orleans, indorse the divisions, the *puncta
taxata*, followed in their instructions by the doctors
of Bologna.[4]

Bolognese jurists went all over Europe. In 1348,
a professor from Bologna was summoned by Charles
IV to the University of Prague. Others went to
Spain. But it was in Italy especially that the disciples of Irnerius propagated the science and methods
of their master, and contributed to the formation of a

---

occurred elsewhere, the clergy favored the study of Roman law,
while the civil power rejected it. It was King Stephen who forbade the lectures of Vacarius.

[1] Placentin, after a first journey to France, returned to Italy;
but he went back again to Montpellier, where he died, February 12,
1192.   [2] A. Germain, *op. cit.*, p. 6.

[3] Crevier, t. i, p. 246.   [4] M. Fournier, t. i, p. 28.

great number of universities, nearly all of them organized on the pattern of the University of Bologna.

Bologna maintained its precedence, none the less, under the successors of Irnerius. It was at Bologna that Accursius taught (1182–1260), who became in his turn the chief of a school, and was surnamed "the idol of jurisconsults." Irnerius had been called "the light of the law." At Bologna, likewise, the famous Bartola studied and received his doctorate (1313–1356); he was, after Accursius, the guide of the Roman lawyers of that time, and taught at Pisa and Perugia. Bartola instituted a new method, more general than that of his predecessors: instead of confining himself to comments on matters of detail, he constructed theories. His authority lasted until the sixteenth century, when Alciat in Italy and Cujas in France replaced him in the direction and general inspiration of legal studies.

What was the method of Irnerius, the dominating method of the twelfth and thirteenth centuries? It consisted, essentially, in submitting the legal texts to very nearly the same laborious explanation and perpetual commentary to which the contemporary professors of logic and philosophy subjected the texts of Aristotle. All obscure terms and vague phrases were interpreted. Marginal notes and interlineations were added to the text. Thence came the name of *glossarists*, makers of *glosse es* (*glossæ*, obscure words), applied to Irnerius.[1] Another process, dear to Irnerius, was

---

[1] See Savigny, *op. cit.*, ch. xxiii, *Les glossateurs considérés comme professeurs.*

that of summaries, of *résumés*.[1] His pupil, Placentin, wrote the *Sum of the Code,* the *Sum of the Institutes,* etc. Doubtless in these earliest studies of civil law in the Middle Ages one discerns no original effort to return to the philosophic sources of laws, or to rise, through comparison of civil and natural law, to new conceptions; but there is, at all events, an interesting and exhaustive work of patient and minute interpretation. The sometimes grotesque, but sometimes penetrating explanations of Irnerius prepared the way for the more certain and complete interpretations given afterwards by Alciat and Cujas, whose originality consisted chiefly in making an appeal to ancient history and literature, and all other aids to interpretation in making their explanations of legal texts. The gravest reproach which can be brought against the school of Irnerius is that, by a phenomenon analogous to that which occurred in the scholastic study of philosophy, where the commentators gradually superseded the author and the text of Aristotle disappeared under the paraphrases of his interpreters, so in the study of law men attached themselves with servility to the *gloss* which came to have greater authority than the text itself.[2]

[1] "The professor began his course by giving the *résumé* or entire title (*summa*)."

[2] E. Petit, professor of the Faculty of Law of Poitiers, *Traité élémentaire du droit romain.* Paris, 1892.

III

Restricting ourselves in the first place to civil law, let us try to form an idea of the order of lectures and exercises in the Faculties of Law during the Middle Ages. For the details I shall go back to the very text of the various regulations published, notably to the statutes established 1339 for the University of Montpellier, and, shortly before that, in the first years of the fourteenth century, for that of Toulouse.[1]

The Faculty of Civil Law, like the Faculty of Arts, had its "ordinary" and its "extraordinary" lessons: the latter appear to have been intended to complete the regular instruction, which was devoted to fundamental questions. The ordinary lectures were absolutely obligatory; it seems that the extraordinary courses were optional up to a certain point. Only the ordinary lectures, says Savigny, were attended by all the students. A simple bachelor might give extraordinary lectures, while the other courses were reserved to licentiates or doctors. At Montpellier, each lecture occupied an hour, and there were four every day; at Bologna, an hour and a half or two hours. The first began at six in the morning[2] (horâ

[1] M. Fournier, *op. cit.*, t. ii, p. 44, and t. i, p. 452. The statutes of 1339 were drawn up by Cardinal Bertrand, in the name of Pope Benedict XII. The statutes of Toulouse had been drawn up, according to M. Fournier, between 1280 and 1320. Père Denifle thinks they date from the second half of the fourteenth century. See on this subject the articles M. Fournier has just published in the *Revue Internationale de l'enseignement supérieur* (February 15, March 1, March 15, 1892) : *L'organisation de l'enseignement du droit dans l'Université de Montpellier.*

[2] At Bologna this course was to begin, at latest, when the *Angelus*

primâ matutinâ); the second at nine (*horâ tertiâ*); the
third at three (*horâ nonâ*); and the last at five (*horâ
vesperarum*). The morning lecture was the essential
one, the one called *ordinary*. At Montpellier and
Bologna, these lectures began on October 19, and
ended on September 29. The other courses were
called extraordinary. At Montpellier, the evening
courses were given by doctors or licentiates; those
at nine in the morning and three in the afternoon
by bachelors. Punctuality was rigidly demanded, at
least by the regulations. At Bologna, a professor
who was tardy in beginning his lesson had to pay a
fine of twenty sous. The number of masters varied
greatly. We find only two in the University of
Poitiers (where there were also two professors of
canon law); a third professor of civil law was instituted in the seventeenth century, at the time of the
reform of 1679. At Orleans, Bimbenet speaks of ten
professors. At Bologna, according to the statutes of
1397, the college of civil lawyers numbered sixteen
ordinary members; and that of the canonists twelve,
plus a certain number of professors *supranumerarii et
extraordinarii*. This number appears considerable,
especially when one recalls that at Bologna, as elsewhere, students and bachelors also took part in the
instruction and had the right to lecture.

The books explained in the ordinary and extraordinary courses were the different works of the *corpus
juris* of Justinian: the *Codex*[1] in the first place; then

was rung at the Cathedral. At Poitiers, in the sixteenth century,
there was a course at five o'clock in the morning.

[1] The *Codex* of Justinian dates from 529.

the *Digestum Vetus,* the *Infortiatum,* the *Digestum Novum,* in other words, the three parts which the glossarists, the Irnerians, had distinguished as the *Pandects* or the *Digest,* the *Institutes,*[1] the *Authenticum* or the *Authentica;* that is to say, extracts from the *Novellæ Constitutinas;*[2] and, finally, what were called the *Tres libri,* a collection composed of books 10, 11, and 12 of the *Codex.*

Nearly all the sources of Roman law, then, were within the reach of the students. But was the study of common law, of modern law, completely forgotten by these Faculties which seem to have been chiefly a revival of the law schools of the Western Empire? No; since we find in the list of classic authors of the school of Montpellier, a book wholly unknown to Roman law, the *Usus feudorum,* that is, a collection of feudal laws. So too, at Bologna, the study of the *Constitutiones* of Frederick I, of Frederick II, and of Conrad, were gradually introduced.[3]

I shall not reproduce in all their details the very precise indications afforded by contemporary documents concerning the distribution of matters taught in the different courses. The statutes of Montpellier, like those of Bologna and Toulouse, determine with minute precision and tyrannous severity what works and what divisions of works shall be studied in both the ordinary and the extraordinary courses. They fix

---

[1] The Institutes (*institutiones*) date from 533, the same year as the Digest.

[2] *Novellæ constitutiones,* collection of the last constitutions by which Justinian had modified certain dispositions of his Code of 529, and which were not published until after his death. Each *Novelle* belonging to the *Authenticum* was called *Authentica.*

[3] Savigny, ch. xxi, 194.

the number of lectures to be devoted to each subject
of instruction. Thus, at Toulouse, the first book of
the *Digestum Vetus* was to be read in thirteen days;
the second, in twenty days; the third, in eighteen
days, etc. The classic works were distinguished into
ordinary and extraordinary books; the first were the
Digestum Vetus and the *Codex*, reserved for the ordinary courses; but extraordinary courses might be
given even on the ordinary books. Another distinction, which we find at Montpellier, if not at Bologna,
consisted in dividing the books into two parts; the
extraordinary books themselves comprised a *pars ordinaria* and a *pars extraordinaria*, confided to different
professors.[1] At Toulouse and at Orleans it was only
the ordinary books which were divided into two parts,
each *pars* having the same importance. The regulations went still farther and put the professors under
very close restrictions; the points (*puncta taxata*) at
which they were to stop their explanations were determined for them in advance. "The *taxatio punctorum*," says M. Fournier, "introduced into each part
a new division, the object of which was to oblige the
professors to teach a certain quantity of matters in a
given time." This *taxatio* varied in each university.
In general, the *punctum* comprised what the professor
could read in the space of fourteen days of lectures
(*dies legibiles*). It is easy to see that this *taxatio
punctorum* had been devised in order to obviate the

---

[1] M. Fournier calls attention to the fact that at Montpellier the
tendency was to abandon the traditional distinction of ordinary
and extraordinary books, and to adopt another which, in all books,
distinguished an ordinary part and an extraordinary part.

caprices or the negligence of masters.[1] By thus binding them down to a far too rigid programme, assurance was at least gained that the programme would be accomplished. Great importance was attached to the observance of these rules. Professors were obliged to take the following oath: "I swear to read, and to finish reading, within the times fixed by the statutes, the books or parts of books which have been assigned for my lectures."[2] Severe penalties were inflicted on those who had not finished their courses at the prescribed time. It is evident that no freedom was left to the professors of those days. One of the vices common to the instruction of the Middle Ages under all its forms, was that of subjecting the masters to rules too minute, too imperative, in such a way as to prevent all originality and engender a merely routine compliance with them. On the other hand, it must be acknowledged that the method pursued secured great order and regularity; it permitted no gaps in the instruction.[3]

What methods were followed? "Sometimes," says Savigny, "the professors spoke extemporaneously and sometimes they read. Among the courses that have been preserved to us, there are certainly some that were improvised; thus, in those of Odofredus,[4] the vivacity and familiarity, but also the carelessness, of oral instruction are recognizable."[5] In any case the

---

[1] It seems that the ordinary courses only were subject to the obligation of the *puncta taxata*.

[2] M. Fournier, t. i, p. 63.

[3] *Libros suos legent in ordine, sine saltu*.

[4] Odofredus taught with distinction in Bologna sometime after Irnerius.   [5] Savigny, ch. xxiii, 204.

instruction was always oral; the professors were forbidden to show their notes to the students or to allow
them to read the notes. One detail which proves
that the courses were not so monotonous as one might
be tempted to believe, is that the students might interrupt the professors and ask them questions, a custom much followed in the evening courses, which thus
became conferences rather than exclusively didactic
lectures.   Another useful practice was that of repetitions (*repetitiones*).[1] "We ordain," said the statutes
of Montpellier, "that all the professors (*ordinarii vel
extraordinarii*) be bound to hold a repetition at least
three times a year (*ter repetere in omni anno*)." At
Bologna, likewise, there were *repetitiones*, to which
the professor frequently relegated the examination
of the *questiones;* that is, of the real or imaginary
lawsuits which might be decided by the legal point
examined in the course.[2]

Finally, the *disputatio*, the argumentation, that
favorite exercise of the Middle Ages, also had its
place in the Faculties of Law. "The argumentations," says Savigny, "could only be participated in
by doctors, or by students aspiring to a salaried chair.
All the bachelors might be present at the disputations,

---

[1] "A repetition," says Savigny, "was the detailed explanation
of a text, with the solution of all difficulties and the reply to all
objections that it might raise."

[2] "The same usage existed everywhere. The statutes of 1303 of
the University of Avignon, said: 'The ordinary doctors of civil
and of canon law shall make a formal repetition two months after
the commencement of the course'" (Fournier, § 11, p. 313). The
repetitions were sometimes entrusted to the doctors themselves
(at Bologna), sometimes to the bachelors by preference (at Montpellier).

and all the students had the right of argumentation. The subject of the disputation was a point of law. . . . The argumentations lasted from Lent to Pentecost."[1]

The duration of the studies varied greatly from one university to another. At Montpellier, the regulation of 1339 declares that the students must be prevented from making too great haste to attain the baccalaureate and the doctorate (*ne quis ad baccalariatum et subsequenter ad doctoratum nimis propere prosilire audeat*). Consequently, six years of study were required for the baccalaureate in civil law, and five for the doctorate: eleven years in all. It is true that dispensations might be granted by the Bishop of Maguelonne to bachelors who had distinguished themselves, after three years of study. "At Bologna," says Savigny, "eight years were required to become a civil lawyer." Petrarch studied seven years at Montpellier and Bologna, and had finished his legal studies at twenty-two. But Petrarch was not an ordinary student, and it is certain that the great majority of his comrades took more time to reach the end of their scholastic life.

How was the work of the students regulated in other respects? We have few details on this point. It is probable that the custom of writing during the courses was as prevalent as in our own day, if not still more so, on account of the scarcity of books.[2] But the

[1] Savigny, ch. xxi, § 100.

[2] The courses were most often dictated. Even when it was attempted, as happened more than once, especially at Paris, to compel the professors to speak extemporaneously, they were permitted to repeat twice what they said, so as to give the students time to write.

regulations of Montpellier, like those of Touıouse, while abounding in recommendations on many subjects, for instance, on the duty of being present at Mass on Sundays, and at the annual Mass for the repose of the dead; on decency in clothing; on the prohibition against dancing outside of one's own house, gaming for money, etc.; are silent as to the obligations of students with regard to their personal tasks. Everything was comprehended, it appears, in following the courses (*audire*), and, when one had become a bachelor, in continuing to attend the lectures of the masters, and giving lectures in their turn (*legere*).

IV

A few words still remain to be said concerning the teaching of canon law, which, in most of the Faculties was done conjointly with that of civil law, but which, at Paris, was the especial object of legal study.

If it were necessary to take the maxim of Seneca literally, "*Timeo hominem unius libri*," nothing could be more awe-inspiring than the Faculties of the Middle Ages. As a matter of fact, hardly any of them had more than one book, or a single author, as the subject of study. The Faculty of Arts had Aristotle, the Faculty of Civil Law had the *Corpus juris* of Justinian, the Faculty of Canon Law had Gratian's Decretal.

The study of canon law, which was at first considered a part of the theological course of study, became

specialized after the appearance of the Decretal of
Gratian, in 1151. And it is to be observed that for
canon law, as well as for civil law, the incentive proceeded from Bologna. Gratian, in fact, was a Bolognese monk. He made a compilation of the canons
of the Councils, papal decrees, and extracts from the
Fathers of the Church, and arranged these matters in
an orderly and methodical manner. The spirit of his
book could not but be agreeable to the Court of Rome,
for Gratian, who was criticised in later times by the
Gallicans, and notably by the Abbé Fleury in the
seventeenth century, "made the power of the Pope
unlimited." [1] Hence his work was approved by Eugenius III, and the School of Bologna, which was teaching Justinian law with great success, adopted also the
Decretal of Gratian.[2] Thence it passed into the other
universities. The Faculty of Paris took the name of
Faculty of Decretal, and the work of the Bolognese
monk became the basis of its instruction.

The other books studied by the canonists were, in
fact, mere complements of the Decretal: the *Decretales,*
the *Sexta,* the *Clementines.* The Decretals had been
put together in 1234, in a collection of five volumes,
by Raymond de Pennafort, General of the Dominicans,
under the title of the *Decretals of Gregory IX,* or
Extra; that is to say, aside from the decretals collected by Gratian. Boniface VIII, in 1298, added a
sixth book, whence its name of *Sexta.* Finally, the

[1] Crevier, t. i, p. 241.

[2] From this time on Bologna had two schools of law, the students
of which formed but one university, although they had distinct
professors.

Clementines, which contained the letters of Clement V, were published in 1313.

In the Faculty of Decretal, as in that of Civil Law, there was a perpetual confusion of ordinary and extraordinary courses.[1] In early times, at Paris, it was enough to have been a civil lawyer for three years in order to be admitted as a student of canon law; but this condition was speedily abolished, because it had the effect of excluding the members of religious orders, to whom the study of civil law was forbidden. In 1370, to become a bachelor it was necessary to have studied canon law during forty-eight months within the space of six years. At Bologna, says Savigny, six years of study were also required to become a canonist.

The Faculty of Canon Law seems to have been one of those in which the studies were least difficult, and wherein professors and pupils had the most leisure. The holidays, so frequent in all the Faculties, were still more so for the *decretists* of Paris, who had, according to Thurot, in addition to the sixty feast days common to the whole university, thirty-four that were special to themselves.[2] In the statutes of Montpellier, which claimed, nevertheless, to reduce the number of holidays, "which have been recognized," say they, "as chiefly occasions of expense," we find the long list

[1] At Bologna the ordinary lessons treated of the *Decretum* and the *Decretals;* at Montpellier, all the books were used, sometimes in the ordinary and sometimes in the extraordinary courses. At Bologna, in other words, such or such a book was considered fundamental; at Montpellier the same book was interpreted in courses of different natures.　　　　　[2] Thurot, p. 173.

of saints whose days the students were called upon to celebrate.[1] But the official holidays were far from being the only ones on which the professors of canon law absented themselves from their lectures. Little by little, they came to consider the doctorate as a sinecure; they entrusted to bachelors the care of instruction in their stead. "The Faculty of Decretal," says Thurot, "was the most corrupt and venal of all the Faculties; it had neither masters nor students: it had only sellers and buyers."[2] The abuses became so crying in the sixteenth century, that the Parliament of Paris, in 1533, decided that thenceforward there should be but six doctor regents, who should be chosen by competition and obliged to give their lectures seriously. This was the *"college sexviral,"* concerning which, ten years later, in spite of the reforms that had been wrought, Ramus was unsparing in his criticism.

There is no disguising the fact that the doctors of law whether canonists or civil lawyers, rich ecclesiastics or rich advocates, formed a class, a caste by themselves, in the universities of the Middle Ages. One recalls what Pope Honorius said about their luxury. At Paris, in order to be a doctor of the Faculty of Decretal, it was necessary to prove an income of eighty livres (about five hundred francs of our money). The *decretists* of Paris constituted a *collegium,* in imitation

---

[1] Fournier, t. ii, p. 53. At Bologna there were about thirty holidays, including fifteen days at Easter, and eleven at Christmas. If no feast day occurred during the week, lessons were suspended on Thursday.   [2] Thurot, p. 183.

of the colleges of Bologna, entrance to which was extremely difficult. The doctors of Bologna bound themselves by oath, towards the middle of the thirteenth
century, not to confer the doctorate on any except
their sons, their brothers, or their nephews, seeking
thus to make it hereditary in their own families; and
in spite of the Rector, and of the opposition of the
inhabitants of the city, they more than once rejected
fit candidates who had the misfortune of not being
their relatives by blood or marriage. If masters of
arts, and even theologians, occasionally showed little
sympathy for the jurists, the latter repaid them with
something of disdain. They really considered themselves as belonging to another race, these professors
of law who, at Poitiers, for example, maintained that
hereditary nobility even, was a prerogative of their
position, and who added in their diffuse style: "The
texts of Roman law have always lavished the most
honorable titles on the professors of law: they are
spoken of as noble, as very noble, as magnificent, as
ministers and priests of justice. . . . The emperors
Theodosius and Valentinian honored them, after
twenty years of service, with the title of counts of
the first rank. In the imperial chamber of Spires,
doctors and nobles enjoy the same prerogatives."
There was an evident pretension on the part of the
doctors of law to place themselves above the rest. In
those days of privilege men had not yet arrived at
regarding equality as the rule both in scientific and
in civil society; they had not as yet come to admit
that in the Republic of Letters there is no primacy
save such as belongs to knowledge and talent. And

particularly were they wanting in that ideal cherished by the moderns, of an university wherein, no rivalry existing between Faculty and Faculty, the representatives of various orders of studies, in the most perfect solidarity and union, each in his own place and with equal rights, shall labor — for the diffusion of universal knowledge.

CHAPTER IV

THE FACULTIES OF MEDICINE

I. Unfavorable attitude of the Middle Ages toward medical studies
— Experience neglected — Nevertheless an important movement
in medical studies began at Salerno — The Abbey of Monte-
Cassino — Constantine the African and his influence — The statutes of King Roger II and of the Emperor Frederick II — The
School of Montpellier — Importance of this university — Influence of Arabian Medicine — Italian physicians in France — II.
Books and Methods — Theoretic teaching — Hippocrates and
Galen — Salernitan books — Other modern text-books — Odd prohibitions — Medicines for the Soul applied first — Lack of practical teaching — Dissection rare — Surgery despised.

I

MEDICAL studies doubtless resulted in nothing very
brilliant during the Middle Ages. The revival of experimental methods and the coming of the sixteenth
and seventeenth centuries were necessary before serious physiological studies modified and transformed
the art of healing, or, at least, the treatment of
disease. Although, in his letters patent of 1396,
relating to the University of Montpellier, Charles VI,
King of France, had already declared that "Experience is the mistress of sciences, especially of medical
science,"[1] yet experience gained little honor in an

[1] " . . . *Experientia quæ in facto medicinali præsertim res est
magistra.* . . . " (Fournier, t. ii, p. 162.)

age when the authority of Aristotle outweighed the authority of nature. Consequently, medical instruction lagged along in the rut of routine, repeating the lessons of Hippocrates and Galen, and as much enslaved to commenting on the texts of Greek or Alexandrian medicine, as juridical instruction was to the task of explaining the monuments of Roman law.

Moreover, it must not be forgotten that the religious and mystical spirit of the Middle Ages, which was too frequently inclined to see in maladies the signs of divine wrath, and to look to the divine will alone for their cure, placed more reliance on spiritual succor, or the intervention of the terrestrial representatives of the Deity, than on the healing virtues of human science. Jesus, healing the sick by the imposition of His hands, giving sight to the blind, movement to paralytics, and by invoking the living God, restoring the dead to life in the name of His Father, seemed to have announced to the world that prayer and faith were the best and most powerful remedies against human infirmities.[1] Hence kings, the delegates of Divine power, attributed to themselves the power to cure scrofulous and other diseased persons simply by touching them. The monks, not disdainful of medicine, and joining that mode of action to all others, yet recommended prayer, pilgrimages to places of devotion, and visits to the relics of saints first of all.

And yet, in spite of all prejudices to the contrary, medical instruction was given in the Middle Ages. The majority of the universities had their Faculty of

[1] Lacroix, *Sciences et arts au moyen âge*, Paris, Didot, 1887. *Sciences médicales*, p. 149.

Medicine. In Italy, Salerno and Naples, Plaisance,
Arezzo, Rome, Perugia, Treviso, Pisa, Florence, Siena,
Pavia, Ferrara; in France, Paris, Montpellier, Toulouse, Avignon, Cahors, Grenoble, Perpignan, Orange;
in England, Oxford; in Ireland, Dublin; in Spain,
Salamanca, Lerida, Huesca; in Portugal, Coimbra; in
Austria, Prague, Cracow, Ofen; in Germany, Heidelberg, Erfurt; more than than thirty cities, in a word,
have had regular bodies of medical professors ever
since the thirteenth and fourteenth centuries.

To explain this movement, apparently so considerable, notice must be taken of a multitude of entirely independent efforts; nor must we forget the
influence exerted by Arabian medicine. But it remains none the less true, that there was an initial
centre of action for medicine, as well as for philosophy,
the arts, and law. The impulse came first of all from
a city, — Salerno; and in that city from a man, —
Constantine, surnamed the African, who merits, all
things considered, to be placed in the same rank as
the other two great initiators of university instruction, Abelard and Irnerius.

It is indisputable that the school of Salerno was
a source of medical studies in the Middle Ages, *fons
medicinæ*, as Petrarch said. And it must be noticed
at once that this school was never erected into a
university. Only a few miles distant from the city
of Naples, it was, one might say, incorporated with
the University of Naples; it became a sort of detached
member when the latter was organized by the Emperor
Frederick II, in 1224.

Let me briefly recall the history of the school of

Salerno,[1] since for medicine it has been what Bologna was for law and Paris for philosophy. It seems that its first beginnings must be sought for in the Abbey of Monte-Cassino, founded by the Benedictines in 528, at some distance from Salerno. Medicine was studied in this monastery with marked devotion. The monks copied and recopied the works of Hippocrates and Galen, which had been translated into Latin as early as the sixth century. The abbots of Monte-Cassino were distinguished for their medical knowledge. About 856, Bertharius compiled a summary of hygienic rules; after him, Alphanus wrote a book on *The Union of Soul and Body,* and another entitled *The Four Humors;* finally, Pope Victor III (1085), who had been previously abbot of Monte-Cassino, is reputed to have been *medicinæ peritissimus.* From the monastery of Monte-Cassino the taste for medical studies spread as far as Salerno; and by the eleventh century, the little town had become an intellectual centre which attracted students from all parts of Western Europe. "I think," says Laurie, "that the school of Salerno may be considered as having been a public school from 1060, and a privileged school after 1100." [2] It was in the latter year that the physicians of Salerno, styling themselves *tota schola Salerni,* dedicated to the King of England their celebrated rules of health, written in Latin verse. It is indubitable, and the fact deserves notice, that medical studies were the first that formed a

[1] See Laurie, *op. cit.,* Lecture VII.

[2] The school seems to me to have been chiefly organized after the Normans had conquered Salerno, that is, after 1075.

regular centre of instruction in the Middle Ages; the
schools of Bologna and Paris, in fact, date from the
twelfth century only.

But, as I have said, the honor of making known the
school of Salerno, of giving it by his personal labors
a vigorous impulse toward higher studies, and of
being, in a word, its veritable founder, was reserved
for one man. Constantine, surnamed the African,
whose works we shall presently find inscribed on the
programmes of the French medical faculties, was a
remarkable man for his time. Born at Carthage, in
the first half of the eleventh century, he travelled
throughout the East, studied in Babylon, visited India
and Egypt, and finally established himself in Carthage
as a physician. But, for one reason or another, perhaps because his compatriots accused him of sorcery,
— an accusation seldom spared the physicians of that
age, — he took refuge in Salerno about the year 1063.
There he became the secretary and favorite of the
Norman, Robert Guiscard, who had just seized possession of Southern Italy.[1] Finally he retired to
Monte-Cassino, where he died in 1087. Constantine
composed a considerable number of works, some of
them original, some mere translations; among others,
the *Viaticum*, translated from the Arabian physician,
Ysaac, which found its way later into all the schools.

The favor extended to Constantine by Robert Guiscard was not improbably connected with the protection granted to the school of Salerno by the Norman
conqueror, who conferred on it privileges that were
confirmed by his successors. Some years later, in

[1] Robert Guiscard (1015–1085).

1137, Roger II, King of Sicily, regulated for the first time, as it seems, the professional examinations in medicine. The doctors of the school, aided by the royal assessors, constituted the jury, and conferred the license — not the right to teach, but the right to practise medicine (*licentia medendi*). Any person pretending to exercise the medical art without having obtained this license, was punished by the confiscation of his property and a year's imprisonment. The edict of King Roger said that these measures were taken in order to prevent *ne in regno nostro subjecti periclitentur imperitia medicorum.*

Statutes analogous to this were promulgated in 1247 by the Emperor Frederick II, then master of Southern Italy. Salerno, thenceforward attached to the University of Naples, remained the privileged school of medicine.[1] Those desiring to pursue a course of medical study, which lasted for five years, must have already followed a course of logic for three years in the school of arts. Moreover, after the five years employed in studying medicine and surgery, "which is," say the statutes, "a part of medicine," the new doctor was bound, for still another year, not to practise his art except under the supervision (*cum consilio*) of an experienced physician. Doctors were enjoined to give advice to the poor gratuitously; and also to visit their patients twice every day and once during the night. The imperial edict also fixed the charge for these visits, when they were to be paid

---

[1] See the text in Duboulay, t. iii, p. 159. . . . "*Nullus in medicina vel in chirurgia nisi apud Salernum vel Neapolem legat in regno.*"

for. Other very detailed rules were established relating to the sale of medicines. The books to be studied were those of Hippocrates and Galen.

Salerno, then, was the initiator of medical studies in the Middle Ages. These studies were held in such honor that even women pursued them, thus taking precedence of the doctresses of the nineteenth century. Mr. Laurie mentions Sichelgaita, a sister of Gisulfe, Duke of Salerno before the Norman Conquest, who "had a medical reputation, especially in the department of poisons." The reputation of Salerno was European. In 1090, Duke Robert, brother of William the Conqueror, repaired thither on his return from the Crusade, in order to be healed of a grievous wound.

But while Salerno was flourishing in Italy, and by its direct influence leading to the foundation of Faculties of Medicine in a great number of Italian universities, another school, that of Montpellier, was developing in France, chiefly under the influence of Spanish and Arabian medicine. The first statutes of the Montpellier Faculty of Medicine date from 1220,[1] about the same time that the statutes of Frederick II were issued for Salerno. But in these very statutes it is said that instruction in medical science had long been held in honor at Montpellier, and had diffused its benefits throughout all parts of the world.

The conditions at Montpellier were specially favorable to its becoming a centre of university studies.

[1] It was Cardinal Conrad, the Pope's legate, who drew up these statutes. Others were drawn up in 1240 and in 1340 (see Fournier, t. ii, pp. 4, 7, 66).

From early times a commercial rendezvous, where Christians and Saracens, Arabs from Spain and merchants from Lombardy, came to traffic, it displayed hospitality to foreigners, and the learned men of Italy and Spain followed the traders thither. "Those who came from Spain," says M. Croiset, "were chiefly Jewish physicians. Montpellier was at that period one of those cities in the world where they had the greatest chance of living a quiet life. Commerce had introduced a relative tolerance in manners and customs which was greatly to their advantage. Disciples of Avicenna and Averroës, they brought with them an Arabian science wholly permeated with Greek tradition. Thanks to their influence, Montpellier, from the twelfth century, had a medical reputation."[1] This reputation increased as time went on; and "while the school of Salerno became extinct, Montpellier has remained great throughout the ages."[2] The medical diplomas of Montpellier are still esteemed by foreigners. Rabelais took his degrees there in the sixteenth century. Locke went there to study in the seventeenth. Throughout the Middle Ages the reputation of Montpellier, like that of Salerno, was universal. "It is at Montpellier," wrote Charles the Bad, King of Navarre, in the fourteenth century, "that common opinion locates the source of medical science; and it is for that reason that popes and kings summon its masters to come and heal them." It was Montpellier

[1] *Les Fêtes du Centenaire de Montpellier*, 1889. Discours de M. Croiset.

[2] *Ibid.* Discours de M. Gaudenzi, professor of the University of Bologna.

that Charles VI, in his Letters Patent of 1396, called
the source (*fons originalis*) of medical science. It
was a professor of Montpellier, Guy de Chauliac, who
published in the fourteenth century (1363) his *Grande
Chirurgie*, of which Victor Leclerc has said that it
"marked a notable progress in studies based on the
observation of nature." [1]

Does it follow that Italian influence did not make
itself felt in Montpellier and other Faculties of
medicine in the west of Europe? No; in what concerns surgery especially, that influence is manifest.
Guy de Chauliac, whom I have just cited, had studied
at Bologna. Says Littré: "There is a fact worthy of
attention in the history of surgery in France during
the second half of the thirteenth century. A number
of Italian doctors, who were at once physicians and
surgeons, having abandoned their country in consequence of the troubles occasioned by the rivalries of
the Guelphs and Ghibellines, took refuge on French
soil, and brought thither the doctrines and works of
Albou Kasis,[2] that famous Arabian physician, born
in Spain, who is regarded as the restorer of surgi-
cal science. This importation seems to date from
the arrival in Paris of a doctor from the school
of Salerno, Roger of Salerno, or Roger of Parma." [3]

[1] Guy de Chauliac published his book under this title: *Inven-
torium sive collectorium partis chirurgicalis medicinæ*. In 1592
this work was translated into French under the title of *Grande
Chirurgie*.

[2] Albou Kasis died in 1107, author of several works on medicine
and surgery which have been several times translated into Latin.
From the fourteenth century his authority was quoted in France as
equal to that of Hippocrates and Galen.

[3] "After him came successively to France, Bruno of Calabria,

It has been claimed, but not proven, that Roger of
Parma (died about 1280) must have been Chancellor
of the University of Montpellier. And this importation of Italian science was not without its uses in
reanimating and enlightening French surgery, if we
may believe Lanfranc of Milan, who, on his arrival
in France, about 1290, said that "French surgeons
were real bunglers, and so ignorant that one could
scarcely find a rational surgeon among them."[1] Another French physician of the end of the thirteenth
century, who had studied at Salerno,[2] John of St.
Paul. Others had doubtless done the same; and,
in any case, it is easy to see, in the writings of the
French physicians of the thirteenth century, that all
of them quote with respect and admiration the authorities of the School of Salerno, not merely Constantine and Ysaac, but Nicolas, Romuald, Bartholomans,
and many others.

Let me attempt a brief sketch of the studies pursued in the medical schools of the Middle Ages, and,
in the first place, of the theoretical instruction given
therein. The most precise indication of the works
that served as text-books for the professors of medicine
is found in a bull of Clement V (1309), concerning the
authors to be studied and the forms to be observed
in conferring degrees in the Faculty of Medicine at
Montpellier.[3] Another document, somewhat earlier
than this (1270–1274), a regulation determining the

Lanfranc of Milan, Thaddeus of Bologna. . . ." And Littré cites
eight additional names, "without counting other less known
authors" (*Histoire littéraire de la France*, t. xxi, p. 514).

[1] *Ibid.*, p. 517.   [2] *Ibid.*, p. 409.   [3] Fournier, t. ii, p. 21.

conditions of a license in medicine and the authors to be studied in the Faculty of Medicine at Paris, proves that the programmes and regulations were everywhere the same.[1]

Hippocrates and Galen are always the basis of the instruction given; their principal works are enumerated under the titles given by their Latin translators.[2] Greek, as is known, was not much cultivated in the Middle Ages; and possibly it is not erroneously related of Rabelais, who studied medicine at Montpellier from 1520 to 1530, that he was the first among his comrades who had read and interpreted the text of the Greek physicians. By the side of Hippocrates and Galen, those two Aristotles of medicine, the programmes of the thirteenth and fourteenth centuries find a place for modern authors. First comes Constantine, the master of Salerno, with his original works and his translations from Arabian physicians. Among these were his *Viaticum,* and the *Theorica et pratica,* from the Arabic of Hali-Abbas. Then follows Rhazès, surnamed "the observer" (850–953), who had been a doctor in the hospital of Bagdad; the Persian Avicenna (980–), who was called the "prince of doctors," but whose works were little more than a compilation of the ideas of Galen; Ysaac, who had written several treatises in Arabic, most of them translated by Constantine, among others, the *Distœ*

---

[1] *Chartularium Univ. Paris.,* t. i, p. 517.

[2] Of Hippocrates, the books of the *Pronosticorum* and the *Aphorismorum;* of Galen, the following: *De Complexionibus, De Malitia complexionis diversæ, De Simplici medicina, De Morbo et Accidente, De Crisis et Criticis diebus.*

universales et particulares, annotated by a famous doctor of the Paris University, John of St. Amand (died about 1300) ; and the *Liber Febrium ;* [1] Johannicus, another Arabian physician, author of a work on the pulse; Nicolas, a doctor of Salerno, whose *Antidotarium* [2] was a classic, and who came to France in the thirteenth century.

Judging from this list of standard medical authors, the influence of the Arabs must have been at least equal to that of the Greeks in the medical schools of the Middle Ages.[3] Mussulman civilization has exerted an influence on the civilization of Christianity whose importance has not been sufficiently recognized. It is rather significant to observe that in the programme of the Faculty of Paris for 1270, neither Hippocrates nor Galen is named, nor is any allusion made to the two famous Greek physicians.

According to the regulation of 1272, the bachelor who desired to obtain his license must prove that he had attended the medical courses for five years, if he had been already licensed in arts, and six years if the contrary were the case. Nothing is said of the baccalaureate. But it is known from other documents

[1] The *Distæ particulares* are inscribed on the programme of Paris; the *Liber Febrium* on that of Montpellier.

[2] *Antidotarium,* which seems properly to signify the "Book of Antidotes," the counter-poisons, became in the Middle Ages synonymous with the " Book of Medicaments." Rhazès also had written an *Antidotarium.* John of St. Amand annotated both of these works.

[3] I have mentioned all of them, excepting a work studied at Paris and Montpellier, the *Liber urinarum,* whose author, Théophile, is unknown to us ; and also the *Versus Egidii.* Egidius of Corbeil taught medicine at Paris under Philip Augustus.

of the same period that the normal duration of
medical studies in their totality was nine years.[1] At
Montpellier, the statutes of 1340 required twenty-four
months of study for the baccalaureate;[2] in other
words, three years, each scholastic year counting eight
months only, by reason of holidays and vacations;[3]
the licentiateship or the doctorate demanded five or
six years more. Rabelais in the sixteenth century
took a still longer time: a bachelor in 1530, he was
not a doctor until 1537; but Rabelais was an erratic
student, who wrote one part of his *Pantagruel* in the
interval between his two diplomas.

The distribution of lessons and the order for the
reading and explanation of texts seem to have been
regulated with less precision and severity in the
Faculty of Medicine than in that of Law. We know
that lessons were given *ordinariè* and *cursoriè*;[4] that
there were *disputationes* and *repetitiones*;[5] and that
here as everywhere, the instruction was a literal interpretation of hallowed texts rather than an appeal
to experience and the individual judgment of the
pupils. " I copied," relates Platter, a student of
Montpellier, in the sixteenth century, " the *loci communes in tota medicina;* I tabulated the most important
books of Galen. Once my comrades and I spent the
night in copying a book, *de componendis medicamentis.*

---

[1] At Montpellier the same, or nearly the same, rules existed:
*quinque annis si in partibus magistri existant alioquin per sex
annos* (Fournier, t. ii, p. 21).

[2] Crevier, t. ii, p. 53.   [3] Fournier, t. ii, p. 71.

[4] See the regulation already cited, of 1270: "*Forma auditionis
librorum est quod bachalarius debet audivisse bis artem medicinæ
ordinaria et semel cursoria. . . .*"   [5] Fournier, t. ii, p. 70.

We were careful not to omit a recipe for making the hair grow. Beardless as yet, we thought mustaches would give us a more respectable appearance."[1]

Texts and their explanations to be listened to; texts to copy and recopy; in a word, a book education: such the character of medical instruction remained at the height of the Renaissance.

I have already had occasion to say that the universities of the Middle Ages had almost no idea of the mutual service which could be rendered by the different orders of studies, and barely suspected the solidarity of the sciences. A curious decree of the Montpellier statutes for 1340, affords another proof of this: "We have decided that no master shall read or permit to be read in the medical schools any book of grammar or logic"; so far so good; but what is to be said of the end of this prohibition? "Nor any book of natural science except *De Animalibus*."[2]

Another citation from the same regulations will show how completely medicine in those days subordinated itself to religion, believing that it could not do its work efficaciously unless it were aided by the medicine of souls: "As bodily evils sometimes proceed from sin, and as God said to the sick man whom He cured: 'Go, and sin no more, lest a worse evil befall thee,' we ordain that when a master is called to a sick person in a critical condition, or suffering from a continuous fever, he shall in the first place counsel the patient to have the physicians of the soul summoned, so that, the spiritual safety of the sick person being already assured, he may afterwards

[1] Valbrigue, *op. cit.*, p. 22.   [2] Fournier, t. ii, p. 70.

proceed with more success to the remedies of bodily medicine." [1]

The regulations, and notably those of Montpellier, forbade the practice of medicine before the course of study had been completed and the doctor's degree obtained. But these prohibitions were not much observed. The newest and most inexperienced bachelors practised their art (and Crevier testifies that the case was the same at Paris), "without hindrance, although without legal authorization." [2] At Montpellier still greater laxness was displayed; bachelors were authorized to practise medicine, with the bizarre restriction, which proves a certain contempt for countrymen, that they should bind themselves by oath not to do so except outside of the city and its suburbs; thus making a sort of first trial of their skill or their clumsiness *in anima vili;* whence the custom, the knowledge of which has been preserved by the historians of the University of Montpellier, that when the promotions to the baccalaureate were made, each new bachelor in medicine was received by his comrades with blows, and cries of *"Vade et occide, Cain!"*

Was there in the Middle Ages, in addition to a very insufficient theoretical instruction based on the hypotheses of ancient medicine, a practical instruction such as presupposes either anatomical study of the cadaver, or clinical lessons given in hospitals beside the beds of the sick? Given the intellectual habits of the Middle Ages, we shall not be surprised to find that in this respect medical apprenticeship was extremely incomplete. It appears that the only custom

[1] Fournier, t. ii, p. 67.   [2] Crevier, t. ii, p. 52.

akin to what we nowadays call the clinic, was the term of probation imposed at Salerno and other schools on young doctors who had taken their degrees, but were forbidden to practise their art for one or two years except under the surveillance and tutelage of an experienced physician.[1] As to anatomy, it was still in its infancy.[2] A dissection was a rare event. At Montpellier, the statutes of 1340 provide that there shall be a dissection once every two years.[3] In 1396 the letters patent of King Charles VI ordained that there should be delivered every year to the faculty of medicine, for purposes of anatomical study, the cadaver of a criminal, "of either sex or of any class, hanged, drowned, or slain in any other manner after legal condemnation."[4] The corpse of the criminal, after dissection, was buried with all the rites and ceremonies of religion.

It was not in Molière's time only that dissections became a real spectacle, to which even ladies thronged as to a festival.[5] At Montpellier the spectators usually included not merely the students, but a great number of curious persons, citizens, nobles, and even women, although it might be the cadaver of a man that was to be dissected. Many monks went likewise. The

[1] At Paris, before presenting himself for the license, a bachelor must have practised medicine during two summers under the guidance of a master regent.

[2] It must not be forgotten that the Arabs, whose labors, as we have seen, had so great an influence upon European medicine, forbade the study of anatomy through religious scruples.

[3] Those of the Faculty of Paris for 1600 say there shall be two anatomical *séances* each year.   [4] Fournier, t. ii, p. 162.

[5] See Molière, *Le Malade Imaginaire.*

dissection was presided over by a professor; the scalpel
was handled by a barber, the surgeon of those days.
The cost of the operation was defrayed by the students.[1]

Even in the sixteenth century, dissections seldom
took place more than once a year. And yet the
following anecdote, related by Platter, proves that
the students were desirous of instruction, and, knowing the value of researches made on the human body,
asked nothing better than to be put in the presence
of cadavers : [2] "We went," he says, "to disinter
secretly, in adjacent cemeteries, the dead who had
been buried the same day. . . . My first expedition
of the sort occurred on December 11, 1554. . . . At
midnight, well armed, and observing the most profound silence, we repaired to the cemetery of St.
Denis ; we disinterred a body, employing nothing but
our hands, because the earth had not had time enough
yet to harden. Then we drew out the corpse by
means of a cord, wrapped it in our mantles, and
carried it on two sticks to the entrance of the city.
There we rapped on the wicket; an old porter presented himself, and opened it; we asked for something to drink, and while he went for wine, three of
us brought in the corpse, and carried it to the neighboring house of one of our comrades. Afterwards the
monks of St. Denis were obliged to guard their cemetery, and they shot arrows from their windows at the
students who came there."

What clearly demonstrates the state of inferiority

[1] Platter, in his account of his stay at Montpellier, quoted by
Valabregue, *op. cit.*, p. 24.   [2] *Ibid.*, p. 25.

in which the practical study of medicine remained throughout the Middle Ages, is the disdain expressed for surgery, which was considered a mean handicraft, and abandoned to barbers. In 1600, at the time of the reform of the University of Paris by Henry IV, surgeons were still excluded from the degrees of the Faculty of Medicine, or were admitted to them only on swearing that they would not practise surgery thereafter.

Actual study, then, was restricted within the narrowest limits in the Faculties of Medicine. Even at Paris, after several centuries of development, there was in 1600 only one professor to teach both anatomy and botany.[1] The Faculty of Medicine which, by the very nature of its studies should have avoided and withdrawn completely from the dialectical fury and mania for discussion which were the great curse of mediæval instruction, was attacked by the same malady as the other Faculties. Thurot says: "It attached much more importance to disputations than to lessons."[2] The ordinary disputations took place

[1] "As our city," said a physician of Montpellier, "was the first where public demonstrations in anatomy were given, so it has been the first to give public lessons in botany, and to possess a royal garden of medicinal plants" (Astruc — *Mémoires*, p. 67). The Montpellier Garden of Plants was not organized until 1593, after those of Pisa (1546), Leyden (1577), and Leipsic (1579).

[2] Thurot, *op. cit.*, p. 197. The lessons were greatly neglected, neither masters nor students forcing themselves to pursue them regularly. "The statutes of 1660 limit themselves to saying: "Students shall *frequently* be present at the public lessons." One Faculty of Medicine, that of Poitiers, during several centuries confined itself to conferring degrees, without giving any instruction whatever.

every Monday and Tuesday from All Saints' Day until Lent; that is, during three or four months. In addition to these, there was one disputation more formal than the others, called *quodlibétaire*, because it might relate indifferently to any subject; and each master was obliged to take part in it in his turn, under penalty of deposition. The supreme end to be attained was not the acquirement of positive knowledge, but skill in dialectic. The idea that man is made to reason, to be a perpetual dialectician, even in medicine, dominated the human mind; and people seemed to think that syllogisms were good for everything, even disease !

Such a programme of studies could hardly form any but mediocre practitioners. Doubtless there were exceptions; and I would not say that all physicians of the Middle Ages deserved the raillery and insults lavished on them by Petrarch in the pamphlet entitled, *Invectives against a Physician.* Nevertheless, it is probable there was some truth in the unfavorable portrait of the doctors of his day, drawn by the same Petrarch, in a letter to Boccaccio, wherein he reproached them, not merely with their noisy charlatanism, but the deadly effects of their incapacity. "They never appear in public," says he, "without being superbly dressed, mounted on magnificent horses, and wearing golden spurs! . . . Next thing you know," he adds, mingling hyperbole with his irony, "they will arrogate the honors of a triumph ! And, in fact, they deserve it; for there is not one among them who has not killed at least five thousand men, and that is the required number to entitle one to those honors!"[1]

There is, of course, no more reason for taking these declamatory exaggerations of Petrarch literally, than there would be for subscribing to all the jests of Molière against the Diafoirus and the Purgons of the seventeenth century. It would be especially unjust to hold responsible for the universal errors, of which they were themselves victims, those men of the Middle Ages who devoted themselves to the art of healing their fellows, so far as they were able to acquire it. It was not their fault if the general system of study rendered them more apt at distinguishing the premises and consequences of a train of reasoning than in diagnosing disease; more skilful in managing an argument than handling the scalpel and the bistoury. To be just, we must take into consideration the fact that the profession of medicine, difficult and dangerous at all times, was especially so at a time when hygiene was a thing almost unknown, and epidemics raged with violence. One is glad to recall, as one instance, that at the time of the plague of 1533 at Montpellier the doctors of that city did their duty bravely, and paid a heavy tribute to death by exposing themselves to contagion.

[1] Quoted by Renan, *Averroës*, p. 262.

Part IV

GENERAL SPIRIT AND INFLUENCE OF THE EARLY UNIVERSITIES

CHAPTER I

MANNERS AND HABITS OF STUDENTS AND TEACHERS

I. Admiration excited among contemporaries — Testimony of John of Salisbury and Petrarch — Habits of the Students — Eagerness for study — Privations endured — Relations between students and masters — Student guilds and associations — Mutual assistance — Tendency towards equality — II. Frequency of disorder in the university associations — Quarrels between students — With masters — With citizens — Turbulent and blustering humor — Examples of riots — Licentiousness of the scholastic life — Lack of elegance and even of cleanliness — Ascetic rules — An oppressive system finally substituted for the original liberty — Discipline of the rod — III. The masters — Habits of pedantry — Some irregularities of conduct — Teachers too dependent on students — Appointed and chosen by them — Salaries of the masters — Their poverty — Consequences of this — Celibacy.

BEFORE leaving the universities of the Middle Ages, we must take a last glance at the internal life of these assemblages of students and masters which, in certain cities, had acquired proportions so considerable. What were their manners and customs, their qualities and defects? What was their general spirit? How was their influence shown in their prosperous days before they dwindled into feeble institutions from which life gradually departed, leaving the movement of thought to slip insensibly out of their hands in order to renew itself beyond them; until, reaching their last stage of decay, they were destined either

263

to disappear or be transformed, that they might be
born anew under the same title, but in forms and
conditions more conformable to the requirements of
the modern spirit ?

I

The first thing to be noted is the enthusiastic
admiration aroused in those who visited them or who
studied there, by these learned cities, these "Latin
quarters," where nothing was taught or spoken save
in Latin, and which were scattered here and there
amidst the uncultivated and barbarous society of the
Middle Ages like oases in a desert. Nothing proves
more conclusively how well the old universities, in
spite of their admitted faults, responded to the aspi-
rations and necessities of their times. Here, for
example, is John of Salisbury, in 1167, saluting
France with veneration as the most hospitable, the
most civilized of Nations (*omnium mitissima et civilis-
sima nationum*). "I saw at Paris," he says, "abundance of life, popular joy, life respected, a crowd
of philosophers absorbed in various occupations. I
seemed to behold Jacob's ladder, with the angels
ascending and descending on it."[1] And here is
Petrarch, in the fourteenth century, recalling in his
old age, the delightful memories which Montpellier
had impressed upon his youth: "On passing out of
childhood, I spent four years at Montpellier, at
that time a very flourishing city. What tranquillity
reigned there ! What peace ! What riches were pos-

[1] *Chartularium Univ. Paris.*, t. i, p. 17.

sessed by the merchants! What a crowd of students! What an abundance of masters."[1]

As Savigny has very justly remarked, the universities of the Middle Ages owed their special importance to the fact of their taking a much more considerable share in education than is done by the universities of our own day. "They had not to dread the competition of the gymnasia, or the multitude of books now published everywhere. Moreover, the scholastic period was much longer and the students often of riper years. Bishops were sometimes seen attending the courses, their rank, functions, and dignity lending an éclat to the university of which they are now deprived."[2] The universities were not merely, as at present, schools of higher education crowning a system of pedagogic institutions; they were the only schools, the only places in the world, where men could study or exercise their minds with a certain degree of freedom. With what joyful enthusiasm must young men, eager for instruction, and glad of an opportunity to acquire learning without immuring themselves in monasteries or submitting to the cloistral yoke, have hastened toward renowned masters whose reputation had penetrated even to distant lands! Then again in an age disturbed by continual wars and unprovided with a regular police, what good fortune it must have seemed, to find in large and well-provided cities, under the protection and safeguard of public authorities, safe places, asylums as it were, where studies might be pursued

[1] Petrarch, *Rer. Sen.*, Lib. x, Epist. 2.
[2] Savigny, *op. cit.*, chap. xxi, § 58.

unmolested, and where, thanks to innumerable privileges, they were honored and respected.

In such a time as ours, when so many facilities are offered to all who desire to study, and when, so far as instruction goes, the supply certainly outruns the demand, it is not easy to form an adequate notion of the spontaneity and ardent zeal for study which animated the thousands of young men who formed the audiences at the mediæval universities. At present, it is most frequently the social condition of young men, their birth and fortune, which destines them, and often without any strong bent, and *invitâ Minervâ*, to pursue the courses of superior instruction. In the Middle Ages the students were all volunteers of science: none frequented the universities but those who had a particular aptitude and a personal taste for study; and, like all volunteers, they brought an extraordinary zeal and enthusiasm to their tasks. Great was the number of those who, destitute of all resources, joyfully braved privation, poverty, and the irksomeness of menial service, in order that they might penetrate at last into the sanctuary of knowledge. "The University of Paris was poor," says Crevier.[1] The majority of the students were so likewise.[2] "Many of them," says Thurot, "begged their bread. They found this no humiliation. The example of the mendicant orders, and especially of the Franciscans, had rendered mendicancy respectable. The bursars of the college of Laon distributed their leavings to poor scholars of

[1] Crevier, t. vii, p. 152.

[2] "There were nobles there, and there were plebeians; there were no rich men" (Lecoy de la Marche, *op. cit.*, p. 461).

their own Nation. Masters gave their old clothes and shoes to their students. To gain the wherewithal to live, scholars copied books, swept, became scavengers. They often entered the service of a college, a wealthy student, or a professor."[1] If, with such a disposition, such a passion to learn, cost what it might, the students of mediæval universities produced nothing marvellous, the fault lay not with their diligence and good will, but with their narrow limitations and sterile methods of the instruction given them.

Moreover, the desire to come in contact with what were then the only sources of knowledge was not all that drew them to the universities. There were also the advantages of every sort guaranteed to them by the university privileges; and, above all, the intimate, affectionate relations which bound them to their masters and their comrades in these corporations and scholastic societies which were like so many families.

"The relations that existed between professors and students," says Savigny, "were then closer and more lasting than in our days.[2] Each student, on arriving at the university, became not simply a new number inscribed on the register of matriculation; he was thenceforward the pupil, the client of such or such a professor, who not only heard his lessons but became his patron, took him under his guardianship, and laid claim to him in case some prank had led the magistrates to put him into prison."[3] In the Faculties of Art more especially, on

---

[1] Thurot, *op. cit.*, p. 39.   [2] Savigny, *op. cit.*, chap. xxi, § 97.

[3] "In the Italian Universities," says Coppi (*op. cit.*, p. 288), "pupils and professors formed as it were one large family, because

account of the slight differences of age existing between licentiates of twenty-one, bachelors of fourteen,
and pupils between ten and thirteen, a real intimacy
and comradeship was established between masters and
students. "Students and masters belonging to the
same Nation," says Thurot, "lodged most frequently
in the same hotel, and often ate at the same table. . . .
The masters frolicked with the pupils and even took
part in their disorder." The scholastic community
as it is found in the colleges of the fifteenth century
was already in existence, but with the addition of
liberty. All there was of good in monastic rules, the
common life of convents, the constant contact between
many minds devoted to the same work and pursuing the same end, all the advantages pertaining to
intellectual association, were to be found in the university, itself a convent after its own fashion, but a
convent enfranchised and restored to liberty.

The special character belonging to the universities
of the Middle Ages is also displayed in the relations
existing between the students. The young men did
not then content themselves, as now, with meeting
each other two or three times a day in the same classes,
for the sake of listening to the lectures of the same
professors. They lived the same life. "United by
profession," said some one, "they could not be dis-
united by sentiment." They formed associations
which amounted to mutual benefit societies. At
Montpellier and elsewhere the corporation relieved
poor students from the payment of the sums owed by

they sought the same goal and were united by the same love of
science and the same habits of life."

them to the University treasury. The exemption, however, was only accorded under condition that the same should be afterwards repaid if the student became rich. If a student could not provide for all his needs, could not pay his barber, for example, some one came to his assistance. On days of festivity and banquetings, sick comrades who could not be present were not forgotten. At Montpellier, "partridges, pigeons, and Muscat wine" were sent to their lodgings, — a bad way to cure them, perhaps, but certainly a touching mark of companionship. The entire corporation was bound to be present at the funeral of any of its members, and those who dispensed themselves from this obligation without a legitimate excuse were fined.[1]

The students' associations were, then, true schools of social solidarity, wherein the young learned their duties as men. They practised mutual help, and were early penetrated, if not by the national and patriotic sentiment, — which had as yet shown itself but dimly, and under its worst aspects, the hatred between races continuing in the quarrels and rivalries between the Nations, — at least by a certain *esprit de corps*, testified to by the solemn oaths taken by the students, them to serve and defend the interests of the university, and maintain its good repute during and after their studies.

Another praiseworthy thing about the spirit of the mediæval universities was their tendency to establish

[1] At Montpellier when any member of the university died, whether professor or student, lessons were suspended, so that everybody might be present at the funeral. If the deceased were poor, the university paid for his obsequies.

equality between all their students, no matter what
might be their birth or condition. Equality before
the law and in civil society had not yet been reached;
but in the university societies a sensible approach to
equality in studies and degrees had been attained.
Thence came the efforts made, both in Italy and France,
to oblige all students to wear the same costume. The
statutes of the University of Florence decreed that
every one, barons, dukes, bishops, and cardinals, as
well as the humblest students, should wear a uniform
vestment." [1] " In the University of Paris, no distinction existed between rich and poor, between nobles
and commoners. . . . In 1311, Clement V put a check
on the prodigalities of newly made doctors, whose
admission was celebrated by illuminations and banquets, by pointing out that these inordinate expenses
were discouraging and ruinous to poor students." [2]

Still, it would be contrary to truth to suppose that
these attempts at equality were everywhere crowned
with success. In many places the privileges of the
nobility were extended even to the common life of
the universities. At Dôle the students were divided
into two classes: nobles and commoners. The nobles
formed a caste apart, and enjoyed certain favors: an
insult offered one of them cost the insulter five francs,
while to insult a commoner cost but one franc. On
the other hand, the nobles were bound by special
obligations: for example, they must have two valets
in their service who were to follow them everywhere

---

[1] . . . " etiam si esset Dux, Princeps, vel Baro, . . . etiam si esset
Cardinalis, vel Episcopus, vel alia dignitate fulgens (Coppi, *op. cit.*,
p. 118).''   [2] Henri Beaune, *op. cit.*, p. xxxii.

and carry their books to class. At Bologna, noble students had a right to occupy the first benches in class. But special charges corresponded to these privileges; they paid two francs to the beadles, while the other students paid only four sous.

II

Nor must we imagine these societies of students, above all in the earliest times, as peaceable, perfectly well-regulated societies in which an admirable order prevailed. As far as scholastic manners are concerned, the Middle Ages present two different sides: that of extreme license at first, and then toward the end, when the scholars had for the most part been shut up in colleges and boarding-schools, that of oppressive discipline.

Peace did not always reign in the collegiate cities; dissensions were frequent, and also violent quarrels, followed usually it is true, by solemn reconciliations which ended in new banquets. Sometimes they arose between the students, sometimes between students and citizens, and sometimes even between the scholars and the masters. Let me cite some examples.

Discord often prevailed between the Faculties. At Montpellier, for instance, the legists, or law students, were frequently at variance with the medical students; perpetual quips, a war of pleasantries went on between, sometimes ending in a resort to arms.[1] Up

[1] It must be added, however, that these incessant divisions may have proceeded partly from the fact that there were two universities in that city, the University of Law and the University of Medicine.

to the sixteenth century we find in the *Liber Procura-toris* several mentions of expenditures for weapons made in advance by medical students, in order to put down by force any legists who might try to assume the privilege of ridiculing them.[1]

The professors were not always respected. Thus, at Poitiers, in 1517, the Gascon students, sword in hand (although they were forbidden to carry weapons), besieged in his chair the professor of law, Longueil, who could only defend himself by flinging at their heads the enormous volumes of the *Digest* which were the subject of his lessons.

But it was above all with the inhabitants of the cities where the universities were situated that the students had frequent quarrels. Though they were a source of honor and revenue to the cities in which they were established, the universities were sometimes viewed with suspicious eyes by the citizens, either on account of the privileges granted to their members, or because of the great number of foreigners included among their pupils. Moreover, by their turbulence and arrogance, the students frequently excited the antipathy, and even the hostility, of the population. Thus, in 1494, at Montpellier, the inhabitants sacked the *Collége des Douze Médecins.*

No one need be surprised at finding in the youth of the Middle Ages the faults common to youth in every age. "The student of the University of Paris," says M. Lecoy de la Marche, "was not always the serious

---

[1] Duels between students were all the fashion, as they still are in German universities; it was for that reason they were forbidden to carry arms.

young person, full of zeal for his tasks, bending over glossaries of the Bible or of Aristotle. He was also, and perhaps one ought to say that he was chiefly, the impudent roisterer who ' runs all night, fully armed, through the streets of the capital, breaks open house doors to commit outrages, and fills the tribunals with the noise of his escapades. Every day,' adds Robert de Sorbon, '*meretriculæ* came to depose against him, complaining of having been struck, of having their clothes torn to pieces and their hair cut off.' His quarrels with the powerful corporation of the citizens of Paris are incessant. The *Pré-aux-clercs*, where one may see the grave students walking with a book in their hands, meditating or argumenting in the language of clerics (*prout inter bonos scholares est fieri consuetum*), is also the theatre of tumultuous scenes." [1]

The rude manners of the Middle Ages, perhaps, too, the scarcity of amusements, the absence of distractions which Rabelais, in the sixteenth century, struggled against in the students of Poitiers, who " knew not," said he, "how to pass the time "; and still other causes, such as the relatively advanced age of many of the students, the isolation which made them independent, the remoteness of their families,[2] — all this contributed to develop the tendency to disorder, the turbulent humor natural to youth, the quarrelsome disposition which often displayed itself in actual riots. The students of Paris always had a bone to pick with the

[1] Lecoy de la Marche, *op. cit.*, p. 460.

[2] One special cause of disorder may be found in the fact that students remained at the university seat even during vacations, on account of the distances from their homes and the difficulties of travelling.

police, and it was with the most sincere determination to keep their word that they hurled this defiance at whoever provoked them : " Come to the *Clos-Bruneau!* You'll find some one there to talk to ! " Nor must it be forgotten that the entire university, as guardian of each of its members, often took sides openly with the most culpable of its students, and encouraged them in their resistance to the authorities and magistrates.[1]

At Dôle, in 1429, six years after the founding of the university, the students fell into all manner of excesses and organized a sort of riot. The bailiff ran to re-establish order. He was badly beaten and obliged to flee. In 1442, the university itself caused the provost to be imprisoned. He was set at liberty by order of the bailiff of Dijon, who imprisoned, in his turn, the rector of Dôle. In 1446, the students made common cause with the inhabitants of one village against those of another, and gave actual battle to their adversaries. A hundred years later, in 1563, a quarrel broke out between two students in the lecture-room of the course of civil law. One of the two received a sword wound ; he summoned his adversary before the rector, who let him off with a reprimand. In 1577, a murderer was acquitted. In 1605, a scholar insulted some children, and was put in prison ; his comrades retaliated by in-carcerating the sergeant who had arrested him. The tocsin sounded ; the citizens armed and came into the street, and fighting was about to begin, when Parliament ordered the aldermen to set the scholar at liberty.[2]

[1] " The audacity and insolence of the students were all the greater because they felt themselves supported by the university." Beaune, *op. cit.*, p. lxxxviii.   [2] Beaune, *op. cit., passim.*

The scholastic world of the Middle Ages, then, was the scene of constant troubles and agitations, a continual ebullition of juvenile passions.[1] More than once violent scenes occurred which entailed terrible reprisals on the students. Thus at Montpellier, relates Jourdain, the students made a disturbance in the neighborhood of the law school, and wounded several persons. "A great uproar ensued. The citizens of Montpellier, who had never liked the students overmuch, determined upon vengeance. The next day, when the bell rang, they lay in wait for the rioters as they came out of school, and hemmed them into a street so narrow that not one of them could escape. In order to distinguish their own countrymen from the foreigners, against whom they had a special grudge, they obliged each of them to say in their local idiom : 'God give you good night, Dieu vous donne *bona nioch,* (bonne nuit). As the strangers were not able to pronounce the last two words of this evening salutation correctly, it was easy to recognize the foreign rioters. Several of them were killed and their bodies cast into neighboring wells. . . . The name of Rue *Bona-nioch* continues to mark the scene of the bloody drama." [2]

It was not in riots only that the students of the Middle Ages took delight. Gallant and amorous adventures played a certain part in their existence. "The misfortune is," says the historian of the University of Angers, "that the morals of the students of

---

[1] This effervescence sometimes went so far as crime. In 1425 six or seven law students of Montpellier, in masks, broke into a house during the night and carried off a young woman. The university hindered the prosecution of these ravishers.

[2] Germain, *op. cit.,* p. 23

that age (thirteenth century) were very profligate.
They fought every day among themselves and with
the citizens. Yet all of these students were clerics,
and some of them already provided with curacies.
But it was not easy to keep this multitude of young
men, just at the most impetuous age, within the bounds
of strict discipline ; these were not children who were
studying. Assembled from different countries, they
were far from their parents, their bishops, and their
seigneurs. They had not the same respect for foreign
masters, to whom they paid a salary, and who were
often of low birth." [1] And Rangeard concludes by
recalling, as applicable to the scholars of Angers, the
very unfavorable portrait drawn by Jacques de Vitry,
in the thirteenth century, of the morals of Parisian
students. From the year 1218 the ecclesiastical judge
of Paris had been complaining of the scholars, who,
said he, force and break open the doors of houses
and carry off girls and women." [2] Jacques de Vitry
denounced the debauched morals of Paris several
years later. " In the same houses," said he, "there
are schools on the first story and infamous resorts
below." [3] If one consults Coppi, for example, he may
convince himself that the morals of the Italian universities were just as bad.[4]

But, in truth, there was nothing in these defects
which was peculiar to the university youth of the

[1] Pierre Rangeard, *Histoire de l'Université d'Angers*, Angers,
1868, p. 174. Rangeard (1692–1786) composed this interesting mono-
graph about 1720, but it was not published until within a few years.

[2] Crevier, t. i, p. 331.   [3] Crevier, t. i, p. 358.

[4] Coppi, *op. cit.*, c. vii, *La vita scolastica nel medio evo.*

Middle Ages. Neither was there in the practical jokes played by the students on new-comers, *bejaunes*[1] or beginners, as they were called; nor in the boyish tricks and jests of every sort permitted to itself by a cosmopolitan youth, at once serious and dissipated, fond of pleasure as well as of study, like youth in every age; nor, in fine, in those habits of idleness with which the scholars were sometimes reproached by their contemporaries: "How far from the example left them by St. Dominic" (a pupil of the University of Palencia), "who devoted entire nights to study, are these scholars whom the slightest labor disheartens, who spend their time drinking in taverns, or building castles in the air (*castella in Hispania*), and who transform their class-rooms into dormitories!"[2]

A more characteristic trait is the lack of good breeding, and it must be owned that the absence, not merely of elegance but of cleanliness, was too frequent among the students of the Middle Ages. John of Salisbury, although so enthusiastic about Paris, wrote a little poem entitled *De Miseriis Scholasticorum,* in which he draws a most uncomplimentary portrait of their sordid way of life. Privation and poverty were doubtless the prime cause of this; but the prejudices of mysticism likewise contributed to it. People still believed that solicitude about the care of the body and the observance of hygienic rules were of slight importance, the care of the soul being all that was needful; they thought it permissible and even suit-

[1] *Bejaune* was at first the name given to a workman who was passing his apprenticeship for master or journeyman.

[2] Lecoy de la Marche, *op. cit.,* p. 163.

able to lodge knowledge in a filthy body, since external uncleanliness and negligence were no hindrance
to the elevation of the mind.

Another thing peculiar to the university regulations
of the Middle Ages is a certain asceticism which tended
to prohibit the most lawful pleasures, and which by
the excessive restraint it put upon the craving for
amusement which is natural to youth, provoked violent reactions. See, for example, what was forbidden
at Montpellier: "Members of the university are forbidden under penalty of expulsion, to dance anywhere
except in their own houses. Forbidden, under the
same penalty, to play dice and other games of chance.
Forbidden to take part in the fêtes of Carnival time,
when it was customary to throw straw and other
things at each other."

It was not by multiplying prohibitions of this kind
that young men could be prepared for the apprenticeship of liberty; nor was it by recommending them,
as was done at Paris, to combat their flighty inclina-
tions by attending sermons and offices, or those evening
instructions called *collations*, which had been expressly
invented in order to keep them from roaming through
the streets of the great city in search of adventures.

It is evident that the spirit of the Middle Ages, with
its tendency to mysticism, its lack of confidence in
human nature, its universal instinct of repression and
constraint, was not adapted to discover, in matters of
discipline, a just medium between license and extreme
severity. It was decidedly toward severity that it
leaned when enclosed colleges and boarding-schools
came to replace the free corporations of students of

earlier days. Then the rod had full sway. The rod, which was the favorite mode of discipline in convents, became the great educational instrument in colleges, "those jails full of young captives." "Children should be brought up to endure severity in all that concerns the body," said a general of the Dominicans, who fortified his opinion by the precepts of St. Bernard and Lycurgus. But the fact that the whip was in constant use, and for the slightest faults, is not the only thing that sheds light on the rigorous discipline of the Middle Ages; the nature of the faults thus punished does the same thing. The regulations drawn up by Gerson, the gentle Gerson, for the Cathedral School of Paris, enumerate the chief faults which the pupils were liable to commit, and which, moreover, their comrades were bound to make known, the giving of secret information being then encouraged as a legitimate means of discipline.[1] Here is the list: "Speaking French,[2] lying, giving the lie, insulting, striking, doing or saying immodest things, rising late, forgetting to recite the canonical hours, and talking in church."

III

It is much more difficult to form an idea of the ordinary habits of professors in the early universities, than of those of the students. Autobiographies were not in

---

[1] A pupil who did not denounce the fault of his comrade was punished like the guilty one.

[2] Even in 1600, pupils were still forbidden, under severe penalties, to speak in their mother tongue.

fashion in the Middle Ages. Absorbed in their professorial duties, the masters of that day did not, as a
rule, provoke much gossip. They did not mingle in
society, and were brilliant only in their chairs. "I
have known," said, in 1444, Æneas Sylvius Picco-
lomini, the future Pope Pius II, "I have known most
of the men of letters in our days. They gorge themselves with science, but there is nothing civil or pol-
ished about them, and they understand absolutely
nothing about the management of affairs, whether
public or private." [1] Thence proceeded the first characteristic of these masters: they were interested exclusively, for the most part, in instruction; hardly to
be called well-bred; blindly attached to their narrow
and restricted science; self-sufficient and intractable,
generally impervious to new ideas; hostile, in consequence, to all whose thoughts differed from theirs;
thorny with syllogisms; and worthy, in fine, of that
reputation for pedantry which history has so justly
guarded for them.

These defects had at least one compensation: the
dignity of a life wholly consecrated to the labor of
instruction. How many obscure but honorable exist-
ences slipped peacefully away beneath the shadows of
the university in the service of youth! Nevertheless,
there were frequent errors of conduct. It must not be
forgotten that, in the Faculty of Arts especially, the

---

[1] What we are saying here may seem to contradict the rôle I
shall assign to the universities a little further on (Chapter II), from
the political point of view. Note, however, that I am now speaking
of the professors as a whole, omitting all mention of the brilliant
exceptions.

masters were not much older than the scholars.[1] Students to-day, they became professors to-morrow, by the mere fact of having attained the licentiate's degree. Leaving the student ranks and becoming masters in a single day, they found some difficulty in shaking off the manners of their comrades of the day before. "The conduct of the masters," says Thurot, "resembled that of the students." Doubtless there was an advantage in that; it enabled them to preserve intimate and familiar relations with their pupils. On the other hand, the regularity of their lives suffered from it. They continued to frequent wineshops, and sometimes headed the scholastic riots; which is proved by the fact that at Paris, for example, in 1335, the Nation of France admitted that detention in prison would be considered as a legitimate excuse for Masters of Arts to omit their lectures.

Another characteristic of the professor of the Middle Ages is that he was too dependent on the students. How was a man to make his authority respected by pupils who perhaps had elected him, and who at all events paid him? There was at that time no superior administration, distinct from the university, and supplying it with professors of its own choice. The universities recruited themselves, and accordingly as they were universities of students as at Bologna, or of masters as at Paris, it was now the students, and again the masters in the exercise of their functions, who

---

[1] Nor must it be forgotten that the Masters of Arts often remained students, after becoming professors, and followed the courses of the Theological Faculty.

chose the new professors.[1] "At Bologna," says Savigny, "there were very soon public chairs, paid for by the city. The city supplied the funds, but the choice of professors was left to the students. The election was for a year only, and the professors were not often re-elected. Doctors were nearly always chosen, but this was not an indispensable condition; many of these professors are found who had not the doctor's title."[2]

The masters were, furthermore, dependent on the students for the payment of their honoraries. "In the Faculty of Arts at Paris," says Thurot, "these honoraries were extremely variable. The sum was fixed by a free contract between master and pupil. Toward 1309, those who gave the morning instruction (the professors of *ordinary* lessons) charged each pupil one franc. In 1450, masters demanded a crown for the explanation and repetition of the books required for the baccalaureate.[3] There were no general rules at Bologna. Sometimes a sum was fixed for which the students as a body were held responsible. Sometimes each student was obliged to pay a specified sum.

In the earliest times there was no question of regular appointments and salaries paid from the public treasury, except in the case of certain universities generously supported and indorsed by the heads of the State. By degrees, however, there appeared, at

[1] In certain universities, Toulouse for example, a mixed system was pursued. The professors were elected there by the Masters in Exercise, and by several students associated with the regents as counsellors.

[2] Savigny, *op. cit.*, chap. xxi, § 83.   [3] Thurot, *op. cit.*, p. 61.

least for a certain number of chairs, the custom of fixed salaries, drawn either from the general revenues of the university, the municipal treasury, or the liberality of princes.[1] Thus, at Montpellier, about the year 1500, the emoluments of the professors of medicine amounted to one hundred livres, those of the professors of law to fifty livres, while the professors of the Faculty of Arts had only thirty livres. At Bologna, where people were richer, the salaries of jurists varied from fifty to nearly five hundred livres.

These were exceptions. In the majority of the universities, especially in the Faculties of Arts, professors continued to receive the fees for their instruction directly from the pupils. "The University of Paris," said one of its rectors at the beginning of the eighteenth century, "finds itself reduced to the sad necessity of demanding a mean and miserable sum from its scholars in order to maintain its masters." The result of this dependence on pupils was, as one can imagine, a tendency on the part of professors to display indulgence and to lower the requirements for passing the examinations, so as neither to discourage the students nor expose themselves to the loss of patronage. In 1412, a rector of Montpellier called the doctors of the Faculty of Law to order for their deplorable laxity in conferring degrees. Poorer universities acquired a sorry reputation for excessive

---

[1] "In the fourteenth century at Bologna," says Savigny, "the majority of the professors were already salaried by the city, and the custom of paying all of them was soon established. Thenceforward, also, the professoriat was considered as a public function, which it had not been before" (*op. cit.*, chap. xxi, § 89).

laxity; the graduates of the University of Orange, for instance, were nicknamed "Orange-flower doctors! *Docteurs à la fleur d'orange!*"

As a rule, the universities of the Middle Ages remained poor institutions, with but moderate resources at their disposal. Historians have long adduced, as a proof of the special opulence of the College of Sorbonne, its exclusive ownership of fifteen silver forks and spoons. In the fourteenth century, the rector and masters of the Paris Faculty of Arts, when dunned for the payment of a university debt, requested a delay in these terms: "We, whose profession it is to have no riches, have difficulty in finding money for the salaries of the procurators and advocates whom our suits oblige us to employ." The University of Paris, however, glories in its poverty. "Opportunities to become opulent have not been wanting in its history," said one of its rectors, in 1715. "But it has remained disinterested; it knows the worth of an honest and modest poverty."[1]

It is none the less true that poverty weighed heavily on the individuals who composed the universities, and that the need of money explains the exactions into which many and many a professor allowed himself to be drawn. At Bologna the doctors were richer, yet occasionally one finds them lending money to their pupils in the same covetous spirit, in order to augment their honoraria and exact all the more because they

---

[1] Jourdain, *Histoire de l'Université de Paris*, p. 330. "The University of Paris," says Vallet de Viriville, "notwithstanding its greed (*son esprit fiscal*) and its exactions, never got anything for itself, as an institution, but poverty.

had made these advances. But this love of gain, if it was perhaps more excusable, was certainly more keen and more developed among the poor professors whose only means of support was to levy on the students.

Another defect in the social status of the professors of the Middle Ages was the celibacy absolutely imposed on them by the regulations. In principle, the law of celibacy was universal, and applied to all graduates indiscriminately. It was permissible to be a layman, but on condition that the layman voluntarily submitted to the rules of the religious state. Up to 1407, Bachelors in Arts presenting themselves for the license had to take oath that they were not married, in order to obtain this degree. It was not until 1452 that the medical professors, and in 1500 the legal professors, attached to the Faculties, were authorized to marry.[1] As to the Masters of Arts, they never obtained this authorization, not even in the eighteenth century. Is it necessary to say what these lay celibates must have needed in order to become true educators? Without a doubt, the university teachers of the Middle Ages were devoted masters who, before entering on their functions, had taken, between the hands of their rectors, high-sounding oaths by which they bound themselves to labor for the welfare of the university, to observe the statutes and regulations, and to fulfil all their duties, and who, let us believe, generally kept these promises. But who does not comprehend that

[1] In 1331, Pope John XXII authorized a married professor to teach in the Faculty of Medicine at Paris. It was an exception. The jurists of Bologna were relieved from the obligation of celibacy earlier than those of Paris.

their spirit would have been enlarged, their authority augmented, and their pedagogic influence increased if, to their other qualities, they had joined that of being fathers of families? Can one believe, for example, that the rude and severe discipline of the rod would have been kept up so long in the schools, if the masters of these schools had had their own children as pupils?

CHAPTER II

EXTERNAL INFLUENCE OF THE UNIVERSITIES AND THEIR SPIRIT OF FREEDOM

I. The universities as a public force — Political and social influence
— Domination of the University of Paris — Democratic rules
of university organization — The habit of perpetual argumentation a preparation for political action — Commentaries on the
Politics of Aristotle — Intervention in public affairs — Political philosophy — Clamor for reforms — Conception of a paternal
government — Intervention in ecclesiastical affairs — Other universities — National character — German universities — II. Spirit
of liberty in the old universities — Free language toward the
Popes themselves — Some examples of independent and bold
opinions — Beginnings of a new spirit — More liberal methods of
study recommended by Robert de Sorbon — Protests against the
discipline of the rod — Preparations for a new era — Decay of the
mediæval universities — Conclusion.

I

A VAST subject, and one that might well furnish the
subject of a special volume, is that of the influence of
the mediæval universities, the part they played in the
history of the human mind, and the political and social
action power that they exercised.

To see in them mere associations of masters and
pupils, exclusively confined to studies, would be to
judge them incorrectly. They were one of the great
public forces of the Middle Ages. Sole depositaries
of the lofty speculations of thought at a time when

academies and other learned bodies were not in existence, when neither books, journals, nor reviews, were
published, — since the art of printing had not yet been
invented, — they represented public opinion, not alone
in scientific matters, but in great political and ecclesiastical questions as well. Permanent centres of propaganda and action when no regularly constituted political
assemblies existed, or when the States-General, as in
France, assembled only at remote intervals, they were
destined to acquire considerable influence.

This is especially true of the University of Paris.
"The authority of the University of Paris," said
Pasquier, "has risen to such a height that it is necessary to satisfy it, no matter on what conditions." [1]
Another contemporary attests the same fact. "The
university men of these days want to meddle with
everything." And again: "The said University had
great power at Paris, so much so that when it un-
dertook any affair it was bound to bring it to a conclusion; it wanted to meddle with the government of
the Pope, the King, and everything else." [2]

With history in our hands, everybody must agree
that the exuberant activity of the universities caused
them constantly to overstep the ordinary limits of
mere educational institutions. We see the universities intimately blended with national life. When
Philip Augustus had just triumphed at Bouvines over
the English and German coalition, he wrote to the
students of Paris: "Praise God, my very dear ones,

[1] Étienne Pasquier, *Rect. de la France*, III, chap. xxix.
[2] Quoted by Coville, *Les Cabochiens et l'ordonnance de* 1413, Paris,
Hachette, 1888, p. 117.

for we have never escaped so grave a danger." Thus
he associates the university with the victory of France.
Later on, from the schools of Orleans, Toulouse, and
Montpellier, come forth those legal knights (*chevaliers
ès lois*),[1] all panoplied in Roman law, who struggle
valiantly against feudalism and assure the progress of
the Third-Estate. They fill the Parliament, they figure
in the States-General; we find them surrounding Stephen Marcel, and again among the authors of the great
Ordinance of the Reformation of 1413. The universities then appeared wholly penetrated by the democratic spirit; they were considered one of the organs
of public opinion in Europe; in great crises, like the
Schism of the West, appeal was made to their intervention.[2] "To tell the truth, they did not wait for it
to be asked; they intervened of themselves."

It has been very justly remarked that by their republican organization, and the character of their instruction
and methods of study, the universities were well fitted
to play a part in politics. On one hand, the exercise
of the elective power, and the frequency of deliberative assemblies, whether of Nations and Faculties, or
of the general assembly of the university, were all
democratic acts which prepared the universities for a
certain liberty of spirit, held them back from passive
obedience, and, in a word, accustomed them in advance

[1] Professors of Law, at Montpellier, for example, were considered
as Knights of Law. After twenty years' practice they became Counts.
Jacques Rabuffi, the famous professor of the fifteenth century, is
styled Count of Laws in his epitaph. At Aix, on receiving a doctorate in law, it was said to him: "*Te comitem et nobilem facimus.*"

[2] Bayet, Rector of the Academy of Lille, *Discours de Rentrée des
Facultés*, 1891.

to political action. On the other hand, the habit of
incessant argumentation ; of discussing the *pros* and
cons of every question ; the exclusively oral character
of instruction in all grades, — all these causes combined
to form numerous debaters and orators among both
students and masters, encouraged them to have an opinion on all subjects, and to put it forward in the assemblies. "Thence arose," says M. Coville, "an inevitable
disposition to talk about everything, discuss everything, intervene in everything." [1]

That the University of Paris had its own ideas and
its political doctrine is indubitable. Following Aristotle, the theologians of the Middle Ages had freely
discussed the constitution of states. In 1307, Siger
de Brabant read and commented on the *Politics* of the
Greek philosopher at Paris. Thomas Aquinas had
composed the *De Regimine principium*, and the *De
eruditione principium*. His disciple, Gilles de Rome,
Archbishop of Bourges, who was tutor to Philip the
Fair, also followed Aristotle in politics, and talked,
like him, of an intermediate class between the nobles
and the villeins, and of its importance in the state.

There is no room for surprise, therefore, at the universities taking part in political agitations. The great
Cabochien ordinance of 1413, one of the best administrative reforms of old France, was the joint work of
the municipal body and the university. [2] But how
many other examples could be cited of university inter-
ference in state affairs? I add several, but with no

---

[1] See in the already cited work of M. Coville, the chapter entitled:
l'Université de Paris au XVᵉ Siècle.

[2] Augustin Thierry, *Histoire du Tiers-État*, p. 60.

thought of exhausting the list.   In 1316, the University of Paris recognized Philip V as the legitimate
king.   In the time of Stephen Marcel, about 1350,
it intervened to re-establish peace: "It negotiated, it
obliged its clients to arm, it sent a deputation to the
Dauphin, who was regent of the kingdom."   In 1374,
"the rectors and several masters of theology, doctors
of law, and other wise clerics of the university," con-
curred with the bishops in establishing the act which
fixed fourteen years as the age when kings attain their
majority.   In 1405, the Duke of Burgundy, then all-
powerful in the kingdom, daily consulted the university on the most secret affairs.   "In 1409, the university
takes an active share in the great labor of reforming
the finances.   It sends ambassadors to the Duke of
Orleans and the Duke of Berry; it is formally received
by the King in the green chamber, and permitted to
expose its grievances and its plans.   The King himself, in 1411, entreats its assistance, writes long letters
to it concerning the state of the realm, and entreats it
to grant him aid and comfort."   Nor does this participation of the university in affairs of state come to an
end in less troublous times, when order is re-established.   In 1465, Louis XI summons to his Council
six members of Parliament, six citizens of Paris, and
six members of the university.   The university is
really an order in the state, and its political powers
decrease and disappear only with the progress of absolute monarchy.   In 1614 it still addressed remonstrances to the States-General; they were its last,
however.

The University of Paris did not employ the politi-

cal power it was so proud of in making opposition to
royalty. Barring a few slight symptoms of insubor-
dination to the royal will, it always remained the
docile child, "the eldest daughter" of the monarchy.
In 1557, Henry II, who had, nevertheless, some grounds
of complaint against it, praised it publicly, "for its
fidelity in upholding the maxims of obedience due
to kings from their subjects." Yet I would not
affirm that the members of the university never
irritated and annoyed princes by the warnings they
gave them, by their zeal in demanding reforms, and,
above all, by the ideal conception of monarchy they
had formed, and which they constantly set forth in
their writings and discourses. Just as Louis XIV
afterwards treated Fénelon as a "fanciful person,"
because he dreamed of perfection in royalty, so these
kings of the older monarchy must have more than
once regarded these university theorizers in politics
as annoying dreamers, full of beautiful chimeras, who
demanded all sorts of virtues from kings, reminded
them of the example of "Monsieur St. Louis," and, in
a word, were bent on the "religious and ecclesiastical
dream of sanctity on the throne." Such, for example,
at the opening of the fifteenth century, was Robert
Courte-Cuisse, pupil, and afterwards famous master of
the College of Navarre, grand-almoner to the King,
and a greatly esteemed orator, who said: "The King
should be to his people like a father to his son."
"The King ought to consider the general welfare
only," and who thus commented Aristotle's maxim:
"Princes are paramount in things not determined by
the laws, but in the laws themselves, *no!*" Such

again was Gerson, who, like Thomas Aquinas, admitted the right of insurrection against vicious and tyrannical kings. "One may judge a tyrannical seigneur," said he, "if he is a sinner in several cases: and finally, this rule of law may be applied against him: *vim vi repellere licet.*" But what Gerson especially desired and hoped for was, that education in the first place, and afterwards the enlightenment of wise counsels, would aid the prince to amend himself and become the father of his people. These disciplined but independent spirits, although profoundly respectful toward constituted authorities, were yet far from dissimulating and holding their peace concerning the impression made on them by the real miseries and vices of their age. The same Gerson who would have desired to reform the character of kings, dared to write concerning the Papacy: "The Court of Rome has created a thousand offices in order to obtain gold; but hardly is one discoverable for the cultivation of virtue. Nothing is talked of there from morning to night but armies, lands, cities, and money; rarely or never do they speak of chastity, alms, justice, fidelity, and good morals."

The University of Paris meddled in religious quarrels as well as in political ones. Under this head, a historian has brilliantly summed up the part it played in the fourteenth and fifteenth centuries: "This vast corporation which represents divine and human science, cannot confine itself within the limits of its lessons and examinations, nor remain a stranger to great exterior events. If it speaks, it knows what weight will attach to its opinion, and how many faithful adherents it will find to support and defend it. We see it busied with, and taking an interest in, everything; but, above all, in the affairs of the Church. It is the epoch of the great Schism of the West, and never has there been such an occasion to display the power and activity of the University of Paris: it inquires into the power of the Schismatical Popes; it causes them to be attacked, ill-treated, and condemned by its orators; it draws up interminable writings, audacious both in matter and form; . . . it appeals to the future Pope; with the concurrence of the king, it prepares and consummates an act of the greatest gravity, the withdrawal of the Church of France from Benedict XIII, the Avignon Pope, whom it had recognized until then, but who would not yield to its requests and exigencies; . . . it suggests the reunion of National Councils to the King, in 1393, 1394, 1398, and 1400; there it manages all the debates; it presides at the tearing up of pontifical bulls; finally, it is the soul of the General Council which was to restore peace and unity to the Church after a disturbance of more than thirty years — the Council of Pisa, in 1409; it is represented there by a formal embassy; more than eighty votes are cast by its members; and the new and only Pope, Alexander V, has been not only one of its pupils but one of its masters." [1] Though it had not always the same brilliancy the ecclesiastical rôle of the University of Paris has, nevertheless, always been considerable; and the popes have always reckoned with the Sorbonne.

Assuredly the other universities have not played a rôle equally important; above all, they did not play

[1] Coville, *op. cit.*, p. 117.

one so soon. It was only in the seventeenth century (in 1603) that Oxford and Cambridge were invested with the right they still have, of returning members to the British Parliament. It was well on in the sixteenth century when Henry VIII consulted the University of Salamanca concerning his divorce from Catherine of Aragon. But, sooner or later, according to circumstances, all the universities have had their day of political or religious influence. The Italian universities seem to be the ones which withdrew most into the isolation of study and speculation. But Louvain, in Belgium, has been one of the fortresses of Catholicism. Oxford has been Royalist and Jacobite by turns, and remains Tory.[1] I have pointed out elsewhere that it was with a view to national consolidation that the kings founded the Universities of Poitiers, Caen, Bordeaux, and Douai.

In Germany particularly, the universities have had a marked tendency to become centres of political and religious action. "The German universities," says M. Lavisse, "have always mingled actively in the national life, since the day when the first of them was founded at Prague, in the fourteenth century, on the model of the flourishing school of Paris. Never have institutions imported from abroad flourished better or thrust deeper roots into a new soil. The universities began to play a part by the fifteenth century; there the new ideas that are agitating minds seek shelter

---

[1] It was to make headway against Oxford, the centre of Toryism, that the Whig party founded the University of London in 1828. It was to struggle against the preponderating Catholic influence at Louvain that the Belgian Liberals founded the University of Brussels in 1834.

against persecution; when the time arrives, they recruit
arms and intelligences there for their defence.   In the
sixteenth century, the universities are the battle fields:
Luther's cry of revolt issues from Wittenberg; there,
and at the same time, the fathers of the new church
are formed, and the first masters who, carrying into
science a liberty of spirit disenthralled from tradition,
discovered new horizons for it.   Nevertheless, Catholicism, surprised at first, defends itself vigorously, and
with the very arms by which it is attacked.   Both
parties found new universities or reform old ones.
Luther thinks that there is no work more worthy of a
pope or an emperor, or, to translate him more exactly,
that 'nothing is more pontifical nor more imperial'
than a good reform of the universities."[1]

II

This external influence of the universities, which ra-
diates throughout all society, would be inexplicable if
the universities had not been intrinsic centres of intellectual development, truly active and living scholastic
institutions.   Whatever judgment may be formed of
the instruction given by them, it must not be forgotten
that they alone gave any; that they had the monopoly
of studies; and that almost no one arrived at high
ecclesiastical dignities, or important positions in the

[1] Lavisse, *La fondation de l'Université de Berlin* (*Revue des
Deux Mondes*, May 15, 1876).   In this article M. Lavisse points out
that in founding the National University of Berlin, in 1810, directly
after its disasters, Germany sought a means of arising after its military and political downfall, by instituting a new organ of intellectual
force.

state, without passing through them. One can imagine what must have been the prestige and power of these schools, which had such an excellent *clientèle* throughout the world, which trained future bishops and popes, as well as the counsellors of lay princes which peopled the Church and the royal and imperial courts with their pupils, and gave preceptors to the heirs-presumptive of crowns. The universities were the privileged source whence in those days emerged all whose knowledge gave them admission to the ruling classes.

Hence we must not be surprised at finding the universities of the Middle Ages frequently expressing their opinions with the hardihood and even arrogance of free and independent corporations, and not with the timidity and humility befitting schools absolutely dependent on Church and State. The University of Paris, however much attached to the Church, did not spare the bishops, or even the popes. It let pass no occasion to assert its rights. Were they liegemen of the clergy, those university men of 1330 or thereabouts, who declared that the Bishop of Paris, Hugues de Besançon, was cut off from the academic body for having broken the oath taken in his youth, when a student of the Faculty of Decretal, an oath of devotion to the privileges of the university, by condemning to a fine a student guilty of rape? Were they the humble servants of the Papacy, those theologians who, towards the end of the fourteenth century, wrote, in a letter to the Pope of Avignon a letter which Clement VI thought full of venom: "Let the pastors do their duty; as for us, we shall do ours.

. . . It is of small consequence how many popes there are; two, three, ten if you like: each kingdom can have its own!"

Nor was it in the domain of practical affairs only that the universities displayed their independence. It is indisputable that in certain universities a real liberty of spirit made itself felt, in spite of the uniformity of studies and the rigidity of methods. M. Renan does not hesitate to affirm, in his book on Averroës, that "the opuscules of Albertus Magnus and of Thomas Aquinas *contra Averroistas* were directly aimed at the professors of the rue du Fouarre." Assuredly the majority of the masters were orthodox, and followed the traditional doctrines with docility. Then, theological professors in especial, all were Thomists. But close beside this obedient and faithful multitude there were independent and adventurous minds. The spirit of free examination had already its adepts. Whom could the condemnations and excommunications pronounced, between 1240 and 1270,[1] against a free and audacious philosophy have had in view, at a time when the university had a monopoly, not merely of instruction, but of thought and speculation, if not members of the university themselves? Abelard's method bore its fruits, and the emancipated reason already ventilated the most daring questions, and accepted the most novel solutions; for example, such as these: "The world is eternal — Human actions are not governed by Divine Providence — One knows nothing more after having learned theology — There are fables and errors in the Christian law as in all other laws — Philoso-

[1] *Chartularium Univ. Paris.*, t. i, pp. 170, 480.

phers are the only sages — The creation of the world is an impossible thing." The mere fact that propositions like these could have attracted the attention of the ecclesiastical power and provoked its anathema, demonstrates that they were wide-spread, and were inculcated: and where could they be so, I repeat, if not in the universities? Moreover, a contemporary testimony, that of a Friar-Preacher of Paris, named Gilles, leaves no room for doubt. Toward the close of the thirteenth century, this monk propounded to Albertus Magnus, inviting him either to refute or to contest them, eleven propositions analogous to those just cited, adding that " they were taught in the schools by the masters of Paris, and by those who are esteemed the most learned in philosophy." [1]

"The orthodoxy of the Middle Ages," says Thurot, " was reconcilable with a liberty that even seems excessive. The custom of not deciding until after having considered the *pros* and *cons*, and the obligation to consider all objections, gave the mind the habitudes of liberty. Men made a boast of not relying on the authority of Scripture, but employing nothing but mere argument. . . . They felt obliged to explain everything; they preferred new and hazardous doctrines to those that were truer, but appeared superannuated. They scorned what seemed too clear." [2] It follows that the period of the Middle Ages, even from the doctrinal point of view, was far from being an epoch of blind servility and absolute traditionalism. [3]

---

[1] Renan, *Averroès*, etc., p. 214.   [2] Thurot, *op. cit.*, p. 161.

[3] Compare this appreciation by M. Bayet, in the discourse already cited: " It must not be believed that the scientific spirit was entirely

So too, we must not believe that the methods of instruction were wholly reduced to the mechanism of the syllogism and mere verbal formalities. A proof to the contrary may be found in a recently published passage from the inedited works of the founder of the Sorbonne. Robert de Sorbon recommended to the scholar who desired to make progress in his studies, the observation of six essential rules, which he summarized thus:

1. To devote a certain hour to a given lesson, as St. Bernard had already counselled;

2. To fix his attention on what he has just read and not pass over it lightly: "between reading and study," said St. Bernard again, "there is the same difference as between a guest and a friend ; between a salutation

lacking in these old universities, nor that they were confined to the study of theology. In their own fashion they desired to extend and co-ordinate all knowledge, and never, perhaps, has man had a prouder confidence in the puissance of reasoning. They were not content to reason merely : men lived in these schools who foresaw the methods of observation and experiment which are the glory of our century. The English monk, Roger Bacon, in the thirteenth century spent long years in the University of Paris, where he was the pupil of a certain Pierre de Maucoint to whom he gives the fine title of 'Master of Experiments, *Dominus experimentorum.*' When he wished to determine the principles of science, he wrote: 'There are three ways of arriving at truth: authority, which can only produce faith, and must, moreover, justify itself in the eye of reason; reasoning, the most certain conclusions of which leave somewhat to be desired, unless one verifies them; and, finally, experiment, which suffices by itself.' And he insists on this fact, that 'above all the speculative sciences and the arts, there is the science of making experiments which shall not be incomplete and feeble.' Roger Bacon speaks the same language that one listens to again in his homonym of the seventeenth century, and certainly Claude Bernard himself has not spoken more confidently of the excellence of experimental methods."

exchanged with a passer-by in the street and an intimate and unchangeable affection";

3. To extract from his daily reading some one thought or truth, and engrave it on his memory with especial care, as prescribed by Seneca;

4. To write a summary of what he has read; for words which are not confided to writing vanish like dust before the wind;

5. To confer with his fellow pupils, either in the *disputationes*, or in familiar conversations; this exercise is still more advantageous than reading, for its effect is to clear up all doubts and obscurities;

6. Finally, to pray, which, according to St. Bernard, is one of the best means to learn.[1]

These pedagogic rules certainly bear the imprint of their age, since they end in extolling a mystical process prayer, and celebrate the benefits arising from discussion, that favorite method of the Middle Ages. But do they not also bear witness to a new spirit when they recommend meditation, that is to say, personal effort, prolonged and patient thought? To these students of the thirteenth century, crushed under a flood of words and an avalanche of dogmas, who left the ordinary lesson only to pass at once into the extraordinary one, who had no time to straighten out or pull

[1] Inedited passage from Robert de Sorbon, quoted by M. Lecoy de la Marche, *op. cit.*, p. 453. "A professor whose school was full was asked: 'What do you do to achieve such a great success?'—'It is very simple,' he replied smiling, 'God studies for me. I merely go to Mass, and when I come back I know by that all I ought to teach'" (*Ibid.*, p. 455). It would be difficult to expect much of the scientific spirit from men who were nourished on these pious prejudices.

themselves together, so bent were they under perpetual dictations, and whose minds never regained elasticity save in complying with the mechanical and routine discipline of syllogistic reasoning, Robert de Sorbon opened the way to individual thought; he invited them to reflect, to choose, to study for themselves, and thus to return to the lost sources of originality. And the intention of our author becomes plain when, long before the critics of the Renaissance, he gibes at the wretched intellectual habits of the students of his time, who thought they had done all they could when they had filled their copy-books with notes. "Not to seem as if they had lost their time," said he, "they collect leaves of parchment, make thick volumes of them, with plenty of blank spaces on the inside, and bind them elegantly in red leather; then they return to the paternal mansion with a little bag crammed full of science but with a mind completely empty." An "empty mind" — was not that the characteristic of an intelligence exercised in purely formal studies, inured to abstract processes of reasoning, but shut away from all positive knowledge concerning the past of humanity and the nature of the world? And if it was not given to Robert de Sorbon to correct the faults which he defined so clearly, at least we owe him thanks for having pointed them out, and, at the same time, as it is permissible to think, for having inspired a certain number of his contemporaries with his more comprehensive and reasonable way of understanding study.

So too, finally, in matters of discipline, it happened more than once in the height of the Middle Ages, that certain minds in advance of their times, protested against the use of corporal chastisements, and demanded gentler and more liberal regulations. Such was Gerson who, in his *opusculum de Parvulis ad Christum trahendis,* enjoined the masters to have a fatherly tenderness for their pupils, and interdicted the employment of the rod. Such also was St. Anselm, whose often quoted protest is well known: "Day and night," said an abbot to him, "we do not cease to chastise the children confided to our care, and they grow worse and worse." Anselm replied: "Indeed! You do not cease to chastise them! And when they are grown up what will they become? Idiotic and stupid. A fine education that, which makes brutes of men! . . . If you were to plant a tree in your garden, and were to enclose it on all sides so that it could not extend its branches, what would you find when, at the end of several years, you set it free from its bonds? A tree whose branches would be bent and crooked; and would it not be your fault, for having so unreasonably confined it?"

Thus there was forming in the very bosom of the routine university, a party of the future, already in possession of the ideas which became the commonplaces of the pedagogy of the Renaissance. Here and there amid the writings of the university men of the fourteenth and fifteenth centuries, we find the germ from which the modern spirit has developed. It must be thoroughly recognized, however, that this evolution took place outside of the old universities although they prepared the way for it; it took place in opposition to them, by virtue of that fatal law which forbids old institutions to reform themselves, and which condemns them to decline and disappear when their time has

come, and the needs which they originally supplied
have given place to other requirements. Born at an
epoch when the only question was to preserve the
deposit of traditional beliefs, the universities were not
armed for the conquests of science. Hence, after days
of brilliancy and glory, came years and centuries of
obscurity. "The ancient universities," has said an
historian of the sciences, M. Biot, "were in the eighteenth century several centuries in arrears of all that
concerns sciences and the arts. Peripatetics when all
the world had renounced the philosophy of Aristotle
with Descartes, they became Cartesians when the rest
were Newtonians. That is the way with learned
bodies which do not make discoveries."

But although they have not had the privilege, refused
to all human institutions, scholastic or other, of brav-
ing the onslaught of time and of being founded for
eternity, the old universities of the Middle Ages have,
nevertheless, rendered immense services. To demonstrate this, it would suffice to draw up the list of their
illustrious professors and pupils. It was not merely
theologians and churchmen that they formed; it was
also literary men and poets; a Petrarch, whom we have
seen studying at Bologna and Montpellier; a Dante who
had visited the schools of the rue du Fouarre. The
very men who have attacked and depreciated them
issued from their schools and were indebted to them,
in part at any rate, for their knowledge. Erasmus
studied at the College of Montaigu in Paris; Montaigne
was a pupil of the College of Guyenne, a dependency
of the Faculty of Arts at Bordeaux; Rabelais had
frequented almost all the French universities; Calvin

was a student of Orleans and Bourges; Bacon studied at the University of Cambridge.

But let us not dwell solely on the famous masters or illustrious students who have been the glory of the universities. Think of those thousands of obscure men, those successive generations of masters, who patiently tilled the field of science. They sowed, it is quite possible, only an inferior sort of grain: they knew neither good processes of tillage nor good methods of scattering seed! But at least, their labor and incessant efforts kept the ground in a state of cultivation; they did not permit it to lie fallow; they did not leave the fields of thought to be overrun by thorns and briars. One may say what he likes of their sterile tasks and wasted pains. They commented, commented, commented. They invented nothing. They ground away at the empty mill of dialectic! They wore themselves out in subtleties, in fine distinctions, in quibblings. A single experiment in chemistry or modern physics, a solitary physiological or anatomical observation does more service to humanity than their enormous folios. But none the less, they have deserved well from science by making ready for the future, by rendering possible the rich harvests of the sixteenth and succeeding centuries. In the chain of humanity's successive progress they have been a link, a ring, less brilliant perhaps, but as solid as the others, as necessary as any for the transmission of the intellectual and moral current of the spiritual life. And the proof that their work has not been wrought in vain, that the scholastic organism, of which they were the springs, was not unworthy to live, is that, even to-day, in all civilized countries, in young America as in old Europe, men labor to maintain and develop where they exist already, and to create or revive where they have disappeared, the universities of modern times, inheritors of the name, and, in many respects, worthy representatives of the traditions of those of the Middle Ages.

BIBLIOGRAPHY[1]

Works relating to the general history of universities

P. Heinrich Denifle, *Die Entsteheung der Universitäten des Mittelalters bis 1400*, erster Band, Berlin, 1885.

F. C. de Savigny, *Geschichte des römischen Rechts im Mittelalter*. 6 vols. 1815–1831.

Vallet de Viriville, *Histoire de l'Instruction publique en Europe*. 1 vol. Paris, 1849.

Henry Malden, *On the Origin of Universities*. 1 vol. London, 1835.

Laurie, *Lectures on the Rise and Early Constitution of Universities*. 1 vol. London, 1886.

Meiners, *Geschichte der Entstehung und Entwickelung der hohen schulen unsers Erdtheils*. Göttingen, 1802–1805. 4 Bande.

Paul Lacroix, *Le moyen âge et la Renaissance*. 5 vols. Paris, 1847–1852.

University of Paris

Bulaeus, *Historia Universitatis parisiensis*. 6 vols. 1665–1673.

Crevier, *Histoire de l'Université de Paris*, 1761. 7 vols.

Jourdain, *Histoire de l'Université de Paris au XVIIe et au XVIIIe siècles*. Paris, 1862–1866.

Histoire littéraire de la France, particularly volume XVI, and the *Discours sur l'état de lèttres au XIIIe, et au XIVe siècle*, in volume XXV de Daunon et de Victor Leclerc.

[1] The books already published on the history of the universities of the Middle Ages would make a large library. I confine myself here to an enumeration of the most important, and those of which I have made use.

Charles de Rémusat, *Abélard*. 2 vols. Paris, 1845.

Hauréau, *Histoire de la philosophie scholastique.* 2 vols.
Paris, 1880.

Thurot, *De l'organisation de l'enseignment dans l' Université
de Paris au moyen âge.* 1 vol. Paris, 1850.

Denifle, *Chartularium Universitatis Parisiensis.* Paris,
Deldain. (Two volumes have been published, 1889–1891.)

Budonsky, *Die Universität Paris und die Fremden an dersel-
ben im Mittelalter.* 1 vol. Berlin, 1875.

Provincial Universities of France

Marcel Fournier, *Les statuts et priviléges des Universités
françaises depuis leur fondation jusque 1789.* (Two volumes
have been published.)

Bimbenet, *Histoire de l' Université de Lois d' Orléans.* 1 vol.
Paris, 1853.

Germain, *Étude historique sur l'école de droit de Montpellier.*
Montpellier, 1877.

Pierre Rangeard, *Histoire de l' Université d'Angers.* 1 vol.
Angers, 1868.

Henri Beaune et d'Arbaurnun, *Les Universités de Franche
Comté.* 1 vol. Dijon, 1870.

Gadien-Arnoult, *De l' Université de Toulouse à l'époque de
vapordation en 1229.* Toulouse, 1866.

Nadal, *Histoire de l' Université de Valence.* 1 vol. Valence,
1861.

Bandel, *Histoire de l' Université de Cahors.* 1 vol. Cahors,
1876.

German Universities

Comek, *Geschichte der Prager Universitäten.* Prag, 1849.

Raumer, *Die deutschen Universitäten.* Stuttgart, 1854.

Kaufmann, *Die Geschichte der deutschen Universitäten.* Vol. I.
Stuttgart, 1888.

English Universities

Mullinger, *The University of Cambridge.* 2 vols. Cambridge, 1873–1884.

Huber, *Die englischen universitäten.* Cassel, 1839–1840.

Newman, *Historical Sketches* (3d vol.). London, 1875.

Italian Universities

Ettore Coppi, *Le Università Italiana nel medio evo.* 1 vol. Firenze, 1880.

Spanish Universities

Vicente de la Fuente, *Historia de las Universidades en España.* 4 vols. Madrid, 1884–1889.

Zarate, *De la instruccion publica en España.* Madrid, 1853.

INDEX

A

Abelard, the real founder of the University of Paris, 3; Victor Cousin on, 4; as a pupil, 6; opens schools of his own, 7; his pre-eminent abilities as a teacher, 9, 16; before the Council of Soissons, 11; at Sens, 12; his self-confidence, 12; his career as a professor, 14; founds the *Paraclete*, 15; by his method the precursor of the modern spirit, 18; his *Sic et Non*, 20; his method reigned supreme in the University, 21; the eminence of his pupils 22; the precursor of the Renaissance, 23; influence of, upon the founding of universities, 24.

Albertus, Magnus, 204.

Aquinas, Thomas, on the specialization of the universities in the thirteenth century, 29, 204.

Aristotle's *Logic* studied in the Faculty of Arts, 176; *Ethics* of, 178; his *Physics*, 179; at Oxford and Cambridge, 181, 182.

Arts, Faculty of, at Paris, 175; works read in, 176, 182; mixed character of, 191; had the lowest rank, 199.

Avignon, University of, 29.

B

Barbarossa, Frederick, and the University of Bologna, 42, 76, 82; the *Habita* of, 76.

Baccalaureate, the, 151 *et seq.*; derivation of the work, 153 note.

Bachelor, signification of the word, 148, 154.

Bachelorship, the test for, 150; significance of, 154.

Bacon, Roger, studied at Paris, 56; a Humanist of the first rank, 59; on the progress of civil law, 219.

Blois, Peter of, 67.

Boethius, *Divisions* and *Topics*, 178, 182.

Bologna, University of, the first in date, 25, 27; at first a school of Roman law, 29; instituted by Frederick Barbarossa, 42, 49, 56, 63; its imitators, 65; the imperial constitution of, 76; the centre of canon and Roman law, 222, 225; the "Nations" at, how constituted, 105; rector of, 123, 125.

Books used in the universities, 182 *et seq.*; method of studying, 183 *et seq.*; scarcity of, 186.

Bordeaux, University of, 43.

Bourges, University of, 44.

C

Caen, University of, 43.

Cahors, University of, 42, 47.

Cambridge, University of, 47, 56; its origin as described by Montalembert, 68; the chancellor of, 124.

Canon law, the study of, 234; Faculty of, 236, a caste by themselves, 237.

311

THE GREAT EDUCATORS.

NOTICES OF THE SERIES.

"Admirably conceived in a truly philosophic spirit and executed with unusual skill. It is rare to find books on pedagogy at once so instructive and so interesting. . . . I hope to read them all, which is more than I can say of any other series."—WILLIAM PRESTON JOHNSTON, *Tulane University.*

"The Scribners are rendering an important service to the cause of education in the production of the ' Great Educators Series.' "—*Journal of Education.*

"We have not too many series devoted to the history and the theory of education, and the one represented at the present moment by the two volumes before us promises to take an important place—a leading place—amongst the few we have."—*London Educational Times.*

ARISTOTLE.

The whole of ancient pedagogy is Professor Davidson's subject, the course of education being traced up to Aristotle,—an account of whose life and system forms, of course, the main portion of the book,—and down from that great teacher, as well as philosopher, through the decline of ancient civilization. An appendix discusses "The Seven Liberal Arts," and paves the way for the next work in chronological sequence,—Professor West's, on Alcuin. The close relations between Greek education and Greek social and political life are kept constantly in view by Professor Davidson. A special and very attractive feature of the work is the citation, chiefly in English translation, of passages from original sources expressing the spirit of the different theories described.

"I am very glad to see this excellent contribution to the history of education. Professor Davidson's work is admirable. His topic is one of the most profitable in the entire history of culture."—W. T. HARRIS, *U. S. Commissioner of Education.*

" 'Aristotle ' is delightful reading. I know nothing in English that covers the field of Greek Education so well. You will find it very hard to maintain this level in the later works of the series, but I can wish you nothing better than that you may do so."—G. STANLEY HALL, *Clark University.*

ALCUIN.

Professor West aims to develop the story of educational institutions in Europe from the beginning of the influence of Christianity on education to the origin of the Universities and the first beginnings of the modern movement. A careful analysis is made of the effects of Greek and Roman thought on the educational theory and practice of the early Christian, and their great system of schools, and its results are studied with care and in detail. The personality of Alcuin enters largely into the story, because of his dominating influence in the movement.

"Die von Ihnen mir freundlichst zugeschickte Schrift des Herrn Professor West über Alcuin habe ich mit lebhaftem Interesse gelesen und bin überrascht davon in Nord America eine so eingehende Beschäftigung mit unserer Vorzeit und eine so ausgebreitete Kenntniss der Literatur über diesen Gegenstand zu finden. Es sind mir wohl Einzelheiten begegnet an denen ich etwas auszusetzen fand, die ganze Auffassung und Darstellung aber kann ich nur als sehr wohl gelungen und zutreffend bezeichnen."—PROFESSOR WATTENBACH, *Berlin.*

"I take pleasure in saying that ' Alcuin ' seems to me to combine careful, scholarly investigation with popularity, and condensation with interest or detail, in a truly admirable way."—Professor G. T. LADD, *of Yale.*

THE GREAT EDUCATORS

ABELARD.

M. Compayré, the well-known French educationist, has prepared in this volume an account of the origin of the great European Universities that is at once the most scientific and the most interesting in the English language. Naturally the University of Paris is the central figure in the account; and the details of its early organization and influence are fully given. Its connection with the other great universities of the Middle Ages and with modern university movement is clearly pointed out. Abelard, whose system of teaching and disputation was one of the earliest signs of the rising universities, is the typical figure of the movement; and M. Compayré has given a sketch of his character and work, from an entirely new point of view, that is most instructive.

"'Abelard' may fairly be called the founder of university education in Europe, and we have in this volume a description of his work and a careful analysis of his character. As the founder of the great Paris University in the thirteenth century the importance of his work can hardly be overestimated. The chapter devoted to Abelard himself is an intensely interesting one, and the other chapters are of marked value, devoted as they are to the origin and early history of universities. . . . The volume is a notable educational work."—*Boston Daily Traveler.*

LOYOLA.

This work is a critical and authoritative statement of the educational principles and method adopted in the Society of Jesus, of which the author is a distinguished member. The first part is a sketch, biographical and historical, of the dominant and directing personality of Ignatius, the Founder of the order, and his comrades, and of the establishment and early administrations of the Society. In the second an elaborate analysis of the system of studies is given, beginning with an account of Aquaviva and the *Ratio Studiorum*, and considering, under the general heading of "the formation of the master," courses of literature and philosophy, of divinity and allied sciences, repetition, disputation, and dictation; and under that of "formation of the scholar," symmetry of the courses pursued, the prelection, classic literatures, school management and control, examinations and graduation, grades and courses.

"This volume on St. Ignatius of 'Loyola and the Educational System of the Jesuits,' by the Rev. Thomas Hughes, will probably be welcomed by others besides those specially interested in the theories and methods of education. Written by a member of the Jesuit Society, it comes to us with authority, and presents a complete and well-arranged survey of the work of educational development carried out by Ignatius and his followers."—*London Saturday Review.*

FROEBEL.

Friedrich Froebel stands for the movement known both in Europe and in this country as the New Education, more completely than any other single name. The kindergarten movement, and the whole development of modern methods of teaching, have been largely stimulated by, if not entirely based upon, his philosophical exposition of education. It is not believed that any other account of Froebel and his work is so complete and exhaustive, as the author has for many years been a student of Froebel's principles and methods not only in books, but also in actual practice in the kindergarten. Mr. Bowen is a frequent examiner of kindergartens, of the children in them, and of students who are trained to be kindergarten teachers.

"No one, in England or America, is fitted to give a more sympathetic or lucid interpretation of Froebel than Mr. Courthope Bowen. . . . Mr. Bowen's book will be a most important addition to any library, and no student of Froebel can afford to do without it."—KATE DOUGLAS WIGGIN, *New York City*.

HERBART.

In this book, President De Garmo has given, for the first time in the English language, a systematic analysis of the Herbartian theory of education, which is now so much studied and discussed in Great Britain and the United States, as well as in Germany. Not only does the volume contain an exposition of the theory as expounded by Herbart himself, but it traces in detail the development of that theory and the additions to it made by such distinguished names as Ziller, Story, Frick, Rein, and the American School of Herbartians. Especially valuable will be found Dr. De Garmo's careful and systematic exposition of the problems that centre around the concentration and correlation of studies. These problems are generally acknowledged to be the most pressing and important at present before the teachers of the country.

"Some one has said there can be no great need without the means of supplying such need, and no sooner did the fraternity realize its need of a knowledge of the essentials of Herbart than Dr. De Garmo's excellent work on 'Herbart and the Herbartians,' by Scribner's Sons of New York, appeared, a book which, costing but a dollar, gives all that the teacher really needs, and gives it with devout loyalty and sensible discrimination. It is the work of a believer, a devotee, an enthusiast, but it is the masterpiece of the writer who has not forgotten what he owes to his reputation as a scholar in his devotion to his master."—*Journal of Education.*

THE ARNOLDS.

No book heretofore published concerning one or both of the Arnolds has accomplished the task performed in the present instance by Sir Joshua Fitch. A long-time colleague of Matthew Arnold in the British Educational Department, the author—leaving biography aside—has, with unusual skill, written a succinct and fascinating account of the important services rendered to the educational interests of Great Britain by the Master of Rugby and his famous son. The varied and successful efforts of the latter in behalf of a better secondary education during his long official career of thirty-five years as Inspector of Training Schools, no less than the notable effect produced at Rugby by the inspiring example of Thomas Arnold's high-minded character and enthusiastic scholarship, are admirably presented. Whatever in the teaching of both seems likely to prove of permanent value has been judiciously selected by the author from the mass of their writings, and incorporated in the present volume. The American educational public, which cannot fail to acknowledge a lasting debt of gratitude to the Arnolds, father and son, will certainly welcome this sympathetic exposition of their influence and opinions.

"The book is opportune, for the Arnoldian tradition, though widely diffused in America, is not well based on accurate knowledge and is pretty much in the air. Dr. Fitch seems the fittest person by reason of his spiritual sympathy with the father and his personal association with the son, to sketch in this brief way the two most typical modern English educators. And he has done his work almost ideally well within his limitations of purpose. . . . The two men live in these pages as they were."—*Educational Review*, New York.

27473